The Beliefs and Experiences of World Language Teachers in the US

PSYCHOLOGY OF LANGUAGE LEARNING AND TEACHING

Series Editors: **Sarah Mercer**, *Universität Graz, Austria* and **Stephen Ryan**, *Waseda University, Japan*

This international, interdisciplinary book series explores the exciting, emerging field of Psychology of Language Learning and Teaching. It is a series that aims to bring together works which address a diverse range of psychological constructs from a multitude of empirical and theoretical perspectives, but always with a clear focus on their applications within the domain of language learning and teaching. The field is one that integrates various areas of research that have been traditionally discussed as distinct entities, such as motivation, identity, beliefs, strategies and self-regulation, and it also explores other less familiar concepts for a language education audience, such as emotions, the self and positive psychology approaches. In theoretical terms, the new field represents a dynamic interface between psychology and foreign language education and books in the series draw on work from diverse branches of psychology, while remaining determinedly focused on their pedagogic value. In methodological terms, sociocultural and complexity perspectives have drawn attention to the relationships between individuals and their social worlds, leading to a field now marked by methodological pluralism. In view of this, books encompassing quantitative, qualitative and mixed methods studies are all welcomed.

All books in this series are externally peer-reviewed.

Full details of all the books in this series and of all our other publications can be found on http://www.multilingual-matters.com, or by writing to Multilingual Matters, St Nicholas House, 31-34 High Street, Bristol, BS1 2AW, UK.

PSYCHOLOGY OF LANGUAGE LEARNING AND TEACHING: 23

The Beliefs and Experiences of World Language Teachers in the US

Pamela M. Wesely

MULTILINGUAL MATTERS
Bristol • Jackson

DOI https://doi.org/10.21832/WESELY5515

Library of Congress Cataloging in Publication Data
A catalog record for this book is available from the Library of Congress.
Names: Wesely, Pamela M., author.
Title: The Beliefs and Experiences of World Language Teachers in the US/
   Pamela M. Wesely.
Description: Bristol; Jackson: Multilingual Matters, 2024. | Series:
   Psychology of Language Learning and Teaching: 23 | Includes
   bibliographical references and index. | Summary: "This book tells the
   stories of 15 world language (WL) teachers in the US through rich
   descriptions of their lived worlds and experiences. It illustrates in
   detail how teacher beliefs relate to their practices and are mediated
   and moderated by their learners, institutional demands, equity and
   access to WL education and other factors"-- Provided by publisher.
Identifiers: LCCN 2023051739 (print) | LCCN 2023051740 (ebook) | ISBN
   9781800415508 (paperback) | ISBN 9781800415515 (hardback) | ISBN
   9781800415539 (epub) | ISBN 9781800415522 (pdf)
Subjects: LCSH: Language teachers--United States--Biography. | Language
   teachers--United States--Interviews. | Language teachers--United
   States--Attitudes. | Language and languages--Study and teaching--United
   States. | LCGFT: Biographies. Classification: LCC P59.3 .W47 2024 (print)
| LCC P59.3 (ebook) | DDC 418.0092/273--dc23/eng/20240116
LC record available at https://lccn.loc.gov/2023051739
LC ebook record available at https://lccn.loc.gov/2023051740

British Library Cataloguing in Publication Data
A catalogue entry for this book is available from the British Library.

ISBN-13: 978-1-80041-551-5 (hbk)
ISBN-13: 978-1-80041-550-8 (pbk)

Multilingual Matters
UK: St Nicholas House, 31-34 High Street, Bristol, BS1 2AW, UK.
USA: Ingram, Jackson, TN, USA.

Website: https://www.multilingual-matters.com
Twitter: Multi_Ling_Mat
Facebook: https://www.facebook.com/multilingualmatters
Blog: https://www.channelviewpublications.wordpress.com

The policy of Multilingual Matters/Channel View Publications is to use papers
that are natural, renewable and recyclable products, made from wood grown in
sustainable forests. In the manufacturing process of our books, and to further
support our policy, preference is given to printers that have FSC and PEFC Chain
of Custody certification. The FSC and/or PEFC logos will appear on those books
where full certification has been granted to the printer concerned.

Typeset by Manila Typesetting Company.

Contents

Acknowledgments

I will start my acknowledgments with the start of this book – thank you to the University of Iowa and the Iowa Board of Regents for providing me with a semester-long professional development award that allowed me to focus on this research and travel around Iowa. Thank you to the Obermann Center at the University of Iowa for providing me with support, space and community as an Obermann Center Faculty Fellow during that time. Thank you to the Iowa World Language Association for helping me to make connections across the state. Finally, thank you so much to my participants for allowing me in their classrooms, for being open to conversations with me, and for continuing to support and promote multilingualism through their daily work. I hope that I did justice to your voices and experiences.

The study took shape with the help of many different people during the analysis and writing process. I enjoyed the support of many colleagues and students in the College of Education and throughout the University of Iowa. I especially want to recognize and thank Diane Neubauer and Bing Gao, who contributed time and effort to this project at important stages. Their attention to detail and thoughtful work are in these pages, too. Thank you to the ACTFL/Middlebury Research Forum in 2021, who offered feedback and insights for this project as my ideas were taking shape for a book. And then of course, thank you to Multilingual Matters and its anonymous reviewers who helped greatly with finalizing and polishing my message.

Finally, thank you to friends, colleagues and family almost too numerous to mention, who supported me and my work throughout the years that I spent on this project. Thank you to Cassandra Glynn and Beth Wassell, the most generous, kind and forgiving collaborators and friends I could ever hope for in my career. And last but not least, thank you to my husband Matt Arnold and children Fiona and Malcolm Arnold, who gave me space, didn't give me space, and inspired me day in and day out, especially as we all braved the pandemic together. I am so lucky and privileged to live my life with them.

1 Introduction

This book offers a window into the world of primary and secondary (K–12) world language (WL) teachers in the United States. Through an investigation of 15 different K–12 classrooms, including in-depth interviews, observations and document analysis, I explore WL teachers' beliefs, actions and experiences in their classrooms.

In this chapter, I begin with a survey of important background information about the educational contexts that I will be exploring. In the first section of the chapter, I offer an overview of K–12 WL education in the US, with a focus on Iowa, the state where the current study takes place. In this overview, I provide a brief history of US K–12 WL education, an explanation of national and state policies related to K–12 WL education, a description of current enrollment trends, a summary of the language outcomes at these levels and, finally, an explanation of how heritage learners (HLs) are considered in the context of K–12 WL education. In the second section of the chapter, I describe the current practices related to K–12 WL teacher preparation, both on national and local levels. I then contextualize some of the US data with comparable data in other countries. Finally, I explore how scholars and experts in WL education in the US are looking to the future in terms of setting goals for the field, identifying and addressing the crucial case of underserved groups without access to K–12 WL education and exploring points of hope such as STARTALK and the Seal of Biliteracy. The chapter ends with an overview of the content of the rest of the book.

I intend in this book for the term 'world language education' to refer to programs and pedagogies that focus on teaching languages other than English in the US. I exclude programs like immersion education and bilingual education from this definition, as they focus on teaching academic content through the non-English language during a large percentage of the school day. World language programs, on the other hand, consist of courses with the primary objective of helping students to learn or acquire a non-English language and culture. These world language courses are customarily separate from content courses in other academic areas, which are taught in English. I do acknowledge that programs exist that bridge the separation that I have identified here between WL and immersion/bilingual education, for instance, WL programs for HLs. I explore that distinction further in this chapter and throughout the book.

Finally, I have chosen not to use the term 'foreign language' in this text in favor of 'world language'. The term 'foreign language' has been pervasive in US educational institutions and scholarship for many decades. However, the word 'foreign' has negative connotations that, in US English, can imply that the language and the community of language speakers is different, other and ultimately negatively considered (Rey Agudo, 2021). Therefore, I use 'foreign' when speaking of historical events or citing other publications and scholars that use that term, as the term was used then. However, I use the term 'world' at all other times. For the purposes of this book, the reader can assume that 'world language' and 'foreign language' are functionally synonyms.

K–12 WL Education in the United States: The State of the Field

A brief history

The record of the United States of teaching non-English languages to English speakers 'follows the ebb and flow of greater social and political forces' (Berbeco, 2016: 3). In the early years of the modern US nation, elite schools and religious institutions taught languages such as Latin and ancient Greek. The growth of comprehensive high schools and public education was accompanied by a growth in teaching world languages, especially German, in the late 1880s (Berbeco, 2016; Pavlenko, 2003). However, after World War II, there was considerable backlash against German, at the time the most commonly taught world language, which increased the public distrust of teaching any languages other than English, and enrollment in world languages dropped (Berbeco, 2016). Prevailing discourses that positioned world language instruction as challenging to the US national identity were reflected in the English-only laws and statutes that were sweeping the country in the 1940s and 1950s (Pavlenko, 2003).

The Cold War between the United States and the Soviet Union gained traction in the 1950s, leading to new awareness of the need to educate the young people in the US in ways that would aid US efforts internationally. In particular, the Soviet Union's success in launching Sputnik in 1957 caused the US to want to overhaul its public education system. This new focus on education led to the 1958 National Defense Education Act (NDEA), which then led to a rise in the nation's world language courses at the secondary as well as the elementary levels (Berbeco, 2016; Met & Brandt, 2017; Terry, 2016). Language teaching approaches at that time were largely focused on Skinnerian behaviorism and operant conditioning. Many students in that era learned language in language labs that offered chances to practice a language and make it into a habit (Met & Brandt, 2017). Soon thereafter, in 1966, an individual-membership organization focused on the quality of world language teaching was created in the US, called ACTFL (originally an abbreviation for American Council on the Teaching of Foreign Languages, but now referred to only by its acronym) (Terry, 2016).

By the mid-1980s, there was considerable variation across the US in how world language study was supported at the K–12 level, since world language education policy was under the purview of the states, not the federal government. K–12 public school programs, especially elementary and middle/junior high school programs, were sometimes created in state legislation but not funded, or were not created at all. In some states, incentive funding was provided to establish and support world language programs. Other states did not institute any requirements, thus leaving decisions about language offerings in the hands of individual school boards. School boards in the US are regional, elected bodies that oversee and govern public school districts, which are geographical bodies that that administrate the local secondary and elementary schools. These bodies and structures do not exist for private schools, which can vary in how they are governed. At the secondary level, high school programs were established and often stayed stable, although elementary and middle/junior high school programs were not as stable and often faced elimination when district budgets were reduced or tightened (Met & Brandt, 2017). At this time in the mid-1980s, ACTFL began to focus on proficiency as the outcome of foreign language study, instead of mastery of grammar rules, with the establishment of proficiency guidelines and, subsequently, tests and measurements that corresponded to those guidelines (Terry, 2016).

In recent decades, as funding for public education has shifted due to changing priorities, enrollment in world language classes has declined, as I explore later in this chapter. Some federal efforts, including the institution of the Foreign Language Assistance Program (FLAP) from 1988 until 2012, promoted world language study through providing grants to establish, improve and expand programs in K–12 schools (O'Rourke *et al.*, 2016). As Dolci (2015) stated, some of these movements stemmed from the concern that '[world language] education imparted in schools and universities was not adequate and could undermine the primacy of the US in various fields' (Dolci, 2015: 2). Other federal funding has followed, although almost none specifically earmarked for K–12 world language programs (Commission on Language Learning, 2017).

In the 1990s, ACTFL developed and disseminated, with several other major language organizations, the *Standards for Foreign Language Learning in the 21st Century* (National Standards Collaborative Board, 1998). These standards offered a new framework for US world language teaching, moving explicitly beyond the focus on grammar learning to the more proficiency-based focus on what was often called the 'Five Cs': Communication, Cultures, Connections, Comparisons and Communities (Terry, 2016). Although the national standards were not always adopted immediately by teachers and teacher education programs (Phillips & Abbott, 2011), they became more and more common in how world language teachers identified their goals and objectives in the classroom from their release in the 1990s until today (Met & Brandt, 2017). The national standards were renamed and revised into the *World-Readiness Standards for Learning Languages* in 2015 (National Standards Collaborative Board, 2015). ACTFL has also released several different position statements outlining its recommendations about how language should be taught that supplement and build on the *World-Readiness Standards*. One notable one has been ACTFL's recommendation that teachers use the target language over 90% of the time in the classroom (ACTFL, 2010b).

The last 25 years of world language education have thus been characterized by changes in techniques and methods, with an emphasis on language proficiency and communication skills in both instructional techniques and in assessments (Berbeco, 2016; Met & Brandt, 2017). Guidelines like the *World-Readiness Standards* (National Standards Collaborative Board, 2015) and recommendations for best practice in world language teaching are widely disseminated through the efforts of national, regional and state organizations for world language teachers.

Current policies about world language education in the United States

As mentioned above, the United States lacks a national policy about world language education at the K–12 level. Dolci (2015) summarized it thusly:

> There is no specific law regulating the use of languages in the United States . . . the current era urges the United States to adopt a language policy in order to meet the challenges caused by internal migration, to remain competitive in the global market, and to guarantee the nation's safety. (Dolci, 2015: 1)

In this quote, Dolci identifies the irony of the lack of a national policy when the cultivation of a multilingual populace would help to address both internal and external needs of the nation. Indeed, this lack of a US national policy has resulted in a desultory set of state-level regulations about language education. In a study of the graduation requirements of all 50 states and the District of Columbia, O'Rourke *et al.* (2016) found that only seven states and the District of Columbia had high school graduation requirements for world languages. Of those, four states required two years of study; three states required one year; and one state required students to demonstrate proficiency in a language other than English. The authors also found that, in 22 states, state law mandated that 'students could use courses in world languages as one way to fulfill a requirement' (O'Rourke *et al.*, 2016: 794). This requirement could be satisfied by other classes in subjects such as the arts or technical career skills. The remaining 21 states, including Iowa, where the current study takes place, did not have high school graduation requirements (O'Rourke *et al.*, 2016). Researchers have investigated the reasons these policies were (or were not) put in place, and they have found that some of the significant factors have been the limited funding sources to sustain language programs (Met & Brandt, 2017), the difficulty of finding language instructors and school scheduling difficulties (Bouabré, 2019).

However, in Iowa, as in several other states, every district was required to offer world languages even if it was not a graduation requirement. Iowa's state policy can serve both as an illustration of the ways that world language education is outlined in state code and as a description of the setting of the current study. At the time of this study, Iowa Code, Section 256.11.5.f (2023), regarding state educational standards, states the following:

> In grades nine through twelve, a unit of credit consists of a course or equivalent related components or partial units taught throughout the academic year. The minimum program to be offered and taught for grades nine through twelve is: . . . Four sequential units of one world language. . . . The department may waive the third and fourth years of the world language requirement on an annual basis upon the request of the board of directors of a school district or the authorities in charge of a nonpublic school if the board or authorities are able to prove that a licensed teacher was employed and assigned a schedule that would have allowed students to enroll in a world language class, the world language class was properly scheduled, students were aware that a world language class was scheduled, and no students enrolled in the class.

This code focuses on determining how many units of course credit are offered in a district, rather than identifying the required language proficiency attained by the students. At the time of this study, two sequential years of a world language had to be offered in grades 9–12 (customarily the high school years) in all districts in the state of Iowa. A third and fourth year of the same language needed to be offered unless a waiver was obtained by the district due to lack of enrollment. All public districts represented in the current study offered four sequential years of a world language in grades 9–12 at the time of the study.

One other component of world language requirements in the US relates to language requirements for students intending to continue with postsecondary education. In Iowa, few colleges and universities require foreign language study at the K–12 level, but many strongly recommend it. My institution, the University of Iowa, is one of the few in the state that requires two years of high school world language study for first-year admission (https://admissions.uiowa.edu/academics/first-year-admission); Iowa State, another large public university in the state, has a similar requirement (https://www.admissions.iastate.edu/freshman/requirements). These individual examples, within one state, illustrate the fact that, although world language study is expected of applicants to many if not most universities, those requirements have had no external regulation and vary considerably by institution.

Enrollment in K–12 world language education in the United States and in Iowa

In the most recent available data, gathered by the American Councils for International Education (ACIE) in 2014–2015, 19.66% of students in K–12 public and private schools in the United States were reported to be taking a world language. These data reflected only school-based programs, and they did not reflect the number of students taking classes, for example, in 'heritage, community-based, afterschool and weekend and summer school programs', which often accounted for much more language instruction outside of the conventional school day (ACIE, 2017: 6). In the state of Iowa, with no state requirement for world language study, the percentage of the population enrolled was 15.23% (ACIE, 2017).

Data on the percentage of public and private K–12 schools in the US that offer any world language programming have not been collected. It is likely, however, based on patterns of known enrollment and language policy in schools, that most schools and districts do offer world language instruction even though students might not take the classes. For instance, data from private K–12 Christian schools in the US gathered in 2016–2017 found that 88% of those schools offered world language instruction (Bouabré, 2019). As shown above, Iowa state educational standards require that Iowa public school districts offer world language classes, so one can assume that Iowa schools also follow this trend.

The top three languages offered and learned in K–12 schools in the US, as measured in 2014–2015, were Spanish, French and German, often called the 'commonly taught languages'. Chinese was the next most instructed and learned language. Table 1.1 illustrates the number of students enrolled in each language as well as the number of programs offered at each level (ACIE, 2017). With this data set, I do not have data on how many schools had many different language programs, or how many students enrolled in more than one language.

Table 1.1 Top K–12 foreign languages in 2014–2015

Language	National enrollment	Iowa enrollment	National high school programs	Iowa high school programs	National K–8 programs	Iowa K–8 programs
Spanish	7,363,125	67,351	8,177	185	112	1
French	1,289,004	7,072	3,738	41	57	0
German	330,898	3,973	1,548	27	15	0
Chinese	227,086	568	1,144	9	34	0

Source: ACIE (2017)

Additionally, one can observe in the rightmost columns of Table 1.1 that high school programs in 2014–2015 were much more common than K–8 programs at both the national and state levels. Other data sources about US K–12 schools in the past 20 years support this finding (Pufahl *et al.*, 2000). For instance, in a study about Massachusetts in 2021, Ritz and Sherf (2021) found that, among the 188 K–12 public school districts in Massachusetts, 20.8% of these school districts offered an elementary world language program, 95% offered a middle/junior high school program and all responding school districts offered a high school world language program.

Data on the types of classes offered at the K–12 level in the US in 2014–2015 are also available at the national level in the ACIE (2017) data. Over 85% of courses in Spanish, French, German and Chinese were offered during the academic year, with the remainder offered in summer, after-school, or Saturday classes offered by the school or district (ACIE, 2017). The format of the classes varied from language to language, although most of the world language classes across all languages were a traditional format in which English-speaking students were taught a world language face-to-face (Spanish [84%]; French [79%]; German [63%]; Chinese [67%]). Other formats included dual language, immersion, hybrid and online courses (ACIE, 2017).

In the 2018 Annual Condition of Education Report in Iowa, data showed that 85.2% of students in the graduating classes of 2017 and 2018 in Iowa public schools had taken at least one high school language course during their four years of high school. Mirroring the 2014–2015 data shown in Table 1.1, about 83% of those students were reported to have taken Spanish, 9% took French, 5% took German, and 1% took Chinese (Iowa Department of Education, 2018).

These data provide a snapshot of the enrollment in K–12 world language education in the US and in Iowa at the time that this study was conducted. Although data of this type are notoriously difficult to gather (ACIE, 2017), the patterns and trends revealed here can provide some needed context for understanding the environment in which the teachers, students and community members live in this study.

Outcomes in K–12 world language education in the United States

Students who learn a world language at the K–12 level in the United States have been shown to advance to a variety of levels of language proficiency, primarily depending on the length of their study (Avant, 2017; Davin *et al.*, 2014; Glisan & Foltz, 1998; Huebner & Jensen, 1992; Kissau *et al.*, 2015; Sparks *et al.*, 2017; Vyn *et al.*, 2019). Studies by Avant (2017), Glisan and Foltz (1998) and Vyn *et al.* (2019) have offered evidence, using three different assessments and three different populations of US K–12 world language students, that the average proficiency rating of students in the US after four years of high school study of one language or the equivalent, across reading, writing, listening and speaking, lies approximately at the Novice-High or Intermediate-Low level according to the ACTFL Proficiency Guidelines (ACTFL, 2012) or A1 or A2 level if using the Common European Framework of Reference for Language (Council of Europe, 2020; see also ACTFL, n.d.). Several other studies have focused on providing distributions of scores and did not provide an overall proficiency level average, but their results have supported the contention that the majority of students, after four years of study of the same language in US secondary schools, test at either the Novice-High or Intermediate-Low Levels (A1/A2 levels) when the four skills are considered together (e.g. CASLS, 2010; Davin *et al.*, 2014; Vyn *et al.*, 2019). Data on the level of proficiency attained by elementary and middle/junior high school learners in traditional world language (nonimmersion) programs has not been available. Most of these studies have omitted HLs from their calculations as well.

One interesting trend that has been identified in several studies is a notable increase in average proficiency score gains between the second-year and third-year courses at the secondary level (Avant, 2017; CASLS, 2010; Davin *et al.*, 2014; Moeller *et al.*, 2012; Vyn *et al.*, 2019). One common explanation for this trend is the fact that, as shown earlier in the investigation of policy in the US, the requirement for language study by states, school districts and even university admissions is often two years of study. This fact then suggests that the classes would be smaller at the upper levels and the students who continue language study after two years have a higher level of interest in world language study overall (Moeller *et al.*, 2012).

If listening, reading, writing and speaking are considered separately, student performance has been found to vary across studies and contexts (Avant, 2017; CASLS, 2010; Davin *et al.*, 2011; Davin *et al.*, 2014). Although in some cases, students test at higher levels of proficiency in the receptive skills of listening and reading (CASLS, 2010), identifying a trend across languages and levels is more difficult. For instance, students learning languages that share an alphabet with English, such as Spanish, French and German, generally have tested at a comparatively higher proficiency level in reading than those learning character-based languages such as Chinese or Japanese (Avant, 2017). Davin *et al.* (2011) found that elementary students performed best on an interpersonal task (speaking and listening), followed by the presentational task (speaking and writing) and then the interpretive task (reading and listening). Thus, although some basic trends in the levels of proficiency reached by US K–12 students can be identified, the amount of variation across contexts, languages and levels limits the interpretation considerably.

Some studies have identified programmatic or instructional factors that contribute to higher levels of proficiency in students in K–12 contexts.

Moeller *et al.* (2012), for example, found that having students consistently set proficiency goals in high school WL classes correlated with stronger performance on proficiency assessments. Kissau *et al.* (2015), in studying students in early levels of Spanish learning in high school, found that those students who had studied Spanish in exploratory programs at the middle/junior high school level consistently outperformed their fellow students on proficiency assessments. Vyn *et al.* (2019) identified that explicit grammar instruction did not benefit high school French and Spanish students in the lower levels, but it did for more advanced students; similarly, more use of the target language in the classroom at the lower levels was a positive factor in proficiency development for those students, but less so at the upper levels. These individual studies, however, are still in need of replication in a variety of contexts and languages in order to generalize more consistently across the varied and diverse world of K–12 world language education in the US.

K–12 heritage language education in the United States

A group of particular interest in this study is that of Spanish heritage learners (HLs). HLs can be defined in a number of ways. The broadest definition identifies them as individuals who have some personal, historical connection to the language, most often because the heritage language is spoken in their home (Bateman & Wilkinson, 2010). The language skills of HLs are not usually assumed to be the same as those who are frequently termed 'native speakers' of the language, who have a full range of mastery of expression. Instead, HLs have been shown to have widely varying academic skills in both English and their heritage language (Bateman & Wilkinson, 2010). Furthermore, these learners have been shown to face complex sociocultural issues relating to their identities as HLs who might not speak a standard form of their heritage language (Carreira & Kagan, 2017; Wang & Green, 2008).

Both the terms 'heritage' and 'native' have been called into question and critiqued by scholars (e.g. García, 2014; Holliday, 2006; Llurda & Calvet-Terré, 2022; Moussu & Llurda, 2008; Ortega, 2019). The term 'heritage', García has argued, risks relegating current speakers of Spanish (for example) and their communities to the past, contributing to the 'silencing of US bilingualism' (García, 2014: 69). 'Native' is often referred to in language education in the context of native speaker bias or native-speakerism, which idealizes the native speaker as the 'ultimate model and source of information about a language, and therefore as the ideal teacher' (Llurda & Calvet-Terré, 2022: 3; see also Holliday, 2006). The distinction between native and non-native speakers of a language, as well as that between HLs and non-HLs, risks cultivating a deficit view of language, where one type of linguistic background is inherently superior to another either as a teacher, learner or user of the language (Ortega, 2019).

However, as with many other terms, these terms and distinctions are 'socially present', as Moussu and Llurda (2008: 316) have stated, and they have a currency in popular discourse that is reflected in the terms used by the participants in this study, their institutions and the surrounding communities. I will thus continue to use these terms in this text, with the caveat and recognition that the terms have been shown to be problematic and flawed in accurately representing the fullness of bilingualism today.

The separation of Spanish instruction for HLs and Spanish instruction as a world language has a long history within the US educational system (Bale, 2014; García, 2014). Where Spanish for HLs was often framed as remedial, often in the context of bilingual or dual language programs where the focus was shared with the teaching of English, Spanish for non-HLs was seen as enrichment and as an enhancement of the WL students' academic and professional profiles. The two teaching fields often did not connect at all (García, 2014). García's 2014 review of the history of the development of Spanish teaching in US schools demonstrates that the history of colonialism, immigration, racism and longstanding discriminatory practices in US K–12 schooling systems all fed into this dynamic through things like prioritizing the teaching of Castilian Spanish over all other forms of Spanish, characterizing Spanish-English bilingual programming as a means to transition Spanish-speaking students to English and ignoring the presence of local Spanish-speaking communities in the development of Spanish education for non-HLs. In this piece, García also argues that current educational practices risk perpetuating this division, although there is hope through the increasing recognition and acceptance of multiple forms of Spanish bilingualism (García, 2014).

Three of the teachers whose classrooms feature in this book (Sarah, Chapter 3; Diana and Gabriel, Chapter 6) either taught specifically Spanish HL classes or identified to me the presence of HLs in their Spanish classes. These practices for integrating HLs into WL programs reflect what scholars have observed elsewhere in the country, where low enrollments of HLs at the K–12 level often mean that they are more commonly integrated into classes for non-HL students (Bateman & Wilkinson, 2010; Carreira & Kagan, 2017). Indeed, scholars in the US have found that heritage language instruction is not commonly institutionalized across educational levels. That is, they observed that heritage language instruction in US schools has frequently not been accepted or seen as legitimately belonging, it was not used widely across districts, there was not a firm expectation that it will continue and it was not stable or routinized through culture or resource allocation (Carreira & Kagan, 2017).

Although, again, little comprehensive national data exists about K–12 Spanish heritage language programs or HLs, a few studies can offer some insights into their prevalence. In a survey of K–12 Spanish teachers in Utah in 2008, Bateman and Wilkinson (2010) found that, out of the

183 respondents, about 10% reported teaching a separate class for HLs. Overall, the authors were able to estimate that about 11% of the students in the respondents' classes were HLs, although a large standard deviation indicated that this varied widely from location to location. These teachers also estimated that 80% of their HL were immigrants (Bateman & Wilkinson, 2010). Pufahl and Rhodes (2011) found that 7% of US elementary schools and 8% of US secondary schools with foreign language programs offered classes for Spanish HLs (Pufahl & Rhodes, 2011).

These issues regarding heritage language education in the US K–12 system will be revisited in the exploration of the classrooms of the three teachers in this book who identify HLs among their students.

Becoming a K–12 World Language Teacher in the United States

Another important consideration in understanding K–12 WL education in the United States is the development and preparation of WL teachers. Learning in extended sequences of instruction is directly related to teachers' professional preparation level and their teaching quality (Donato & Tucker, 2007). Unfortunately, there is a lack of trained world language teachers at the K–12 level in the US, a fact that has consistently been mentioned as a barrier to providing widespread and comprehensive world language instruction that meets the national need (Commission on Language Learning, 2017; Egnatz, 2016). In the 2017–2018 academic year, 41 US states, plus the District of Columbia, Guam and the Virgin Islands, all listed world language teachers as a Teacher Shortage Area (US Department of Education, n.d.b). In Iowa, world language teachers have been identified as a shortage area every year since the records were made publicly available, from 1990 to the present (US Department of Education, n.d.b).

The process of teacher credentialing in the US takes place at the postsecondary level. Institutions of higher education have offered a variety of programs to credential language teachers, sometimes concurrent with a four-year BA program, other times as a degree program that takes place after receiving a BA, such as a post-bac program that only provides licensure or a graduate program that gives students an MEd or MAT degree along with their teacher licensure (Egnatz, 2016). Each individual state, usually via the governor-appointed state board of education with the cooperation of the administrative arm of the government in the department of education, determines the coursework and field experience requirements for teacher candidates. When teachers who are credentialed in one state move to another state and wish to teach, they sometimes are required to complete additional coursework or pass additional tests in order to be able to do so, depending on the requirements of that individual state.

As Tedick (2009) outlined, the coursework that is required in US K–12 world language teacher preparation customarily has included the following:

- coursework in the language, usually about linguistics or literature;
- coursework in world language pedagogy (usually between one and three courses), usually not language-specific in order to include teacher candidates preparing to teach any language;
- field experiences that go along with the WL methods coursework, where teacher candidates work with teachers of the languages that they are seeking to teach; and
- student-teaching experiences.

To these, I add:

- Foundations courses required of all teacher candidates, regardless of content area, in topics like technology, special education or the history of education – as determined by state boards of education.

Whether academic language or pedagogy courses or classroom field experiences should be prioritized in language teacher preparation courses has long been debated in the field (e.g. Kubanyiova & Crookes, 2016; Tarone & Allwright, 2005), and programs can differ significantly in this proportion depending on state and institutional guidelines. Additionally, teacher education programs require a variety of assessments for admission as well as for completion of their programs. These have varied considerably from state to state, and indeed even from institution to institution.

The major accrediting body for teacher education programs in the US, the Council for the Accreditation of Educator Preparation (CAEP), sets standards for teacher preparation programs. In world language teacher preparation programs, CAEP works with ACTFL to establish these standards and to provide program reviews (ACTFL/CAEP, 2015). Although several hundred teacher education programs across the US adhere to the ACTFL/CAEP standards, importantly for this study, none of those programs exist in the state of Iowa, as evidenced by a search on the CAEP website (http://www.caepnet.org/provider-search).

In Iowa, teacher licensure is governed by the Iowa Board of Educational Examiners. This board determined that Iowa's teacher preparation programs would have to meet state accreditation standards, but they would not have to meet or face accreditation reviews with CAEP (281 IAC 77, 2017). Approved teacher preparation programs must face a state review every seven years in Iowa, to be sure that they are meeting the state standards for teacher preparation (281 IAC 79.8[256], 2017). The INTASC Standards provide the framework for the in-state accreditation process (Council of Chief State School Officers, 2013).

One important factor in ACTFL/CAEP accredited world language teacher preparation programs is the requirement that the teacher candidates test at advanced-low or intermediate-high level on the Oral Proficiency Interview (OPI) and the Writing Proficiency Test (WPT; see also Egnatz, 2016). The value of this requirement has been debated by scholars in the field (e.g. Burke, 2013; Tedick, 2013). In the state of Iowa, there is no specific language proficiency requirement placed on world language teachers, although they are required to have completed 24–30 semester hours (approximately 7–10 classes) in the target language at the postsecondary level (https://educate.iowa.gov/educator-licensure/endorsements-list). Different teacher preparation programs have instituted their own proficiency requirements, however. Although there is a mechanism for native speakers of the target language to become world language teachers in Iowa, called the Native Speaker Authorization, it requires that the teacher candidate already have a job offer from a specific district to qualify (Iowa Board of Educational Examiners, n.d.).

Finally, some documented gaps in US K–12 world language teacher preparation are important to point out. Pufahl and Rhodes found in 2011 that most language teachers in elementary schools did not have the proper credentials to teach. In contrast, the majority of secondary teachers had certifications (Pufahl & Rhodes, 2011). Scholars of heritage language teaching have found that there is a lack of teacher training that is specific to the needs of HLs (Bateman & Wilkinson, 2010; Carreira & Kagan, 2017). However, Bateman and Wilkinson (2010) did find that teachers who taught HL-only classes reported much higher levels of training in teaching HLs.

International Comparisons

Comparing the United States to other countries in the world, there are some stark differences in K–12 world language programming. Most notably, students in the US have been shown to be much less likely to begin formal world language instruction in the early grades. Pufahl *et al.* (2000) found in a comparison of 19 countries that students in Australia, Austria, Germany, Italy, Luxembourg, Morocco, Spain and Thailand started studying world languages by age eight. Students in other countries, such as the Czech Republic, Finland, Canada, Denmark, Israel and the Netherlands, were offered world language classes in upper elementary grades. In the same study, the authors found that most students in the US did not start studying world language until age 14 even though the number of early language programs in the US had been increasing at that time in the early 2000s (Pufahl *et al.*, 2000; see also Commission on Language Learning, 2017).

A comparison with European countries can offer a perspective on some of these differences. Although the age at which students begin to study a world language varies in these countries, it is notable that this guideline has most frequently been governed and regulated by the national government, not left to local or regional governments to decide (Devlin, 2018). Recall that 19.66% of students in the US in 2014–2015 were currently enrolled in a world language class (ACIE, 2017); this overall number contrasts with the 92% of European students who were learning a language in 2018 (Devlin, 2018). English is currently the most studied language in Europe, followed by French, German, Spanish and Russian. Additionally, more than 20 countries in Europe have required students to study a second world language for at least one year (Devlin, 2018). Although no data are available to measure the frequency with which students study a second world language at the K–12 level in the US, there are no recorded mandates at the federal, state, or district level that require this of US students.

In China, a national policy for English education was instituted in 2001, called 'The Ministry of Education Guidelines for Vigorously Promoting the Teaching of English in Primary Schools' (Hu, 2007). In this policy, all Chinese students in the country were required to begin English study in the 3rd grade, following the general belief among government officials that earlier is better. However, this policy was seen in many ways to not be successful, largely due to the top-down imposition of instruction in some cases where the resources needed, notably qualified teachers, were not available to implement the change (Li, 2017). This perspective offers an interesting implication for US WL education, where, as already shown, there is a critical lack of qualified WL teachers to carry out policies that have already been put in place.

Countries and regions that were colonized by Western imperialists have socially, culturally and politically different relationships with the teaching of languages than do countries that were the colonizers. One example can be found in the countries of the Middle East and North Africa (Al-Khatib, 2008). Where rules about what languages could be taught and spoken in schools shifted considerably during and after colonial presence, modern WL study has tended to focus both on the local languages and the international language of English (Al-Khatib, 2008). In Jordan, English study has been compulsory for all students in elementary and secondary schools. Other languages like German and Italian, however, have not been found as much in instructional contexts in schools. Multilingualism is much more common in many of these countries, for instance, in Tunisia, where students might enter university study with fluency in standard Arabic, Tunisian Arabic, French and English (Al-Khatib, 2008).

Although this brief overview does not include data about parts of the world such as sub-Saharan Africa and South America, it is evident that the US is a clear outlier in terms of the amount of world language instruction at the K–12 level compared with many countries in the world. The teachers in this study, teaching Spanish, French, German and Chinese in Iowa, clearly might have experienced their jobs differently from teachers of the same languages in other countries.

Looking to the Future

National goals for US K–12 world language education

There has been a call for increased world language education in the United States for many years, from many different governmental, educational and non-profit institutions. In a 2012 policy memorandum written by the Council on Foreign Relations, a nonprofit think tank specializing in US foreign policy and international affairs, several leaders in the field made the argument that the promotion of world language instruction 'should be a national priority' (Wiley *et al.*, 2012: 1). They articulated that the US does not offer enough language instruction to meet important national economic, military and diplomatic needs, an argument repeated by many prominent organizations and scholars (e.g. ACTFL, 2010a; Commission on Language Learning, 2017; Met & Brandt, 2017). Furthermore, the authors stated that the languages taught in US K–12 schools did not match the 'fastest-growing foreign markets' (Wiley *et al.*, 2012: 2). Where Spanish has been by far the most common language taught and learned in US K–12 schools, languages such as Portuguese and Hindi have been severely underrepresented in world language programs. Even Chinese, the authors argue, although corresponding to one of the world's largest economies, has rarely been taught in US K–12 schools (Wiley *et al.*, 2012).

Much of the rhetoric and the principles circulating around the need for world language study in the US have focused on concepts like addressing migration, the global market and national safety. ACTFL, in a 2010 publication titled *Foreign Language Enrollments in K-12 Public Schools: Are Students Prepared for a Global Society*, stated: 'economic, military, and humanitarian needs require a multilingual population that begins with foreign language education throughout grades K–12' (ACTFL, 2010a: X). To do this, the publication's three recommendations for the development of foreign language education were to set standards to make US students competitive with other nations, to enroll students in foreign language classes as early as possible and to get more opportunities and resources for that learning (ACTFL, 2010a).

Similarly, Brecht (2007) stated that a national language policy in the US should target three main goals:

> (a) an educated citizenry aware of the role of language and culture in the world and in human cognition, (b) a broad base of school graduates with functional foreign language skills, and (c) a cadre of advanced language specialists capable of the highest level of linguistic and cultural performance. (Brecht, 2007: 264)

This focus on developing graduates with skills, awareness and specializations echoes some of the 1960s rhetoric in the US around supporting language study to compete with the Soviet Union. When speaking about

K–12 language programs, Brecht (2007) also suggested that those programs should focus at the K–8 level on 'receiving an appreciation of the role of language and culture in society' and to 'launch language careers of selected students', with a continuation of those goals at the secondary level (Brecht, 2007: 264).

In the last decade, goals such as global competence have entered the discourse among world language teachers in the US. ACTFL's publication of a Global Competence Position Statement in 2014 identified five needs associated with communicating with someone of a different language or culture, including the need in the global economy, the need in diplomacy/defense, the need in global problem-solving, the need in diverse communities and the need in personal growth or development (ACTFL, 2014). The latter two needs, focusing more on connecting with others and developing individual skills, offer a counterpoint to the prevailing goals of language study as focusing on economic, political or diplomatic advantages for society.

The goals of creating a multilingual, multicultural, globally competent populace through world language education has been inconsistent in its consideration of the linguistic diversity already present in US society. HLs, for example, have sometimes been invisible in how these goals for world language learners were framed, with little consideration given to how they might leverage their own knowledge and cultural backgrounds in their contributions (Bale, 2014; Carreira & Kagan, 2017; García, 2014; Wang & Green, 2008). As the Council on Foreign Relations articulated, 'Even though bilingualism/multilingualism is widespread in the US, it must be nurtured and cultivated. It cannot be considered an obstacle, but rather must serve as a resource that needs to be properly utilized' (Wiley *et al.*, 2012: 21).

Key tensions thus exist prominently in the discourse surrounding the goals of world language education in the US. First, there is a mismatch between school offerings, US domestic education policy and the exigencies of international markets and governments. The decentralization of policy related to world language education in the US has reduced the ability for educational systems to be responsive to national needs in world language education, in the form of offering the languages most in need in the country. Secondly, the instrumental reasons of diplomacy, economics and military security contrast with some of the ideals of intercultural competence and understanding of others that can also be centered in the goals of language learning. Finally, world language education is often characterized as a way of enriching a monolingual English citizenry, but the reality of HLs and other multilinguals has been shown to be vital to consider. These tensions play out in the classrooms of K–12 world language teachers, as this study's investigations will show.

'Who gets to play?'

> In order to provide greater access for all U.S. students to become bilingual and bicultural, we must continue to examine the institutional and individual policies and practices that make world language study open to only a select group of students. (Glynn & Wassell, 2018)

In their article 'Who Gets to Play? Issues of Access and Social Justice in World Language Study in the United States', Cassandra Glynn and Beth Wassell explored the evidence that, in world language education in the US, many students are systematically excluded from study (Glynn & Wassell, 2018). As previously shown, in contrast to other parts of the world, the US has positioned world language learning as a largely voluntary enterprise for elementary and secondary students (Met & Brandt, 2017). In some cases, especially in lower grades, students do not have the opportunity to learn a world language in public schools. In other cases, world language education is completely optional, with students able to complete all their K–12 education without ever studying another language.

Then the question becomes, who gets to be in these classes? A component that has been notably absent in many discussions of today's world language program policies and enrollment is the identities or language backgrounds of the students in those classes. One source of such data was gathered by the National Center for Education Statistics, which looked at average high school credits earned in foreign language in 2013. Their study revealed that Asian students earned more credits in foreign language (2.4 credits) than white students (1.9 credits), followed by Hispanic students (1.8 credits) and Black students (1.6 credits) (de Brey *et al.*, 2019). Similar data have been collected in previous years from K–12 contexts (Glynn & Wassell, 2018). Considerable evidence from studies of world language programs has suggested that students from minoritized groups, especially Black students, have often been advised out of pursuing study in a world language (Anya & Randolph, 2019; Baggett, 2016; Glynn, 2012; Glynn & Wassell, 2018).

Furthermore, students in rural and low socioeconomic status (SES) schools have been shown to have fewer opportunities to take world language courses (Pufahl & Rhodes, 2011). Students with Individualized Educational Plans (IEPs), students who were struggling with the language and English learners (ELs) were often excluded from the world language programming. In Massachusetts, Ritz and Sherf (2012) found that the exclusions commonly happened at the middle/junior high school level.

In examining paths forward into the future in K–12 world language study, therefore, many voices have been calling for a diversification of how students from all backgrounds are recruited, retained and cultivated in these classes. The time for world language education as the domain of the elite (Glynn & Wassell, 2018) has passed, and continued transformation in the field will hopefully lead to new access and equity for more students.

New points of hope

Before concluding this chapter with an overview of the book's structure and contents, I wish to offer two distinct points of hope in the world of K–12 world language education in the US, as represented by two new national initiatives that have enjoyed wide support with policymakers, teachers and students of world languages.

The first such initiative is STARTALK. In 2006, then president George W. Bush established the National Security Language Initiative (NSLI), designed to increase the number of people in the US who were learning languages deemed critical to national security. The STARTALK programs were one outcome of the NSLI. These programs had the following three goals for language education in levels K–16: increase the number of students enrolled in the study of those languages; increase the number of highly effective teachers of those languages; and increase the number of highly effective materials and curricula in those languages (Ellis, 2016; Ingold & Hart, 2010). STARTALK programs take place in the summer across the US, as supplementary programs with considerable latitude for implementation (Ingold & Hart, 2010). In its first year, 2007, 34 programs in Chinese and Arabic were implemented across the US. By 2014, 90 student programs and 56 teacher programs received funding in 11 languages (Arabic, Chinese, Dari, Hindu, Korean, Persian, Portuguese, Russian, Swahili, Turkish and Urdu) (Ellis, 2016).

The documented outcomes of participation in the STARTALK programs from 2007 to 2019 have suggested that the programs were effective in encouraging long-term study of critical languages and development of appreciation of other cultures (NFLC & NSA, 2020a). Evidence from the teacher education programs has suggested that most of the teacher participants were native speakers of the languages that they sought to teach. After participating in a STARTALK program, many of the teachers sought certification and further qualifications to teach their critical language, and many participated multiple times in STARTALK programs (NFLC & NSA, 2020b). Further, the teachers reported an improvement in their teaching techniques and approaches from their participation. Importantly, the goals of STARTALK in recent years have been to expand it to areas and populations in the US that might not normally have access to the study of critical languages. STARTALK has been a strong force in the US in encouraging the study of critical languages, both in inspiring students and in educating teachers.

The second initiative is the Seal of Biliteracy (SoBL). Offered in 49 states in the US and the District of Columbia, the SoBL is a high school graduation credential designed to recognize students who have reached high levels of language proficiency in English and one or more other language. The movement began with legislation in California in 2011 that established the SoBL in the state, and every year has seen new states adopt the SoBL. Most states have instituted the SoBL through the efforts of grassroots movements led by the language education community, followed either by legislation that was approved by the state governor, policy resolution that went through the state board of education or policy resolution that went through the state department of education (Heineke & Davin, 2020). The criteria for earning the SoBL and verifying students' language proficiency vary from state to state. Most criteria require students to provide evidence of their attainment of the state-designated level of proficiency via a standardized test or graded portfolio (ACTFL *et al.*, 2020; Black *et al.*, 2020; Heineke & Davin, 2020).

The SoBL is rooted in a collaboration between the world language, bilingual and English learner (EL) teaching communities. Where some state and local schools and districts have emphasized the world language students as recipients of the SoBL, others have focused more on bilingual or HLs as well as English learners (Heineke & Davin, 2020). Issues of equity in access to the SoBL have been debated in the scholarship, with important questions raised about how the SoBL can best be used to honor all multilingual students, not just those who learned a world language (Heineke & Davin, 2020). However, the SoBL has the potential to move world language education in the US to an even clearer focus on proficiency, to raise the visibility of world language education and to affect public opinion about the value and benefits of bilingualism in the US (Davin & Heineke, 2017).

In Iowa, the SoBL was voted into law in April 2018, at the same time the data for this study were being collected. Therefore, as mentioned above, the teachers were aware of this recent change in the field and the possibilities that it represented for their students and their programs. Indeed, the next year, in spring 2019, 775 high school seniors in Iowa were awarded the SoBL from districts across the state (Black *et al.*, 2020). The SoBL, thus, is another point of hope for the continued development of and focus on proficiency in K–12 WL education in the US.

Overview of the Book

Purpose and aims

This book tells the stories of 15 different WL teachers in the US at the elementary and secondary levels (K–12) through rich descriptions of their lived worlds and experiences. By incorporating interviews with teachers with extensive observations, learner interviews and document and environment analysis across 15 distinct contexts, the study investigates in detail (1) how teacher beliefs relate to their practices and (2) how that relationship is mediated and moderated by their learners, institutional demands, equity and access to WL education and other factors.

The chapters provide a deep, rich and robust explanation of individual teachers' teaching lives as well as a cross-contextual comparison of their experiences. Above all, this book aims to contextualize and situate WL teachers and learners in real environments, embedded in the realities and demands of modern US schools. Grounded in the research literature about language teacher beliefs and cognition (e.g. Borg, 2003), this book takes the stance that all teaching is situated and contextual, and that teaching about methods, practices and knowledges in ways that are divorced from their setting and environment has serious limitations (Farrell & Guz, 2019; Wesely *et al.*, 2021).

With several possible applications, this book offers insights to researchers, teacher educators and pre-service and in-service teachers. WL teachers at the K–12 levels in the US are understudied, and their stories are often difficult to access for individuals outside of their schools. However, what happens in those classrooms is key to understanding how individuals learn world languages in the US today. Although this book is not intended to evaluate the success of the teachers' instructional practices, their stories serve to illustrate a variety of ways to approach language instruction in context. As a work of research, the book offers qualitative description, trace connections and identification of patterns across contexts to provide a credible, transparent and trustworthy analysis of how WL teachers make their decisions and enact their beliefs in the classroom. As an aid to teacher development, it gives readers a structure to reflect on current and former experiences in teaching and learning languages. For all readers, this book illustrates the diversity as well as the shared characteristics among WL teachers, identifying and describing the US K–12 WL classroom today.

Structure of the book

The second chapter of this book continues the introductory material from this chapter, focusing on establishing the theoretical background of the book with an explanation of key concepts like teacher beliefs, the relationship between teacher beliefs and practices and how learners and institutional factors have been shown to mediate that relationship. I review the scholarship about these issues as investigated in other works of research in the field. The second section of the chapter describes the research methods used throughout the book, providing a comprehensive overview of the setting, participants, data sources, data collection procedures and data analysis procedures.

Chapters 3 through 7 of the book present the case studies of teachers and classrooms, organized according to their contexts and languages.

First, in Chapter 3, I focus on elementary and middle/junior high school WL teachers, including a Spanish teacher from Latin America who taught in a private urban K–8 school; a US-born Spanish teacher who taught both heritage and non-heritage Spanish classes in a public middle school in a large urban district; and a US-born French teacher in a smaller urban district who divided her time between teaching courses at the junior high school and the high school.

In Chapter 4, I investigate the experiences of teachers in four districts who are 'singletons', meaning that they were the only WL teacher in their school and district, usually teaching at least levels 1–4 at the high school level. All four districts were small and rural, with a student body between 90% and 95% white and US-born, with English as their first language. All of these teachers were US-born native English speaking Spanish high school teachers. In Chapter 5, I examine the world of three Spanish teachers in small to mid-sized WL programs, where they were not the only teacher in the district, but where they only had a few colleagues and no other world languages offered in the district. In Chapters 6 and 7, I describe the teaching lives of teachers of Spanish (Chapter 6), French, German and Chinese (Chapter 7) in large world language high school programs. These teachers worked in programs in large high schools that featured multiple languages, and their classes and students were diverse in their racial, socioeconomic and linguistic backgrounds. Chapter 6 addresses the complexities of teaching HLs alongside non-HLs; Chapter 7 also addresses different issues surrounding teaching and advocating for languages other than Spanish in the US.

Chapter 8 offers a summary of all 15 school settings presented throughout the book, revisiting and restructuring their presentation in order to provide new insights. A synthesis of the findings and their contributions to research on teacher beliefs and practices is provided. A substantive section summarizing the implications for practitioners at all levels of WL education and WL teacher education is the culminating point of the chapter.

Every chapter will conclude with a reference section as well as a short set of discussion/reflection questions designed to guide you in thinking through how the readings connect with your own practice, interests and context. These questions offer insights whether you are a member of the research community, a graduate student in language education or applied linguistics, a university language educator or a K–12 pre-service or in-service WL teacher.

Questions for Discussion and Reflection

(1) How does the information in this chapter conform to what you already know about K–12 WL education in the US? Did any information surprise you?

(2) What do you see as the biggest challenges facing K–12 WL education in the US?

(3) What would you recommend to policymakers, scholars or other leaders in the language education field to address the challenges to K–12 WL education in the US?

(4) If you are based in the US, how do the policy and enrollment patterns in Iowa compare with where you are? If you are based outside of the US, how do the policy and enrollment patterns in the US compare with where you are?

(5) What goals do you have as you read this book?

2 Studying the World Language Classroom

This chapter has two main parts. In the first section, I establish the theoretical background of the book with an explanation of key concepts like teacher beliefs, the relationship between teacher beliefs and practices, and how learners and institutional factors have been shown to mediate that relationship. I review the scholarship about these issues as investigated in other works of research in the field. In the second section of the chapter, I describe the research methods used throughout the book, providing a comprehensive overview of the settings, participants, data sources, data collection procedures and data analysis procedures.

Theoretical Background of the Book

Sociocultural perspective

A substantial body of scholarship on language teacher beliefs has focused on characterizing and categorizing those beliefs in general (e.g. Gatbonton, 2000; Horwitz, 1985), as well as in relation to specific topics, for instance, curricular standards (Allen, 2002), effective teaching (Bell, 2005) and the English language (Pan & Block, 2011). I would argue that many of these studies are at their heart cognitivist, focused on characterizing beliefs as the result of internal processes and complex mental lives (Gabillon, 2013). This book examines language teacher beliefs from a sociocultural perspective (Borg, 2019; Gabillon, 2013; Johnson, 2009). In this, I am considering these beliefs as social and situated in specific contexts. I explore beliefs as 'contextually situated social meanings emerging in specific sense-making activities' (Negueruela-Azarola, 2011: 369). I see beliefs as inextricably linked to action; actions both guide and influence beliefs (Barcelos & Kalaja, 2013).

This study examines the connection between teacher beliefs, teacher practices and how that connection between belief and practice might be mediated by other contextual factors, such as learners and institutions. I thus adopt the perspective of Borg (2017), who stated:

> Social perspectives on the study of teacher cognition argue that teachers' beliefs and practices are socially and historically constructed and dynamic and that it is not possible to adequately understand them without reference to interactions the teacher has with students, colleagues,

professional learning, and institutional structures more generally over time. (Borg, 2017: 88)

As such, Borg argued that considering beliefs as separate from practice is problematic. Other scholars, like Negueruela-Azarola (2011), have agreed, suggesting a dialectical view that identifies beliefs as transformative and not metacognitive. In this view, beliefs and actions have to be considered together, and instead of focusing on a mismatch between beliefs and actions, scholars should engage with 'conceptualizing beliefs and their contradictions as ideas that emerge in the very act of making sense of actions: beliefs-in-action-on-actions' (Negueruela-Azarola, 2011: 361). Burns *et al.* (2015) similarly called this view on teacher cognition as 'situated, dynamic, mediated, and inherently complex, [shifting] us toward a complex, chaotic systems ontology' (Burns *et al.*, 2015: 597).

In this review of the literature, I examine what is known about teacher beliefs in the literature from this sociocultural, dialectical perspective. After further reviewing some of the conceptual framing of teacher beliefs, I identify the main components of the relationship between teacher beliefs and practices. Finally, I synthesize the literature about the relationship between teacher beliefs and learner beliefs and between teacher beliefs and institutional influences.

Teacher beliefs

As Borg (2006: 35) has argued, the field of teacher cognition is characterized by an 'overwhelming array of concepts', including but not limited to teacher beliefs, knowledge, mental constructs and other psychological labels (see also Barcelos & Kalaja, 2013). I primarily focus on teacher beliefs in this book, for which I use this general definition: 'attitudes and values about teaching, students, and the education process' (Pajares, 1993: 46). Furthermore, in this book, teacher beliefs are considered to have several key characteristics (Barcelos & Kalaja, 2013; Barcelos & Ruohotie-Lyhty, 2018; Borg, 2017). I review those characteristics in this section.

Teacher beliefs are dynamic

In this component of beliefs, I hold that beliefs are 'subject to change over time in response to experience', as Borg (2017: 85) has stated. As shown above, the sociocultural perspective on teacher beliefs and cognitions unequivocally prioritizes the complexity and dynamism in the consideration of those beliefs (Burns *et al.*, 2015).

Teacher beliefs can be identified as either core or peripheral

Just as beliefs might change over time, they also might overlap, contradict and relate with one another in different ways. Some beliefs might be more frequently embodied in practice (core beliefs), while others might have less influence and be less consistently connected to practice (peripheral beliefs) (Borg, 2017). Teacher beliefs can thus be characterized as a system of beliefs, including subsystems. Core beliefs can be characterized as 'deeper' and 'more general' (Phipps & Borg, 2009: 387), or 'based on tried and true, concrete, dominant activities' (Oranje & Smith, 2018: 326). Peripheral beliefs might be more easily changed in the face of student or contextual pressures (Phipps & Borg, 2009) or are 'new, abstract, and not well-supported' (Oranje & Smith, 2018: 326; see also Watson, 2015a). This component of teacher beliefs conforms with the sociocultural perspective on beliefs, insofar as the nature of core and peripheral beliefs can only be seen when considered with teacher practice in their specific context.

Teacher beliefs are connected to emotion

Many scholars have described the relationship between beliefs and emotions as being reciprocal and mutually constitutive, with emotions shaping beliefs and beliefs giving rise to emotions when enacted in the classroom (Barcelos & Ruohotie-Lyhty, 2018). Like beliefs, emotions are contextual, embedded, complex and dynamic (Barcelos, 2015). Often categorized as a part of the affective domain in applied linguistics research, emotions can be behavioral, physiological, phenomenological, cognitive and social. Some examples include anxiety, motivation, nervousness, boredom and introversion and extraversion (Barcelos, 2015). Emotions are experienced as feelings that guide individuals, relating intimately with practices and actions in the classroom. In this study, emotions will be addressed as they are expressed by the teacher participants, often in relation to their beliefs but sometimes just as a way of understanding their experiences and thoughts.

Teacher beliefs are connected to their identities

Similarly, identity and beliefs have often been intertwined, with beliefs contributing to how teachers have articulated their identities (Barcelos, 2015, 2017; Barcelos & Ruohotie-Lyhty, 2018). Language teacher identities are both internal and external to the individual teacher, contested and harmonious, hybrid, changeable and dependent on social and material interaction with others (Barkhuizen, 2017). In part of his comprehensive definition of language teacher identity, Barkhuizen (2017: 4) explained that language teacher identities are 'cognitive, social, emotional, ideological, and historical', and, within the cognitive component, are connected closely to 'teachers' beliefs, theories, and philosophies about language teaching'. The scholarship of Kubanyiova and Crookes (2016: 124) has presented the 'identity-relevant vision' of teachers as grounded in teacher beliefs and knowledge, and yet more influential than them as well. The current study's focus on the relationship between teacher beliefs and practices thus potentially can offer some insights about the nature of language teacher identity.

Farrell (2017: 184) conceptualized a professional teacher role identity that comprises 'the different roles and activities that language teachers play or are asked to play while they carry out their duties'. This type of identity role is thus particularly relevant to the study at hand, as it relates specifically to the job and classroom practice. A study by Flores and Day (2006), for instance, found that the interaction between beliefs and practices often made new teachers reconsider their own professional teacher identities. In this study, the aspect of professional teacher role identity that relates to the participants' beliefs is explored as it emerges in the data. Other aspects of teachers' identities, for instance, their histories as teachers and language learners and their linguistic and cultural backgrounds, is similarly addressed as the teachers referenced them.

Teacher beliefs are socially constructed

Out of these five components, this one is perhaps the least studied in the context of teacher beliefs; Borg (2017: 85) has suggested that this area 'merits much more attention'. Teacher beliefs are seen here to not just come from training or prior experience, but also to continue to be influenced by social groups and communities (Borg, 2017). The nature and membership of these social groups and communities is a major part of the inquiry in this study. The participant teachers often spoke about their belonging in online communities and connecting with other teachers at conferences, so this component is certainly relevant to this investigation.

Teacher beliefs and practices

The relationship between language teacher beliefs and teacher practices has been described across contexts and teaching approaches as being complex, discrepant, contradictory and unclear (Assen *et al.*, 2016; Basturkmen *et al.*, 2004; Farrell & Bennis, 2013; Farrell & Guz, 2019). These studies have examined topics as varied as pronunciation (Baker, 2014), focus on form (Basturkmen *et al.*, 2004), grammar instruction (Phipps & Borg, 2009; Watson, 2015b) and communicative language teaching (Rahman *et al.*, 2018; Woods & Cakir, 2011). Breen *et al.* (2001) suggested that even shared beliefs by teachers in the same context might lead to different practices.

This is not to say that language teacher beliefs and practices have never been shown to align. Several notable in-depth studies of individual teachers have shown a connection between the teachers' beliefs and practices. For instance, Farrell and Ives (2015), in a study of one second language teaching teacher, found that his beliefs were largely aligned with his practices. The authors attributed this coherence to the teacher's consistent use of reflection. Farrell and Yang (2019) also found in a case study of one teacher that her beliefs and practices overall were aligned, with only minor instances when the influence of the teaching context required her to shift her focus. Watson (2015b), in investigating one teacher's grammar beliefs, found that the teacher was able to align the beliefs and practices particularly when she reflected on her practices in retrospect, thinking about what had already happened in her classroom.

Many studies have examined how contextual factors play a role in the complex and contradictory relationship between language teacher beliefs and practices. Some have argued that the contextual constraints in a given context consistently influence, mediate and mitigate the relationship between teacher beliefs and practices (Basturkmen, 2012; Borg, 1998, 2003, 2017; Farrell & Bennis, 2013; Farrell & Guz, 2019; Farrell & Lim, 2005; Farrell & Yang, 2019; Mason & Payant, 2019). Two of these primary contextual constraints have been shown to be learners and institutions (Wesely *et al.*, 2021). In the next section, I review what the research has shown about these two mediating factors between teacher beliefs and practices.

Mediating and moderating factors

Learners and learner beliefs

The study of learner beliefs has been primarily depicted as vital to an understanding of the language learner and their internal processes, what Kalaja and Barcelos (2019) explained as 'a more complete picture of the language learner and his or her learning' (2019: 6). Studies about learner beliefs have related those beliefs, for example, to learner motivation and reasons for taking a class (Gabillon, 2007); learner socialization in becoming members of specific communities (Kalaja *et al.*, 2017) and learner beliefs about language in general (Pan & Block, 2011). Although the studies have depicted learner beliefs as being influenced, created and coconstructed in their environment, the scholarship has tended to focus on learner beliefs as being influenced and not influential, as affected by (teacher) action and not as affecting action (Kalaja & Barcelos, 2019; Kalaja *et al.*, 2017). Learners and their beliefs are acted upon and are not actors in much of this research, suggesting a potential gap that merits some further exploration.

A significant body of literature has identified the frequent existence of a mismatch or tension between teacher beliefs and learner beliefs in the language classroom (e.g. Barcelos & Kalaja, 2013; Bernat, 2008; Brown, 2009; Gabillon, 2012; Hawkey, 2006; Kumaravadivelu, 1991; Mackey *et al.*, 2007; Wan *et al.*, 2011; Weibe & Kabata, 2010). Some mismatch studies have focused on specific components of the language classroom and how teachers and learners have viewed them. However, not all studies in all contexts have consistently identified the presence of a mismatch between teacher and learner beliefs (Griffiths, 2007; Kern, 1995; Pan & Block, 2011). These studies, like the mismatch studies, have focused on specific components of the language classroom or about language learning in general. An example is Pan and Block's 2011 study of teachers and learners of English in China, who expressed similar beliefs about the English language. Although this book is not specifically investigating the relationship between learner and teacher beliefs, it is important to recognize that learner and teacher beliefs are identified in the literature as often being interrelated and even in tension.

As such, learners and their beliefs are an important part of the context of language teaching, one area that will be explored in this study. As mentioned above, in the studies that look at teacher beliefs and student beliefs, the predominant focus has been on how teacher beliefs influence or do not influence learner beliefs. As Bernat (2008: 8) stated, 'while much has been reported on the nature and strength of learner beliefs, less has been said about their actual impact in the classroom and beyond'. Some studies have made a general claim that learners affected teachers but have not focused on presenting substantive data to that effect (e.g. Baker, 2014; Barcelos & Kalaja, 2013).

Other studies have presented evidence that teachers were affected by learner characteristics or behaviors. Teachers have been shown to be affected in their practice by their desire to build positive relationships or otherwise promote good behavior among students. In these studies, scholars documented that when certain tasks produced negative interactions, even if they conformed to the teachers' beliefs, the teachers avoided them (Borg, 1998; Breen et al., 2001; Farrell & Bennis, 2013; Gatbonton, 2000). Another common factor that mediated the relationship between teacher beliefs and practices was student performance (Borg, 1998; Farrell & Bennis, 2013; Farrell & Guz, 2019; Gatbonton, 2000; Graden, 1996). These studies demonstrated that teachers made decisions for their instructional practices based on what helped their students to meet their academic goals. Finally, a few studies identified specific student characteristics as affecting teachers' instructional decisions, for instance, teachers' interpretation of the students' maturity (Breen et al., 2001; Farrell & Guz, 2019).

Teachers have also been shown to be affected by their interpretation of how learners were experiencing their teaching and their class. Similar to studies that showed that teachers changed their teaching when students responded negatively, Kennedy and Kennedy (1996) documented the 'power' that learners could have in an educational context, and that 'power can override teachers' positive attitudes towards a change' (1996: 356). Phipps and Borg's (2009) study about teacher beliefs and grammar presented a strong argument about how teachers were influenced by students. As they presented in one section:

> The tension in the teacher's work was between ideal and actual ways of teaching grammar; she approached grammar through exposition not because she felt this was ideal but because she felt it was what her higher level students expected. . . . [Another teacher's] perceptions of students' expectations here seemed to be overriding his beliefs about how best to teach grammar. (Phipps & Borg, 2009: 384)

Thus, these researchers identified learners' expectations as being key factors in how teachers' beliefs about the best teaching techniques transformed in context. Kim (2011) found that teachers often consciously recognized learner beliefs, learning experiences and expectations. Those observations sometimes resulted in teachers consciously imposing their convictions on learners, but at other times, the teachers were shown to adapt to accommodate learners, even when their own beliefs did not change. Nishino (2012) found in quantitative data about teacher beliefs and practices that 'Student-Related Communicative Expectations' directly affected classroom practices, a finding that was supported by her qualitative data, which also showed that teachers regularly thought about their students' conditions and perspectives.

Johnson and Golombek (2020: 125) argued for a more ecological view of teachers' 'inner lives' that connects teacher learning and student learning. That relationship of influence should be seen as a dialectic where the two processes 'mutually shape one another'. Although, as they argued, demonstrating this relationship through research is somewhat difficult, that is what I attempt to do throughout this book.

Institutional factors

Scholars have found that another significant mediator of the relationship between teacher beliefs and practices is institutional factors. Most frequently, the scholarship has focused on institutional factors that directly impacted day-to-day classroom procedures, such as standardized curricula (Assen *et al.*, 2016; Borg, 2017; Farrell & Lim, 2005; Farrell & Guz, 2019; Farrell & Yang, 2019; Mason & Payant, 2019; Rahman *et al.*, 2018), mandatory assessments (Nishino, 2012; Pan & Block, 2011; Rahman *et al.*, 2018; Watson, 2015b; Wesely *et al.*, 2021) or the influence of teacher supervisors (Borg & Sanchez, 2020; Flores & Day, 2006; Kennedy & Kennedy, 1996; Priestley *et al.*, 2010).

As Borg (2017) argued, curricular factors have in most cases been explained in the research as a cause of inconsistencies between teachers' beliefs and their practices; they have been identified as a factor that 'limits teachers' ability to enact their beliefs' (Borg, 2017: 86). In several studies, teachers reported that their curriculum or textbooks dictated the way that they should teach, sometimes in contrast with their beliefs (Assen *et al.*, 2016; Farrell & Yang, 2015). In other cases, the time constraints imposed by a predetermined curriculum were identified as a primary factor in teachers altering their practice so that it did not reflect their beliefs. Farrell and Lim (2005: 9) found that teachers often had to plan around 'the time they perceived they would have to complete an activity as outlined in the syllabus' (see also Farrell & Guz, 2019; Rahman *et al.*, 2018).

Interestingly, the lack of curricular support was also cited in one study as an impediment to some teachers in enacting their beliefs in their instructional practices. Mason and Payant (2019) found that three English as a Foreign Language (EFL) teachers in Ukraine lacked access to the resources, in the form of textbooks, supporting materials and training, that would help them to enact communicative language teaching (CLT) effectively in their classrooms. However, these teachers believed that CLT was the right approach, and they were asked to carry it out despite the lack of support. Borg and Sanchez (2020) identified the opposite in a study of successful teachers; their access to resources helped them align their beliefs and practices. Mason and Payant (2019) concluded that 'CLT does not work in a vacuum and requires that we reflect on the realities of individual classrooms, schools, cities, and countries' (2019: 11). This work reminds us that teachers do not always have the means to enact their beliefs in their instructional practices for a variety of reasons.

Some studies, conducted in contexts with mandatory language assessments, found that teachers often felt that their practices had to conform to preparing the students for the assessments, even when those assessments did not match what the teachers believed that they should be teaching (Wesely *et al.*, 2021). Several studies described contexts where teachers were encouraged to teach and align their beliefs with CLT, but their students were to be assessed purely on their knowledge of grammar structures (Nishino, 2012; Pan & Block, 2011; Rahman *et al.*, 2018; for an example using a language teacher identity framework, see Robertson & Yazan, 2022). For instance, Rahman and colleagues (2018) found that two English as a Second Language (ESL) teachers in Bangladesh, working with a curriculum based in CLT, professed to have beliefs in line with CLT principles, but rarely actually taught according to CLT principles. The authors attributed this discrepancy to the emphasis on the high-stakes language tests, which did not measure students' communicative ability but rather focused on grammar. Although CLT was enshrined in ESL policy, the skills that it was designed to develop were not assessed, so the teachers taught according to what was tested, often contrary to their beliefs. Interestingly, in a study by Watson (2015b), the researcher identified a close alignment of beliefs and practices observed, but she attributed that in part to the lack of high-stakes tests in that particular year.

Teachers' beliefs and practices sometimes did not align due to the pressure and influence from individuals other than their students, for instance their managers or supervisors. Priestley *et al.* (2012), in a general study of teachers, found that 'quality assurance, including procedures for identifying and addressing poor performance by teachers and departments', could strongly affect teacher agency about their own classroom practices (Priestley *et al.*, 2012: 209). Flores and Day (2006), in looking at teacher professional identity, suggested that school culture and leadership strongly influenced how teachers viewed their jobs. Kennedy and Kennedy (1996), in a conceptual review of several studies on teacher intentions, saw that supervisors were an important factor. Although few studies on language teachers have looked at this directly, Borg and Sanchez (2020), in their study of three successful teachers, discovered that the teachers who trusted their managers had an easier time aligning their beliefs and practices. Some teachers in the current study spoke about the role of their supervisors and managers in their professional practice, while others did not; this area will be explored further as a potential mediator between teacher beliefs and practices.

Finally, several studies and scholars have offered counterexamples and counterarguments that suggest that institutional factors are not as important as some studies have shown. These works of research are also important to consider. For example, Borg (1998), in a study of one EFL teacher and looking at how his instructional decisions about the teaching of grammar were affected by the context of instruction, found that the teacher did not rationalize his behavior 'in terms of external forces he had no control over' (1998: 30). This idea that teachers were constrained by their institutions or contexts from putting their beliefs into practice was also contested in a literature review by Basturkmen (2012), who suggested that sometimes teachers in the studies reviewed might have been using those situational constraints as an excuse to justify their practices. Indeed, one important characteristic of many of the studies referenced above is that they are almost all case studies of fewer than three teachers, examined in depth. A study of 18 teachers by Breen and colleagues (2001) argued that teachers in the same context could be quite different in the classroom and that the diversity was greater than expected in how their beliefs related to practice. This study thus suggests that institutional context does not always mediate the relationship between belief and practice in a predicable or identical way. In this book, I look across multiple contexts to trace this relationship between belief and practice for many teachers, grouping them contextually and analyzing them individually, to search for more insights about this complex interplay.

Research Methods

The purpose of this study is to investigate in detail (1) how teacher beliefs relate to their practices and (2) how that relationship is mediated and moderated by their learners, institutional demands, equity and access to WL education and other factors. Many researchers have argued that any investigation that seeks to address teacher beliefs and teacher prac-tices must do so not only theoretically, but also methodologically and as a purposeful part of the research design (Baker, 2014; Borg, 2017, 2019; Kern, 1996). For example, Baker (2014) found that teachers' self-reports of their beliefs, knowledge and practices did not offer an accurate picture of their cognitions. Only through both self-reports and classroom obser-vation, Baker argued, was she able to see complementary information that allowed her to develop 'a sufficiently detailed picture' in her study (Baker, 2014: 155). Furthermore, as Kern (1996) argued, classroom observation is necessary to examine how beliefs appear in teachers' instructional and assessment practices, as well as how those beliefs and practices relate to students (Kern, 1996). Borg's 2019 review of 15 teacher cognition studies conducted in 2016 and 2017 found that most studies used talk as a way of addressing teacher cognition, often supplemented by observation.

The current study follows in that paradigm, with attention also paid to establishing rigor through extensive interviewing with teachers and, in some cases, students, as well as observations of multiple classes, as recom-mended by Borg (2017).

Qualitative multiple case study

Qualitative case studies, like all qualitative research, include the fol-lowing criteria, as outlined by Merriam and Tisdell (2015: 37): 'the search for meaning and understanding, the researcher as the primary instrument of data collection and analysis, an inductive investigation strategy, and the end product being richly descriptive'. Perhaps the most important com-ponent that makes a qualitative study a case study is the identification of a specific case as the unit of analysis, or the delimited object of study (Merriam & Tisdell, 2015). This study is a qualitative multiple case study, with each teacher serving as one case. Fifteen teachers in all are included in the study.

In the within-case analyses, each teacher is described fully in their context, using multiple sources of data. The teachers are also grouped in the chapters by similarity of teaching context. This allows for one type of cross-case analysis after each case is presented and described individ-ually. The last chapter of the book offers a cross-case analysis across all 15 cases. This comparative component, as recommended by Basturkmen (2012), helps the reader to move beyond description to investigate and cre-ate inferences about relationships between beliefs and practices and influ-ences like learners and contexts.

Setting

This study is set in Iowa, a state of about 3 million people in the mid-western region of the US. Iowa's education system in 2018 included 333 public school districts, with an overall enrollment of 486,264 students in 2017–2018 (Iowa Department of Education, 2018). Of these students in the state, 40.5% were eligible for free or reduced-price lunches, an indication of poverty. In public and nonpublic schools, 23.8% of students represented racial or ethnic minorities. The percentage was slightly higher in public schools, with 24.3% minority students. Of these, 10.9% identified as Hispanic, 6.2% were African American, 4.0% were two or more races, 2.5% were Asian, 0.4% were American Indian and 0.3% were Hawaiian/Pacific Islander. English learners were identified as being 6.1% of the public school population and 2.8% of the nonpublic school population. The languages spoken by these English learners in their homes was reported to be primarily Spanish, followed by Arabic and Karen languages (Iowa Department of Education, 2018).

As explained in Chapter 1, the state of Iowa has no requirement for language study at any level. About 15% of K–12 students in the state of Iowa in 2014–2015 were reported to be enrolled in a world language class (ACIE, 2017). In the 2018 Annual Condition of Education Report, 85.2% of the graduating classes of 2017 and 2018 were reported to have taken at least one high school language course at some time, with 83% having taken a Spanish class, 9% a French class, 5% a German class and 1% a Chinese class (Iowa Department of Education, 2018). These are the four languages that are taught by the 15 teachers in this study.

The schools of each teacher in the study are described in depth in each chapter as each case is presented, including more details on the student population and the location of the school. Table 2.1 offers an overview of the schools presented in each of the chapters of the book (all school and teacher names are aliases). Note that a few teacher participants taught in the same school and/or district (Toby and Gabriel in the same school with Sarah in another school in the same district; Veronica and Marlene in the same school) and one teacher taught in two schools (Evie in a junior high school and a high school).

Participants

Teachers

Of the studies reviewed in the first part of this chapter about teacher beliefs and practices, few were set at the K–12 level in the US world language classroom. Graden's (1996) study of six high school language teachers in the US is one of the few examples of a study set at this level. Most of the research related to teacher beliefs in applied linguistics has been conducted in countries other than the US, most frequently focusing on ESL or EFL contexts of study. Therefore, the setting and the participants included in this book have the potential to offer a new perspective based on context alone.

Table 2.1 Overview of participant schools organized by chapter (2017–2018 school year)

School name	Grades	School size	District size	Teacher	Language
Chapter 3: Elementary and Middle/Junior School World Language Teaching Life					
Manfred Academy	K–8	250	N/A	Calvin	Spanish
Allston Middle School	6–8	750	34,000	Sarah	Spanish
Winter Junior High	7–9	600	5500	Evie	French*
Chapter 4: The Singleton World Language Teaching Life					
Granite Hills Jr/Sr High School	7–12	300	600	Lydia	Spanish
South Fork High School	9–12	200	750	Bryanna	Spanish
Ravenwood High School	9–12	200	800	Wade	Spanish
Pioneer Secondary School	6–12	250	450	Abbie	Spanish
Chapter 5: Experiences in Small to Mid-Sized World Language Programs					
Littlerock Middle/High School	6–12	400	850	Caitlyn	Spanish
White Mountain High School	9–12	450	1600	Veronica	Spanish
White Mountain High School	9–12	450	1600	Marlene	Spanish
Chapter 6: Large World Language High School Programs: The Spanish Teachers					
Oak Leaf High School	9–12	1700	14,500	Diana	Spanish
Little Valley High School	9–12	1100	34,000	Gabriel	Spanish
Chapter 7: Large World Language High School Programs: Languages Other Than Spanish					
Winter High School	10–12	1100	5500	Evie	French*
Vista High School	9–12	1500	5300	Molly	French
Little Valley High School	9–12	1100	34,000	Toby	Chinese
Springfield High School	9–12	1500	5200	Demi	German

*Evie is included in two different parts of the book because she taught two classes at the junior high school level and three at the high school level. The nature of these classes and contexts was different enough to merit a separate analysis for each setting.

There were two groups of participants in this study: teachers and students. The teachers were the primary focus of the study, with students providing secondary information. The teachers had the following inclusion criteria:

- They were teaching half-time or more in an accredited public or private school.
- They were world language teachers, teaching languages other than English.
- They taught in Iowa.
- They taught any grade from kindergarten through 12th grade.

After obtaining preliminary permission through our Institutional Review Board (IRB), I recruited teachers for the study through four main venues.

First, I recruited teachers through personal connections. Due to my work at the University of Iowa as a teacher educator and my volunteer efforts in the Iowa World Language Association, I knew many teachers in the state. I sent the link to the recruitment materials in personal emails to many of those teachers. I contacted this list of teachers two times. Second, I contacted teachers through about four targeted tweets on my X account (formerly known as Twitter) that included appropriate hashtags that I knew were popular with state teachers (#langchat, notably). Those tweets also included links to my recruitment material. Third, I contacted teachers through the Iowa World Language Association, via its website, its Facebook announcement page, its Facebook group page and its email blast. The Iowa World Language Association sent out materials for me about three times. Fourth, I posted to other Facebook groups that targeted world language teachers in Iowa, for instance, Iowa World Language Teachers and CI in the Heartland. I posted to each of their Facebook pages about three times.

Twenty teachers who met the criteria responded to my recruitment efforts and completed the consent materials for this first step. At that point, I worked through the process to seek school or district permission to conduct research. In some cases, particularly in smaller districts, this process simply entailed notifying their superintendent or principal with a short summary of the study information. Those individuals then responded via email with their approval, and I was able to submit that to our IRB to obtain school- and district-specific approval to conduct human subject research. In larger districts, I had to undergo their internal research approval process according to directions that the district provided to me.

In two cases, I was unable to obtain this permission from the teacher's district, so those two teachers were removed from my participant list. I then returned to the other 18 teachers to secure their informed consent via email. At this point, two other teachers withdrew from the study. For one additional teacher, I was unable to schedule the classroom observations due to conflicts in our schedules. That left me with 15 teachers as my final group of participants. I obtained their written consent when I first visited their schools, reviewing the nature of the consent process and the fact that they were able to stop their participation in the study at any time. None of the 15 participants had a professional relationship with me that gave me power over them, although I had previously taught several of them either in the teacher education program at my university or in teacher workshops. Table 2.1 also summarizes the schools and languages taught by the final list of participants.

The 15 teachers who participated in every stage of this study were compensated $100 for their time and effort in the study. They were given a gift card from Amazon.com in this amount once all the classroom observations were completed.

Students

Student interviews were an important secondary source of data in this study. I conducted student interviews to access rich information about the context of language teaching for the participant teachers. As explored earlier in this chapter, learners and learner beliefs have been shown to be important factors for teachers and their decisions about practice, yet they are often subject to assumptions on the part of the teachers and researchers. In this study, I chose to interview students in order to, when possible, get a first-hand account from the other key player in the language classroom. These interviews allowed me to provide a more in-depth description of what was happening in the classrooms from a variety of perspectives, including more information on how teachers' beliefs appeared in their instructional and assessment practices and how students saw those beliefs and practices relating to them.

Students were recruited via their teachers. Once the teacher had provided informed consent to participate in the study and during my first visit to their school, I asked them to select students to participate in the study. For the students, the inclusion criteria were the following:

- They were students identified by the teacher to be good representatives of learners in their classes and to be likely to respond to participate.
- They were fluent speakers of English and did not need an interpreter to communicate with a researcher.

I asked the teacher to distribute recruitment materials to 5–10 students who met the inclusion criteria in their classes. The packets of hard-copy materials included full consent information and information about the study, including parental consent forms. The packets also included an envelope addressed to me so that, if they consented, they could send it directly to my work without the teacher knowing who they were. Of those five to ten students who received the packets, I expected that one or two would consent/assent to be interviewed at each school. I received 40 consent packets across the 15 teachers, and I was able to secure, schedule and carry out interviews with 16 students. This low response and yield rate was probably in part because the end of the school year coincided with this part of the data collection, and some students might no longer have been checking their email. Table 2.2 summarizes the student participants.

When I interviewed each student on the telephone, I started by verifying their consent to be interviewed. I described the content of the interview, and I repeated the fact that they could stop the interview or skip questions at any time. This information was already included in the parent consent document, but it was repeated individually with potential interviewees as some time had passed. The student participants were not compensated for their participation.

Table 2.2 Distribution of student participants across teacher participants

Teacher	Students
Chapter 3	
Calvin	3
Sarah	1
Evie	0*
Chapter 4	
Lydia	0
Bryanna	0
Wade	3
Abbie	0
Chapter 5	
Caitlyn	1
Veronica	0
Marlene	2
Chapter 6	
Diana	1
Gabriel	1
Chapter 7	
Evie	4*
Molly	0
Toby	0
Demi	0

*Evie did have four interviewees, but they were all from her high school and not her junior high context, so they are numbered among her high school students only.

Researcher positionality statement

The positionality of the researcher affects how research is conducted, its outcomes, and its results. It is unique to the researcher and yet is not fixed, and it affects the totality of the research process (Holmes, 2020). Thus, disclosing and addressing the positionality of the researcher is a vital part of any research enterprise. However, talking about the researcher and bringing in extensive reflective strategies to inform a statement of positionality can risk making the entire work self-absorbed (Pillow, 2003). The reflexivity required in describing one's positionality, scholars have warned, has both advantages and disadvantages (Holmes, 2020; Pillow, 2003).

I thus enter into this positionality statement somewhat warily, wanting to disclose and interrogate my own self in the work, but also wanting to avoid centering my own experiences above those of my participants.

I find myself with this work bound up in an insider-outsider positionality debate (Holmes, 2020), where I appreciate the connection and the membership to the same groups as many of my participants, but I also need to acknowledge where I am an outsider. Furthermore, I recognize that I am sharing a relatively uneventful, positive and privileged professional history where others have experienced trauma, marginalization and violence related to their identities, languages and cultures. I give tribute to my colleagues and contemporaries for whom writing a positionality statement might be profoundly difficult.

I am writing this book because I believe that the stories of K–12 world language teachers are not told enough, and they are often subsumed in applied linguistics by the stories of instructors at the postsecondary level. I see fundamental differences between these contexts, and I challenge the assumption that findings about postsecondary institutions, instructors and students can be applied easily to the K–12 context. I embrace a research process that privileges the voice of the participants and attempts to echo them as closely as possible before offering an interpretive lens on the data. I appreciate the importance of keeping stories whole and not dividing narratives into themes that then preclude individual voices from being intelligible from one another. However, I also know that identifying themes and patterns in qualitative data offers key insights. I conduct and have published qualitative, quantitative and mixed methods research, but I feel that this project requires an interpretivist lens to best highlight the voices and experiences of teachers.

I am a white, middle-class, educated, cisgender woman with English as my first language and the language that I taught (French) as my second language. I studied French across all years of my schooling, from elementary through graduate school. I learned this language in school and not in my home or community. This background fits 11 of the 15 participants in this study. This positionality gave me an insider perspective on many of their experiences.

One reason I came to this work was indeed due to my own experiences in the US as a K–12 world language teacher. I was a French teacher, primarily of students in grades 5, 6, 7 and 8 (ages 10–14) for eight years. One of those years was in Massachusetts, and the other seven were in Minnesota. Both schools were independent schools, where students had to pay to be educated; the first was a single-gender (female) school, and the second was co-ed and affiliated with the Episcopal Church. Both were relatively small with graduating classes of about 100 students, but both were located in large suburbs of major metropolitan areas. For the last three of my years as a teacher, I simultaneously took graduate courses for my doctorate in Second Languages and Cultures at the University of Minnesota. I worked during this time to marry research and practice, often being introduced to concepts in my evening classes that I was then able to put into practice in my own classroom the next day.

However, I was an outsider to the experiences of teaching in Iowa or teaching in their specific schools. Fourteen of the 15 teachers were public school teachers, which was not my familiar teaching context, although I had attended public schools K–12 as a student. Furthermore, I was working as a teacher educator and researcher at the university at the time when I was collecting data, and it had been 12 years since I had been in the K–12 world language classroom full time at the time of data collection. Many things had changed in the world language classroom, including the increased integration of technology and availability of resources on the internet. Things like cellphones and smartphones were just emerging in 2006 when I left the classroom. Although some of my students had their own laptops in my last year teaching, it was a very new phenomenon at that moment in time.

I knew many of the participants prior to data collection, and several of them had attended workshops or talks that I had given. One of the teachers had been my student in my teacher education program several years prior to the study. I believe I was viewed as an expert in the field by many of the teacher participants, both because of my work situation and my role in our state language teacher organization, of which I was at the time serving as the president. In this sense, although I may have felt that I had an insider's perspective on some aspects of their lives and stories as K–12 language teachers, they likely saw me primarily as an outsider. Additionally, this position in this study often led me to conversations where I was helping or advising the participants informally, sometimes in the form of providing resources or connections.

My own perspective on language teaching and teacher beliefs in many ways echoes the literature. Although I have strong opinions on what does and does not make good language teaching, I also believe profoundly in the existence of a post-method condition in modern world language teaching in the US, where teachers are above all responsive to their contexts in making their classroom choices. This belief comes in large part from my prior research, as in my 2021 study with Vyn and Neubauer about the post-method condition (Wesely *et al.*, 2021). Ultimately, I feel that I have been out of the classroom long enough to have been in these teachers' classrooms as an agnostic to their teaching methods, seeking only to depict the relationship between their beliefs and practices as mediated by their contexts.

Of course, my positionality has affected this project in several ways, even beyond what I have mentioned above. First, I see these teachers and their work as important and relevant to enhancing the multilingual citizenry in the US, even when the teachers are working with young, novice-level students in a midwestern state that is largely white and English-speaking. I thus attribute meaning to their actions and intentions perhaps differently than another researcher who focuses only on older or more proficient learners, or learners in more typically culturally and linguistically diverse contexts. Secondly, I identify with these teachers, and I see myself in the instructional decisions that they make, the relationships that they have with their students, and even in details like how they decorate their classrooms. I still imagine and literally have dreams about returning to the K–12 world language classroom, and I stay strongly connected with world language teachers across the state and the country. My view of the teachers is as a friend to their work. This perspective and position will certainly lead me to a less critical view of their work, and I might sometimes miss or underestimate issues, discrepancies or inconsistencies that other researchers would highlight more. The iterative structure of my data analysis is intended in part to address this.

Finally, my positionality as a white, cisgender, heterosexual, middle-class woman with a first language of English who was born and raised in a midwestern state bordering Iowa has undoubtedly affected this project. Although critical theories and critical pedagogies have long been a part of my scholarship, I know that there are things that I simply do not see due to my own privilege and perspective. I am more likely to overlook aspects of teacher and student experience that differ from my own. Again, I hope to avoid this through iteratively structuring my data analysis.

Data sources

Teacher interviews

The first type of data collected for each participant was the formal teacher interview. The main topics addressed in the formal interview included their background as a teacher, their description of their own teaching, their opinions and thoughts about teaching and their students, their ways of learning and connecting about teaching and their ways of changing or innovating as a teacher. The interview protocol (see Appendix A) also included questions about the use of technology that largely have not been relevant to the topic of this book but will be presented as needed. In the interviews, I made attempts to avoid methodology-related issues, where data collection would be impeded by teachers' unfamiliarity with terms or their difficulty articulating beliefs (Basturkmen, 2012). Instead, I asked them questions that elicited belief statements (e.g 'How do you feel that students learn language best?') or reflections on their context (e.g 'How do you know when to make changes or depart from your lesson plan?').

This formal teacher interview was accompanied by a more informal set of short conversations that took place during my day-long observations. These conversations happened during passing periods, planning periods, before or after school or during student work time; the timing was dictated by the teacher's availability and willingness to talk. These short interviews were intended to capture the in-the-moment reactions to specific observed events and to capture the attitudes and beliefs of the teacher *in situ* as they were teaching. I had a list of prompts in mind, although they often were not asked in exactly the way that they were worded (see Appendix A). In fact, most informal teacher conversations were started by the teachers, often to explain their actions or to describe their students to me. These informal interviews were not audio or video recorded.

In the text of each chapter, many quotes from each teacher are included. Unless otherwise indicated, these direct quotes are from the formal interview, as that interview was audio recorded and transcribed. Occasionally, I include quotes from informal conversations or comments made in class by the teacher; in those cases, I indicate their source.

Classroom observations

I observed each teacher for two full, uninterrupted, nonsequential days. To gain access to the K–12 schools for research, I had to schedule these days in advance. The teachers thus knew ahead of time which days and which classes I was going to be observing. This forewarning might have affected the nature of the data that I was able to collect in the observations. However, since I was observing several different classes and lessons, I believe that the observed classes were an accurate representation of the teachers' instructional practices. Having done research like this in the past, I was sensitized to moments in the classes when students seemed unfamiliar with the procedures or when they commented on the different practices. Among the 15 teachers, I rarely if ever observed moments that led me to believe that the instructional practices were not authentic.

During these visits, I observed classes taught by the teacher participant. As I observed, I took extensive notes for each class observed. A series of prompts guided my notetaking (Figure 2.1). These prompts were focused on recording events in the classroom that could characterize the teacher's

---

What does the classroom look like?

How is the class organized? Teacher-directed, student-directed?

How much target language is used?

Who is talking/communicating, and who is not?

Is the focus on form or meaning?

What communicative mode is targeted – interpersonal, interpretive, presentational?

Are students engaged, paying attention, looking at the teacher?

If there is group work, are the students doing the work?

How does the teacher interact with the students?

Figure 2.1 Observation prompts

teaching practices, the culture of their classroom and their relationships with students. My notes did not focus on individual student actions, and I only reported general information about student interaction and engagement in the observed classes. No audio or video recordings were made of the classes. I wrote my notes on paper to be as inobtrusive as possible.

I organized my notes chronologically, and I marked the time for each different major activity in each class. As the observation prompts suggested, I noted details such as the number of students in each class, the layout of the classroom furniture and, for every activity, the percentage of students who seemed engaged and the amount of the target language that was used. As a fluent speaker of French, an intermediate-mid speaker of Spanish, and a novice-mid speaker of German and Chinese, I was able to understand most of the language content in the classes that I observed. I thus noted phrases in both English and the target language when appropriate. I also wrote down phrases that the teachers said to their students that I felt had bearing on their beliefs about language learning.

During and after the visit, I collected course documents and took pictures of the walls and resources in the classroom. The documents did not include student work, and the pictures did not include people or identifiable parts of the school (like labeled schedules or student work).

Student interviews

The student interviews took place over the telephone, several weeks after I had observed their classes. This delay was largely because of the nature of the student recruitment, which required several steps after my observation days: the teacher needed to hand out the packets, the students needed to reply and mail me their consent and I needed to follow up and schedule a time. The interview protocol was adapted from other qualitative studies involving world language student interviews (Wesely, 2009, 2010; Wesely & Plummer, 2021). Even more than in the teacher interviews, I avoided using terminology like 'beliefs' or even 'attitudes', because I wanted to avoid confusing the students with specialized lingo or jargon that might mislead them about the nature of my questions. My experiences and research in interviewing adolescents revealed that they often responded differently based on how they were asked about their attitudes and beliefs, and I wanted to approach the topic from a number of perspectives and with a variety of questions (Wesely, 2009).

The student interviews had roughly four areas of questioning adapted from Wesely (2009), which in turn came from Gardner's socioeducational model (1985) (see Appendix B). The first area of questioning was a general discussion of their attitudes about language learning, largely to start with an approachable topic rather than to provide data for analysis in this study. The second section focused on having the student describe their language class, where they were asked to identify what they liked the best and least in the class, and what helped them learn the most. This section offered indirect data on how the student responded to the teacher's instructional practices. The last set of questions directed them explicitly to describe their teacher and their teacher's goals for their class, their memories of the class, and finally, a few hypothetical situations where they had to, for instance, give advice to another student entering their language class. The questions overall were intended to get students to identify their primary thoughts and opinions about learning language, focusing them to reflect on their teacher's instructional practices as much as possible as the interview continued. The interviews also helped me to identify how students might have expressed themselves and their beliefs to their teachers.

Data collection

Data collection for this study took place in spring 2018 (January–June), with a follow-up member check with each teacher conducted in spring 2019. I sent out the first messages to recruit teacher participants in late January 2018, and I received the first response a few days later. Interested teacher participants responded one by one over the next few months as I sent out repeated recruitment messages. The recruitment process, described earlier in the Participants section, lasted different amounts of time depending on the district procedures and the responsiveness of the different offices and people involved. Thus, my data collection for each of the 15 participants began at different times. Data collection across the 15 participants also differed in duration, as scheduling the observation dates was dependent on a variety of factors. The two observation dates ranged from three days to three months apart, depending on teacher preference and availability.

Obtaining responses from teachers and permissions from their districts, as well as scheduling interviews and observations, took different amounts of time, so this process was staggered over the six months of data collection. However, the process for each individual teacher was parallel. The data collection sequence is detailed in Figure 2.2.

In all cases except one, I conducted the formal interview with the teacher on the phone or via videoconferencing prior to the first observation. In that one anomalous case, I interviewed the teacher face-to-face during their school day during the first observation due to difficulties in scheduling. All student interviews were on the phone. The teacher and student interviews were audiotaped. The teacher interviews lasted between 45 minutes and an hour, and the student interviews lasted between 15 minutes and 50 minutes.

The member-check procedure took place in spring 2019, after I had conducted an initial analysis of the rest of the data. I explain that process further in the next section.

January–June 2018
1. Recruitment, permission and consent process with teacher and district
2. Teacher formal interview (one per teacher)
3. Two classroom observation days and informal teacher interviews
4. Student recruitment and consent process
5. Student interview(s) (if applicable) (one per student participant)
Spring 2019
6. Member check

Figure 2.2 Data collection sequence

Data analysis

Phase One: Data Collection and Preparation [all data]

In qualitative studies, data analysis begins with the initiation of data collection (Merriam & Tisdell, 2015). As I began data collection by interviewing the different teachers and visiting their classrooms, I allowed myself to create categories and find patterns in what they were saying to me and what I saw in their classrooms and schools. I noted these themes in the margins of my observation notes and in my notes on each case. As I proceeded with the overlapping data collection described above, where I might have visited three different classrooms in one week while also interviewing other teachers, I made connections and noted them in my informal researcher notes.

Once I had conducted the interviews, my graduate research assistants transcribed the interviews and conducted some initial analyses. Although I collected all data and was responsible for all formal analysis and writing procedures, I had several graduate research assistants who transcribed interviews, read and commented on themes in the data and helped with data organization, management and preparation. We created folders where we organized the documents, photos and collected data from each data site. I had conversations with these colleagues both during and after data collection to generate and identify patterns collectively. These initial impressions and conversations helped me as I began the process of more formal coding.

Phase Two: Descriptive Casewise Coding and Member
Checks [teacher interviews, observation notes]

The process of descriptive coding began in fall 2018, once all data collection had ended. During this time, I focused first on the teacher interview transcripts. I read through all of the transcripts and assigned descriptive codes. One body of descriptive codes was about the teachers' *instructional practices*, where they talked about how they structured their teaching and what their most common classroom activities were. I also coded for *change*, meaning where each teacher talked about change and growth as a teacher.

Additionally, during this early coding process, I looked primarily for statements or observations about or suggesting *teacher beliefs* and *influences on teacher beliefs*. For instance, if a teacher said something like 'I never teach lists of vocabulary', I would code that as relating to a belief about instruction. If a teacher mentioned a specific research study during their class, I would code that relating to an influence on their beliefs focused on research. These codes formed the basis of much of the next phase of interpretive coding.

I then looked at my observation notes for each teacher. Each set of two days of observation notes consisted of about seven pages of handwritten notes. I worked from these notes to create a narrative description of each teacher's instructional practices as I had observed them. I focused on both identifying patterns and common practices as well as example lessons and activities that illustrated their practices in more detail. I also examined my notes for informal comments that teachers had expressed during my observations that reflected their beliefs and the influences on their beliefs.

After doing this with the teacher interview and observation data, I prepared a two-page 'Teacher Summary' document to send to each of the participants. Each participant was just sent the Teacher Summary for their own case; no cross-case analysis or themes were identified. Each Teacher Summary included the following:

(1) a description of the teacher's teaching responsibilities and classroom in spring 2018;
(2) an outline of major patterns in their teaching;
(3) a summary of their beliefs and attitudes about teaching language;
(4) a summary of their expressed thoughts and observed actions about making changes;
(5) other key quotes and paraphrases (in some cases).

Part 1 was based on my notes and drawings of the classrooms and school. Part 2 was primarily created from my observation notes, but it was also influenced by what they had said during their interviews if pertinent. Part 3 included bullet points that had quotes from the interview and things they said during my observations both to me and to their students. Part 4 included both interview and observation data. Part 5 was purely quotes that I thought were interesting but did not fit into one of the other categories. I did not use the student interview data in this phase of analysis, both to preserve the students' confidentiality and because one does not have someone member check data generated by a different participant in the study.

I asked the teacher participants to read through what I had written and to react either by writing a response in an email, by setting up an appointment to talk with me, or by declining to respond. I posed the following three questions to them:

(1) Is there any place where you would interpret or state something differently from how I wrote or framed it? Where? How would you interpret it?
(2) Are there any themes or ideas that are missing from my analysis? What? Why do you think that they should be included?
(3) Are there any themes or ideas in the document that you think are unimportant, trivial, or of little effect? What? Why do you think this?

After receiving their member check documents, one participant sent me written clarification of some comments I had put in their Teacher Summary. A few other participants responded and said that they were fine with what I had written. The other participants did not respond.

Phase Three: Interpretive Casewise Coding [all data]

The next phase of the analysis entailed an interpretive casewise coding procedure. I began this phase by analyzing the student interview data for each case, as I had not looked at it in detail yet. As Table 2.2 indicates, I was not able to interview students for each teacher in the study, so not all cases included this data source in the casewise analysis.

The analysis of the student interviews began with descriptive coding, similar to the process undertaken in the analysis of the teacher data. I looked for student statements of their *beliefs about language learning and language instruction* and coded them accordingly as 'language learning belief' or 'language instruction belief'. I wrote a short comment to describe how these beliefs connected to the students' learning experiences in their classroom. Additionally, I identified places in the student interviews where I could see evidence that *teachers shared their beliefs* with the students, often by explaining or justifying their reasons for doing something in the classroom. For instance, a student might have said something like, 'The teacher always says that we need to drill the language in order to learn'. Lastly, I marked down where *students explained how they expressed themselves and their beliefs to teachers*, identifying how they said that they might have influenced the teacher or at least shared their thoughts with them.

Once that descriptive coding of the student interviews was completed, I turned to the Teacher Summaries as well as the original transcripts of the teacher interviews and the original handwritten observation notes. I considered these different documents together, using the themes and patterns that I identified in the Teacher Summaries as a key to identifying patterns across all documents. For each case, considered individually, I focused primarily on establishing (1) a clear description of teacher practices in the classroom, (2) two or three main core teacher beliefs and related peripheral beliefs, (3) the relationship between the beliefs and practices and (4) the factors that mediated that relationship. Those four areas eventually served as the structure of my reporting on each case, which can be seen in the next chapters. In referring both to the prewritten Teacher Summaries and the original raw data sources of the interview transcripts and observation notes, I allowed new themes to emerge that I might have overlooked in earlier phases of analysis. The inclusion of student interview data and descriptive coding assisted in this new look at the case. As I read through all the data sources together, I took notes in all these areas on each case. Once I had these notes, I continued to the next phase of analysis.

Phase Four: Writing Each Case [all data]

Writing is often seen as a vital step in the process of qualitative analysis, particularly when writing the narratives included in individual case studies (Bazeley, 2013; Merriam & Tisdell, 2015). Therefore, after creating my detailed casewise notes, I drafted the full, complete reports on each case. I had determined early in the process that I was likely to group the cases by contextual similarity, which the reader can observe in the structure of the chapters in this book. Although I was still focusing on a casewise analysis, I found it beneficial to write each case in order next to other cases that shared a context. During this time, I took informal notes to draw parallels among the cases, but that was not the focus of my work.

The focus of writing each case, in fact, was to craft a narrative for each teacher relating to their beliefs and practices and then, in turn, connect that narrative to some of the teacher beliefs frameworks and scholarship reviewed earlier in this chapter (Bazeley, 2013). With the notes written in Phase Three, I worked to refine my analysis to be in conversation with that other work, while considering things only on a case-wise basis.

Phase Five: Cross-Case Analysis [all data]

The cross-case analysis was the final phase of analysis. Represented in the concluding paragraphs of each chapter and in Chapter 8 of this book, this cross-case analysis identified how teachers in the same contexts (chapter conclusions) and across all 15 cases (Chapter 8) shared or did not share similar narratives about teacher beliefs and practices. To make these connections, I worked from the case reports created in Phase Four, identifying the common and divergent beliefs and practices, as well as the common and divergent ways that the relationship between beliefs and practices was mediated by other factors, including students and institutional factors. I created analysis tables that summarized each case and put each component of each case next to the others. I consulted the scholarship on teacher beliefs and practices to ensure that I was in dialogue with the field. These analyses opened this study to broader contributions to what is known about teachers and their beliefs and practices as a whole.

Conclusion

In this chapter, I have provided some important theoretical, empirical and methodological context for the presentation of the rest of the book. These foundational elements offer a starting point for the main descriptions, inferences and arguments that create the bulk of this study.

Questions for Discussion and Reflection

(1) Research gaps can be defined in a number of different ways. What is the research gap that this book proposes to address? Do you feel that the proposal is effective? Why or why not?
(2) How do the findings about teacher beliefs conform to your knowledge of world language teachers or your personal experience in your context?
(3) What do you think still needs to be studied related to teacher beliefs and practices? What are areas about which you want to know more?
(4) What are the strengths in this study's research design and/or methodology?
(5) What are the risks presented by this study's research design? What changes would you make if you were able to do so?

3 Elementary and Middle/ Junior High School World Language Teaching Life

This chapter presents three case studies of teachers who work at the elementary and middle/junior high school levels. These teachers include a Spanish teacher from Latin America teaching in an urban private K–8 school (Calvin), a US-born Spanish teacher teaching both heritage and non-heritage Spanish classes in a public middle school in a large urban district (Sarah) and a US-born French teacher in a smaller urban district who divides her time between teaching courses at the junior high school and the high school (Evie). Three other participants in the study (Lydia, Abbie, and Caitlyn) taught one or two seventh- or eighth-grade classes in addition to high school classes in their small combined junior and senior high schools; their cases will be presented in Chapters 4 and 5.

Case One: Calvin

School context

Calvin was born in Colombia and had come to the US to study biology. As he characterized it, during his first years in the US, 'the world kept pushing him' to become a teacher of Spanish, so he switched in college and got a degree in education. At the time of the study, Calvin worked at a small independent K–8 school with about 250 students in an urban area of Iowa. The school was at the end of a wooded road in a park, giving the feel of entering an oasis. When I entered the school, all four adults in the office looked at me expectantly; one knew who I was and introduced herself as a school administrator. I got the impression of a well-connected, intimate learning setting. There were many small children around, and the rooms and hallways were bright and modern with big windows looking out into the woods.

The school's demographics in 2018 included over 75% white students, with about 10% Asian students and less than 5% of all other ethnicities. The school's website advertised the fact that families at the school hailed from countries all over the world, as well as many different parts of the local urban area. As an independent school, Calvin's school did not report or provide information about free and reduced-price lunches, so there are no indicators of socioeconomic status available for the school. The school charged tuition, but also advertised the availability of tuition assistance, so few conclusions can be made about that aspect of the students' lives. Students who graduated from this school in eighth grade continued in a high school in the area, and there was no designated independent or public high school that was linked with this K–8 school. Calvin shared that in the past, students sometimes had been placed in Spanish 1 in high school because the placement tests focused on grammar, which did not conform to his proficiency-oriented approach in the classroom. However, he changed his practice in the years prior to the study so that students were more commonly placed in Spanish 2 and above when they continued in high school.

In this section, I present data from two full days of class observations, one formal interview with Calvin as well as several informal conversations during my observations and interviews with three of his students: a seventh grader, a second grader and a third grader.

Teaching environment

During the semester when data were collected for this study, Calvin taught a different schedule from day to day, for students in second through eighth grades. He saw each grade multiple times per week in a Foreign Language in the Elementary School (FLES) model where students take regular WL classes designed to build their language proficiency. He had a break midmorning every day, and he had another break for lunch. His responsibilities sometimes included supervising recess. His classes were 20–30 minutes long, and his classes contained between 6 and 16 students. Students filed in and out of his classroom on a predetermined schedule, sometimes ushered by a different teacher, sometimes independently, depending on their ages. Because he taught elementary students, he did not assign homework or give formal assessments as a part of the class. He gave informal assessments in the form of monitoring participation.

Calvin's classroom was a large, square, high-ceilinged room with cinder block walls painted white. It was decorated with a variety of posters and miscellaneous images, including posters of frequently used phrases in Spanish with pictures or English translations. As he said to me during the first observation, 'If it's on the wall, it's for a reason'. Supplies and books were on carts and shelves around the room. The student desks were in rows, facing a large whiteboard and a space where images could be projected. There were two teacher desks behind the student desks, including Calvin's desk and a desk for his partner teacher who was not often in the room during my observation days, as she taught in another classroom. When projecting images from his computer, Calvin stood or sat at his desk behind the students who were facing front, while he managed the computer and guided the discussion. There was a tall window on the left side wall covered with a large curtain, and the door was on the opposite wall.

Classroom activities

During his short time with each group of students, Calvin engaged them actively. There was a lot of energy in the classroom, and the students acted silly, giggling and wiggling around. However, Calvin was very much in control, moving around the classroom with purpose, telling stories engagingly, drawing on the board or projecting images from his computer. He made a lot of jokes and prompted a lot of laughter from students. Students felt empowered by their interactions in his class; as one student attested, 'He will teach anybody and everyone he probably ever meets that "todo es possible en la clase de español" ["everything is possible in Spanish class"]'. While remaining playful and engaging actively with his students, Calvin maintained a certain authoritative reserve, and it was always clear who was in charge and who was directing the class.

Every class that I observed was very different, in no small part due to the varied ages and developmental levels of Calvin's students, something that he explained always affected his planning. However, these activities were clearly connected by the thread of Calvin's belief that providing Spanish language input to students was most effective way to teach. As he stated, 'I think that the most effective thing for me is to tell stories in the class. And to include students' lives in the story. To ask them, and to have them help me . . . construct these stories'. At another moment of the interview, he said, 'I get up there, and I talk, and I listen to them, and we just tell stories and talk, and tell stories and talk!'. Some of the ways that he engaged students in talk included telling stories with pictures, asking the students repeatedly what was going on and encouraging them to respond in full sentences. He varied the complexity of his questions between either-or ('Is he happy or sad?'), or more complex questions like, 'What does he say?' or 'Does he want to?' or 'Why didn't she do this?'. Some of the activities involved reviewing stories that had already been told in the class, so the student answers were about recalling what they had discussed on another day. Other times, the stories and images were new to the students, so Calvin guided them more by telling them things, and then having them answer questions about what he had just said. He rarely corrected students' language throughout these activities, although he did prompt students to self-correct when the error was more pronounced.

Calvin also had his students narrate and act out stories. During these collective retells, all students participated and acted out roles while a student narrated and Calvin prompted, corrected, or, occasionally, distracted them and tried to jokingly prompt them to make errors. Many of the stories had been written together, often based on vocabulary that had been carefully selected by the teacher, which he called target structures. Very little non-targeted vocabulary appeared in these stories. One interviewee noticed this technique and praised it, saying that 'you hear that word so much in that context, that it's just kind of in your head. And so the repetition is very helpful'.

Calvin planned by writing himself small notes for lesson plans: 'We're going to focus on this, we're going to do this, it's very simple'. However, as he said, '[if] the story is leading somewhere else . . . [and] the target structures are starting to get in the way', he would not necessarily force the students to adhere to them. Calvin saw his planning as flexible, and he centered it on some general ideas rather than specific steps. The unexpressed part of his planning was the years of knowledge of young people and learners, and his innate ability to know how to sequence lessons and learning experiences without writing anything down. He was responsive to his instincts about where the collaborative 'story' was 'leading'.

The students responded positively to these stories, with one student saying, 'I like the stories so much more, they make so much more sense' following it up with the observation that the stories really '[get] into your brain'. Clearly, Calvin's work to incorporate the stories effectively into his teaching worked for this student. Another student agreed that the thing that really helped them learn was telling 'the Renata story' over and over again.

In another repeated activity, Calvin narrated a short film clip in Spanish, asking students to respond to questions about the content of the film, make predictions and react to the clip. During some of these activities, he would give students 'strikes' if they said anything in English. Calvin also had students work on big arts and crafts projects in preparation for the Hispanic Festival, which took place every spring at his school. The older students had their own laptops and were sometimes assigned short videos or exercises from a website, or they were asked to illustrate stories using online software.

Themes and patterns in teaching and connection to beliefs

Providing comprehensible input: 'I don't slow down. I speak my normal speed Spanish.'

The images decorating the walls in Calvin's classroom offered evidence of the extensive use of Spanish that characterized many interactions. There were many aides to comprehension, including posters with words in Spanish and their English translations. Calvin spoke only in Spanish with his students, except for when he directly translated individual words from Spanish to English to help with comprehension. When he did that, he often asked students to repeat the word chorally in Spanish. Overall, he stated, 'I'm focused on speaking in a comprehensible way in the classroom and on producing results, and if I stick to this, I'll hit the standards, and my students will be right in line'. I saw in my observations that Calvin clearly and consistently chose vocabulary and checked for comprehension in a way that helped me to understand everything that took place in Spanish.

Indeed, Calvin regularly included many supports for the students' comprehension of Spanish. His main goal was not necessarily to speak Spanish 100% of the time, rather, as he said, 'it's about making it comprehensible'. He disagreed with the belief that language classes need to be challenging, stating, 'I think they need to be interesting, interesting and comprehensible. These kids are acquiring language'. Calvin enacted this belief through maintaining consistent interaction with students as he looked at texts with them. Calvin checked for comprehension almost without ceasing as they read and reviewed material. He drew on the whiteboard, sometimes quite furiously, to illustrate ideas and vocabulary so that students could follow along with the stories. One younger student, who did not have a lot to say in the interview, did mention that he liked when Calvin 'stops in the stories, so to review some words that we said in the stories'. Calvin believed that pictures really helped with comprehension in a story, and they helped students translate ideas into the bigger picture of what the story is saying. There was evidence that even the youngest students agreed. Calvin would also use translation to help with clarifying vocabulary as needed.

Expecting student output: 'He teaches us to speak in the way that people from that culture speak it'

Calvin strongly encouraged his students to speak only Spanish. Even small incidental interactions (e.g commands to turn off the light) took place in Spanish. However, he was very clear that output happens after sufficient input, 'when they're ready'. Calvin connected this practice with his belief that speaking at normal speed in the target language with students prepared them for talking to people in real life. One student echoed their interpretation of Calvin's philosophy of Spanish-speaking during class: 'He doesn't want us to learn how to say it completely, absolutely perfectly . . . he teaches us to speak in the way that people from that culture speak it'. The student also attributed this quality in Calvin's teaching to the fact that Spanish was his first language, a quality that all three interviewees mentioned as important in how they saw Calvin as a teacher.

Calvin argued that the shift to output can be 'one of the hardest things' for the students. Indeed, Calvin also acknowledged that his focus on input and deemphasis on output and knowledge of grammar sometimes produced students who demonstrated fluency in immersion or comprehensible input-focused classrooms but were then placed in very low levels of language class due to the testing that focuses on grammar details or grammar terminology.

Culture: 'I didn't even think it was a cultural unit'

Calvin believed that culture was naturally ingrained in his classroom, and it did not require a set of independent objectives. As he stated:

> You know, we work a lot with culture. And I don't even realize it, you know. And I get congratulations, oh, I love this cultural unit that you're doing. And I didn't even call it culture, I didn't even think it was a cultural unit. It's just something that comes so natural to me, because it – you know.

By 'you know' here, Calvin was explicitly referring to what we had discussed at other times in the interview, specifically his status as a native speaker of the language who was raised in a Spanish-speaking country. However, there were times, notably during the preparation for the Hispanic Festival, where Calvin was explicit in his emphasis on teaching students about other cultures, primarily in the form of cultural products and practices.

In my observations, I saw that Calvin gave a few cultural notes about stories in English, especially if the cultural note required a broader vocabulary than the students knew. Students recognized this, with one saying, 'since he knows a lot of Spanish since he was . . . born in a Spanish culture, so . . . he just has like a different perspective and the way he teaches'. All three student interviewees knew that Calvin was a native speaker of Spanish and came from another country. Calvin also represented a certain belief that students were understanding and mimicking cultural aspects without realizing it, stating, 'They are producing, imitating, and unconsciously, they don't know this, they have no clue, but many are speaking Spanish with a [national] melody or accent. Kids imitate sounds and rhythms that us as adults can't'. Although events like the Hispanic Festival were important to Calvin, where activities about culture were explicit, these implicit instructional practices seemed to be closer to his overall beliefs about how culture should be taught in the elementary classroom.

Factors influencing beliefs and practices

Calvin reflected repeatedly through our conversations on how he selected his teaching methodologies through his observations of his students. He found that focusing on providing students with comprehensible input and making sure that they understood through a variety of supports helped him with classroom management: 'All of a sudden, everyone was interested'. As he stated, 'I can tell by their eyes, I can tell by their face' if they are following along. He also gauged how long to stay on a topic and how long to question them about stories or videos by whether he was 'losing them' – 'Students, you know, after a few times [asking repeated questions] . . . you start losing them'. But ultimately, he reiterated his position that he was in charge in the classroom, something which I also observed, stating that 'they don't know, they don't have a clue' about what was most effective in the classroom.

In trying new techniques with students, Calvin also observed carefully to judge if they were engaged. He was inspired and energized when he saw that his students enjoyed an activity. One example of this was using leveled readers to teach. He found that 'the engagement went woof! Incredible!' which surprised him, because it was 'just paper, a paper book thing'. But when he found that the students experienced such excitement from simply reading a book, he made reading a more consistent part of his class.

Calvin also explained that he got refreshed from working with and learning from other teachers, specifically teachers who, like him, focused on giving students comprehensible input in the classroom. His pursuit of results in his students' learning has led him to imitate teachers whose results, he found, were 'shocking' in their effectiveness. He was able to attend conferences, watch teaching demonstrations and observe teachers in their classrooms. During these experiences, he brought things back to try with his own students. It was not necessarily a matter of doing exactly what the other teachers did, but rather, 'you just try it out and see if it fits with you, and at the end, you get something that works because it's now you, it's gone through your personality, your style'. Indeed, Calvin also shared that several techniques that he observed did not fit with his own personality, notably one called 'circling', where the teacher asks a variety of questions on a specific topic, repeating targeted vocabulary. He found that technique 'very strange and boring for me as a native speaker', even though he agreed that it showed good results in other contexts. Thus, although he did find inspiration from other teachers, he considered their recommendations carefully, and indeed did not always implement them if he felt that they were not congruent with his thinking or his background.

Case Two: Sarah

School context

Sarah, a white, US-born, native speaker of English, came to teaching Spanish as a second career after starting her professional life in one of the helping professions. She spent some time as a long-term substitute teacher, then was hired in a full-time position. Sarah taught at a middle school in a large urban district in the state. The school was located in a quiet neighborhood off of a main street in a large city. The main street, a few blocks from the school, had significant commercial activity with fast-food restaurants and shops. With a large U-shaped driveway in front, the school building was low with only two floors. After entering and car-rying out a complex check-in process, I walked through the tumultuous hallways, where students jostled each other and teachers monitored very carefully in the halls. A few teachers greeted students. I heard Spanish in the hallways, and many Spanish or bilingual Spanish-English posters decorated the walls.

The school had about 750 students in grades 6, 7 and 8 (aged roughly 12–14) in 2017–2018. Just over half of the students qualified for free or reduced-price lunches in the school, and about 10% were identified as English Learners (ELs). About 25% of the students in the school were Hispanic, about 10% were Black, 60% were white and the rest were of varied races and ethnicities. Students who graduated from this middle school continued in one of the high schools in the large district.

In this section, I present data from two full days of class observations, one formal interview with Sarah as well as several informal conversations during my observations and interviews with one of her students, a 6th-grade student who was not a Spanish heritage learner (HL).

Teaching environment

At the time of data collection, Sarah taught Spanish classes on a two-day rotation ('A' days and 'B' days). Every day, she taught a combination of 6th, 7th, and 8th grade classes, including both heritage and non-heritage classes at each grade level. Additionally, the heritage Spanish classes were divided in the sixth grade between Spanish-literate and Spanish-nonliterate Spanish speakers, a separation which, Sarah explained, would no longer be made in future years. The goal for Sarah's students was to be well-prepared to start Spanish 1 (which would be a review of some of the material) or Spanish 2 when they entered the high school. Her classes were 45 minutes long, and each class contained between 15 and 20 students. She taught six classes total every day with one planning period that overlapped with lunch and a tutorial period, thus resulting in one two-hour break per day for planning, eating lunch and working with students individually as needed.

Sarah's classroom had tile floors, bright orange-red chairs and new-looking desks grouped in pods of two or three. The desk pods were lined up in three columns with a generous space between each pod. The walls were decorated with flags, words and student drawings. Well-organized buckets full of supplies lined shelving along one of the walls. There was a whiteboard in front of the room, windows along one side, and a teacher desk in the back of the room. Other small unoccupied tables were also in the back of the room.

Classroom activities

Sarah included a wide variety of classroom activities during every class, allowing students to work independently, in all-class activities and in small groups. She worked hard to come up with a variety of creative activities for her students that would still meet district goals or guidelines in her curriculum. Indeed, her instructional activities were often marked by clear differentiation for learners, and I frequently observed students engaging in different tasks to meet the same objectives. For instance, in a part of class where the goal was to review vocabulary, some students illustrated pictures individually, others collaborated and talked through creating comics, others completed worksheets, yet others read through lists of words. Sarah said that she did this to make Spanish 'attainable' to all students, hoping that she would be 'differentiating in a way that is highly effective'. In addition to language-learning activities, Sarah explicitly focused on teaching life skills, such as taking care of the classroom, working in groups, completing work and being on time.

Activities were designed to cultivate student engagement and excitement about Spanish, as Sarah was working with early adolescent students who easily lost attention or got distracted by one another or their phones. She carried out small-group activities and games designed to help students develop their comprehension of new vocabulary, such as charades, logic puzzles and running dictation (a game where a passage in Spanish was posted on the wall, and students had to run back and forth to the posted passage and tell one another what to write to 'dictate' it on their own paper). During these games, Sarah walked around the classroom, answered questions from students and kept them on task. These games kept students active, and I observed between 70% and 100% of the class engaged at any given moment.

Sarah also read books to her non-HLs, sometimes acting out the parts dramatically and using silly and engaging voices. The sole student interviewed from Sarah's classes, who had just finished 6th grade in the non-heritage class, said that this part of class was very fun, and the students '[have] a competition going on, so like who translates it first and says it first'. After listening to the story, the students filled out worksheets or completed pictures to demonstrate that they understood the story. In her heritage classes, Sarah introduced a reading in Spanish with some background information, then she assigned students to read a chapter simultaneously and discuss it. In some cases, she simply instructed the students to have silent reading time. Students in both heritage and non-heritage classes worked individually and in small groups on performance assessments like visual dictionaries that included cut out pictures and extensive labeling in Spanish, or on individual journaling that could include doodling and scrapbooking about a chapter or a reading. When students finished early, Sarah would direct them to work online to watch short videos or songs in Spanish accompanied by comprehension activities. The student interviewee explained how these varied options allowed for him to accelerate his study: 'I also was doing a separate book my teacher gave me, 'cause . . . she thought I was more advanced . . . there was a dictionary at the back that would help me out with the words. [Reading that book] helped me learn a lot'.

Sarah did not assign homework, so in-class worksheets and projects determined grades in her classes. During my observations, I saw her check in frequently with all the students in her classes to see if they had completed work correctly. If they had not, she would send them back to fix their work.

Themes and patterns in teaching and connection to beliefs

Behavior and encouragement: 'Clear expectations and high achievement goals'

Given Sarah's stated interest in teaching skills as well as language, it was not surprising that I observed her regularly correcting students' behavior during class. As she said, 'I like to be very consistent in my approach to misbehavior or success'. She prioritized being 'firm, consistent and fun' while still setting 'very clear expectations and high achievement goals for my kids'. She articulated several times that classroom management was a persistent issue in teaching, adding that teaching could be difficult due to the trauma lived by some of her students.

Sarah regularly projected warmth and support for students as she taught, even as she worked to correct their behavior and set them on paths that were appropriate for communication. As she stated, students needed to 'feel valued and . . . realize how important they actually are'. She encouraged students by having them cheer for one another, urging them to applaud by saying 'aplauso!' ['applause!']. She called students 'queridos' ['my dears/my darlings'] in both her heritage and non-heritage classes. Her support for her students was clearly felt by the student interviewee, who said that 'everybody gets along with one another, and . . . my Spanish class does really well together'. Additionally, he explained that he got the message that 'the Spanish teacher will never give up on you', and that her class was a constant 'confidence booster'. Sarah also explained that she liked being 'silly and fun' while also giving students 'a really good base of language', calling herself the 'self-proclaimed crazy charades lady when we read a structured reader or novel in class'. I observed this sense of fun in Sarah's use of silly voices, creative activities and otherwise joking with students.

Navigating HLs and non-HLs: 'Making the culture connection and personal experience to our material'

As a teacher of both heritage and non-heritage classes, Sarah navigated regularly among the diverse needs of very different groups of Spanish students. As she explained, her school often made errors in differentiating students into HLs and non-HLs, which in turn had a negative effect on the development of the heritage language program. As mentioned above, her 6th-grade heritage classes were divided into literate and nonliterate students, a distinction which would no longer exist after that year.

In her non-heritage classes, Sarah used English and Spanish in a balanced way, often translating from Spanish to English immediately after saying something in Spanish and repeating the phrase in both languages several times. She used translation to help her students to complete worksheets and other activities. She found that some of her non-HLs were not interested in Spanish, as they believed that it was not important to learn Spanish in the US. She identified this as a major struggle for a Spanish teacher. Since she found that drive and genuine curiosity made a good language student, when students discounted the importance of Spanish, they had more of a tendency to struggle in her classes.

In her heritage classes, she used Spanish more frequently, still featuring some translation into English. She implemented word games, where students could teach her 'their words' and she could 'help them through the spelling of things, and I can teach them some more formal terms if it applies to the situation'. In her plans for the next year, Sarah said that she planned to 'build the foundational level language skills' in her first-semester 7th-grade heritage class, and then her Latinx colleague who was a native Spanish speaker would teach the second-semester 7th-grade heritage class as well as the 8th-grade heritage class, where they could 'really start making the culture connection and personal experience to our material'.

Indeed, Sarah thought carefully about how she, as a white woman who learned Spanish as a second language during formal schooling, could be an effective instructor to her HLs with whom she did not share a linguistic or cultural background. She revealed that her heritage classes were sometimes a struggle for her, but that she also was able to see 'so many gains in so many aspects of their lives'. During the interview, she told a story of how the students were talking in her class one day when half of the class was on a field trip:

> They were maintaining conversations in a respectful and deep way . . . they were reflecting on their experiences as being brown. And what brown means to them. Um, because I'm not. And, they've created a safe space where we can talk about things, and I was just, I was really moved. I cried at one point.

Sarah's experience as a teacher of both HLs and non-HLs thus gave her very different perspectives on teaching and learning Spanish in the US today. Her work with HLs disrupted her ideas about what being a language teacher was, and the work caused her to think through the purpose of creating a classroom community.

Focus on goals: 'How do we help them get there?'

Sarah considered having clear goals to be a central part of her approach to teaching. She believed that it was important to define what the goals of a program were, and to be sure the teaching methods and assessments aligned with that. She incorporated competencies and standards into her classes, an act which helped her to balance and to move beyond staying in her comfort zone through repeating successful practices without altera-tion. As the student interviewee identified, Sarah offered students multiple ways to meet the same goals, but the goals were the focus. She saw her repeated efforts to connect with standards and competencies in the field as a way of pushing herself to be professional and to connect with the professional community. Overall, she stated that she wanted students to be 'ready for Spanish 1 or 2' in high school after taking her classes.

On a day-to-day basis, Sarah displayed the goals of each class at the start. I observed this in her classes, and her student noticed this practice as well, saying, 'She always tells us what we have to accomplish that day, and for the last five minutes of class, she tells us like tomorrow's plan'. She focused on language goals and not grammar patterns in planning, stating, 'We want students to be able to do [X]'. And then, she used back-ward planning to determine 'how do we help them get there'. She focused on providing comprehensible input to students, which she stated allowed her to '[value] what they have to say in class, instead of talking at them about . . . grammar'. Her belief that students learned through meaningful, impactful language that is comprehensible connected with her belief that students were more likely to acquire and retain language when they saw how it connected to their own lived experiences.

Factors influencing beliefs and practices

Sarah was a self-motivated individual who drew her energy from her belief in the power of education to be impactful and a change agent in both 'lives and systems'. As indicated above, goal setting was vital to how she approached her classes, but it was also vital to how she saw herself as a teacher. She built her goals through prioritizing reflection and self-evaluation, including receiving and incorporating input from her students. She consulted regularly with students to see what might work for them. She explained in the interview that she often asked them questions, for instance: 'How do you think this day went? Tell me, what can I do differently? Oh, this? We did not do well on this. What do I need to do differently?'. She also conducted regular self-evaluation through acts like recording herself to make sure that she varied the students that she interacted with, critically examined her classroom materials and avoided stereotypes. Furthermore, Sarah set goals for change each year. When I was observing, she shared that her goals that year were to use the whole room, to be more culturally aware and to look more at student behaviors and her responses. The next year, she thought that she would reconsider how she asked questions to her students. These goals were generated from student feedback, but also through her personal observations about her own work, which she then recorded on her own initiative in a bulleted set of journal entries.

Sarah also looked to others for support and inspiration. She conferred regularly with the other Spanish teacher across the hall, with whom she said that she shared a similar philosophy and who taught the same grades of students. As she said, 'We push and pull each other'. Although much of the two teachers' interactions occurred during their shared planning period, their relationship extended outside of the workday and the corridors of the school. As Sarah described, she and her colleague were 'constantly texting each other . . . pretty much seven days a week' and sending messages about resources they had found or things that they wanted to try. Beyond this local support, Sarah connected with teachers outside of her school via blogs, Facebook groups and the state conference for language educators. She stated:

> We all know that when we work together, and steal the great things from other people, and build on those, that's when real teaching happens. And real teaching happens cause that's also when we're learning . . . if I see something successful, I try to replicate that.

As with her own goal setting, she saw her work in teacher communities as ways to get ideas and, again, move out of her comfort zone and access more creativity. Even her use of techniques with telling stories in the classroom came from her work in social work and observing speech therapists in her previous career.

Case Three: Evie

School context

Evie, a white, US-born, native speaker of English, was in her third year of full-time French teaching at the time of data collection for this study. Evie shared her time between a junior high school and a high school in the same large urban district. In this chapter, I focus on her junior high school context; I discuss her high school context in Chapter 7. These two contexts were different enough to merit separate descriptions. Because I only observed two classes at the junior high level for this teacher, this section will be somewhat abbreviated compared to my examinations of Calvin and Sarah.

The junior high school where Evie worked included about 600 students in grades 7, 8 and 9 (ages approximately 13–15). About 25% of the students in the school qualified for assistance for free or reduced-price lunches in 2017–2018. The school was over 80% white, with about 5% each of Asian, Black and multiracial students. About 5% of the students were identified as English learners. The students in this junior high school continued to 10th grade in one of the high schools in the large urban district. The school itself was a sprawling building in a populated area in a large town, with many entrances, with a clean, well-maintained and generally positive feel. The students moved fast through the halls. Murals decorated the hallways above the lockers.

In this section, I present data from two full days of class observations and one formal interview with Evie as well as several informal conversations during my observations. Although I interviewed several of Evie's high school students, I did not interview any of her junior high students. Some of the older students' comments did inform my analysis, however, and are mentioned as appropriate.

Teaching environment

In the junior high school, Evie taught one 7th-grade world cultures exploratory class and one French language class that included both 8th and 9th graders. The classes were just under 50 minutes long, and both classes contained about 18 students. In the exploratory class, Evie introduced students to culture, society and some beginning language phrases in French, Spanish and German. This program model is often called a Foreign Language Exploratory (FLEX) model in the lower grades, in which language proficiency is not the goal and classes are taught about other languages and cultures in English. The 8th- and 9th-grade class was a French 1 class, equivalent to a French 1 class taught at the high school. The year I collected data was the first year 8th graders were allowed in the French 1 class, and five of the 18 students in that class were 8th graders. Evie reported that the 8th-grade enrollment would increase to 14 students in the class in the next year.

During her time at the junior high, Evie taught her two classes in two different classrooms. The first classroom, where she taught the exploratory class, was used primarily by an English Language Arts teacher in the school, so it was decorated and busy with English-related materials and posters. The room had rows of student desks facing the center aisle, with windows on one side. The second classroom was next door to the first one, and it had student desks in the room all facing front in rows, in a more traditional classroom set-up. There were very few decorations on the walls, and one side of the room was a row of windows.

Classroom activities

The two classes taught by Evie were quite different in their content and focus, primarily because the world cultures class featured Spanish,

French and German as the languages and cultures of focus, and the French 1 class had a stronger emphasis on the French language.

Technology featured heavily in Evie's world cultures exploratory class, because, as she said, 'I can't lead the class like I do with my French classes' because of her lack of fluency in Spanish and German. Instead, she offered the students opportunities to conduct 'independent work and investigating online' when it involved languages that she did not know. This statement was backed up by my observation, where I saw her guide students through an activity where they were able to go online to visit other countries and navigate virtually around their scenery on their laptops. Evie shifted between that type of individual work and discussions about related topics such as, 'If there are so many benefits to traveling, why do you think that some people don't visit a lot of places?'. The focus in this class was not on language acquisition, but rather on getting students to engage more generally with topics related to language and culture.

Each French 1 class began with a warm-up question in French. Students prepared their responses individually, and then Evie called on each student to respond, giving some short feedback in French to expand on their response. She corrected students when they used the incorrect French form, especially if it was targeted in the question. Her customary pattern of instruction throughout her French 1 class was to present or review a grammar rule or concept, have students practice with a set of translation questions for which they could often use their notes then check students' answers individually and then as a group. Her formative assessments, most frequently focused on grammar rules and vocabulary, included online competitive quiz games, student note taking and book listening exercises. When appropriate, she reviewed the responses and explained common errors. Homework was not a regular part of her French 1 class.

Another resource that Evie used in these introductory classes was to bring in guest speakers to respond to questions in French and English. During my observation of one of the sessions of her French 1 class, she brought in a teacher who currently worked in France to show pictures, describe her life and answer questions in French from the students about schools and teenage life in her town.

Themes and patterns in teaching and connection to beliefs

Drawing students into language study: 'New ideas to kind of hook kids'

Evie designed her two junior high school classes with the primary aim of drawing her students in to language study and 'hooking' them into learning languages while using the resources that were available to her. Although technology was a main component of these activities in general, Evie said that she resisted changing class procedures to include more technology in some cases if there was a risk of cheating or if it didn't bring anything new to the class. She reported asking herself, 'Is it just replacing something or is it enhancing it?'. In both classes (as well as in her high school classes, as Chapter 7 will show), Evie regularly used an online team quizzing game, which required students to work together to answer multiple-choice questions in competition with other groups. In the world cultures class, the questions were in English about topics like foods and restaurants in the target culture.

Some of the ways that Evie 'hooked' her students included connecting with their own life experiences and their culture(s). For instance, in her world cultures class, she asked them to look at what was 'similar and what was surprising' between a video about French food and their own experiences with food. She had them reflect on traveling and their own experiences, encouraging them to think through challenging their own barriers to travel whenever possible. In the French 1 class, she had them practice a grammar concept by asking them where their house was and having them respond. When the guest speaker came, the woman spoke primarily about schooling in her town in France, so students made consistent connections with their own experiences.

In general, Evie's work in these two junior high school classes showed a desire to engage students above all through whatever resources she had available.

Culture and language instruction as separate enterprises: 'A little bit of a taste of each of the language, culture, foods'

The two classes that Evie taught at the junior high school level demonstrated how she conceived of culture teaching and language teaching as two separate enterprises. Both classes featured a wide variety of different activities. Evie sometimes had students work in small groups, and sometimes she asked questions of them in the large group, often letting them compare or prepare with a partner before sharing in the large group. However, the learning experiences in the two classes clearly had very different objectives and learning targets. In the world cultures exploratory class, Evie's focus was squarely on making cultural connections and comparisons. Although some minor phrases were taught in French, Spanish and German, it was clear from observing and talking with Evie that the students were assessed on their culture knowledge and not their knowledge of any of the languages. Projects, activities and assignments were all about thinking about culture, often in a very sophisticated and engaging way.

Evie concentrated on teaching about the French language in the French 1 class, a marked contrast to the world cultures class. She kept a careful eye on keeping the students engaged in their practice of different vocabulary and grammar concepts. The students' activities were focused on drilling and practicing language structures. Evie explained that she believed that students learn language best in a variety of ways, often depending on the student 'which [activities] speak to them'. Some students, she explained, liked the formula of language, some liked to be able to make mistakes, and some told her that they learned the most from drilling, or talking. Although I did not have any interviewees among Evie's junior high school students, her high school students (whom I discuss in Chapter 7) corroborated this observation of hers. She did bring in a guest speaker to this class who focused on sharing information about French culture, but this speaker was clearly a break from the usual curriculum, and the students were held accountable only minimally for the knowledge that the guest shared with the class.

Factors influencing beliefs and practices

The contrast between Evie's two junior high school classes was largely attributable to the structures that were put in place in her district and the language department. Culture and language were deliberately divided between these two classes, with the world cultures exploratory class focusing on culture and the French 1 class focusing on language. Evie did not question this division or discuss it as an issue during our conversations. The separation of culture and language was a reality of her teaching experience, and her beliefs about language teaching did not prevent her from continuing that separation in her practice.

Evie paced her classes with a knowledge of the age and capabilities of her students. She said, 'If they're at their seats by themselves for more than 15 minutes, I think it's time to find a new activity'. She was clearly dedicated to creating dynamic, varied learning experiences for her students. She also worked to keep things novel for her students and to meet them where they were. She disagreed with people who told her that middle/junior high school students were 'terrible', instead saying that, yes, they required a lot of work and were sometimes exhausting, but they're 'so funny' and easy to enjoy. As she said:

> It's really fun for me to teach introductory courses, because before they have me, they know nothing. And at the end of the year, I see all the progress that they've made. They can say things, and they can understand things, and that's a lot of fun for me.

Evie repeated the word 'fun' a number of times in our conversations, often connecting it with her students being funny, and other times, as above, connecting it to how she could inspire and observe growth in her students.

Evie also capitalized on her familiarity with her students and her young age to make connections. As she said, 'I'm young, so I can relate to them in different ways . . . I know what they're talking about . . . on TV or what have you . . . that's fun as well'. She used her proximity to her young students to motivate her to change her practices. She knew it was time to change when she got bored with the class:

> If I'm bored, probably the students are bored with it, too! [laughs] . . .
> that's kind of the barometer as far as I go, like, oh my God, I'm so tired of
> this activity. And I am the teacher and this is my thing, so I think it's time
> to find a new one.

Evie's responsiveness to her students, her close connection with them and her appreciation for the fun that she could have in the classroom all demonstrated the importance of the ecology of the classroom in how she experienced her teaching.

This is not to say that Evie avoided other forms of interaction and inspiration. She explained several times that she shared a lot with other teachers in her district, especially other teachers of French who taught the same levels as her. She saw this as necessary due to her newness to the job and the fact that she had to travel between schools and classrooms. As she said, 'Because I'm still relatively new to the profession . . . any sharing that can happen I appreciate'. This perspective can be seen more when she discusses her high school classes later in the book.

Looking across Three Cases

These three teachers, located in very different schools and districts, teaching different languages to different ages of students, demonstrated the diversity in modes of delivery that exists in the US at the elementary and middle/junior high school levels (Table 3.1; Davin *et al.*, 2011; Kissau *et al.*, 2014; Pufahl & Rhodes, 2011). The relationship between teachers' beliefs and their classroom practices was strongly influenced by their district and school context, particularly the mitigating factors like the structure and length of their classes, the ways that students were assigned to classes, and the curricular expectations in the school. The example of the

Table 3.1 Comparison of Calvin, Sarah and Evie's contexts

	Calvin	Sarah	Evie	
			World Cultures	**French 1**
Grades	2–8	6–8	7	8–9
Focus	Building proficiency	Building proficiency	Culture/language exposure	Building proficiency
Placement goal	Spanish 2 or 3 in 9th grade	Spanish 1 or 2 in 9th grade	(none)	French 2 in 10th grade
Program model	FLES	Middle school	FLEX	Jr High school

separation of language and culture instruction in Evie's two junior high school classes is one instance of how larger curricular decisions influence teacher instructional decisions, regardless of the teacher beliefs about teaching and learning. As elementary and middle/junior high school WL programs are less common than high school WL programs in the US (ACIE, 2017), teachers at those levels are perhaps more likely to have to adjust their practice because the program structure can vary so broadly across contexts.

Additionally, I can connect these three cases to what other studies have shown about teacher beliefs in the contexts of their classrooms. Calvin's case was the only one where there was a significant amount of student interview data to consider, and it was clear that his students were inspired by his personal identity as a native speaker and his techniques in the classroom. The students' words and descriptions of his class mirrored his own incorporation of his personal history and his reliance on the creative opportunities for comprehensible input. The students had clearly internalized the predominant ideology of the native speaker as an ideal teacher identified in the literature, and Calvin drew upon that as a major part of his professional identity with them (Llurda & Calvet-Terré, 2022). On the other hand, but not unrelatedly, Sarah and Evie spoke at length about how they self-evaluated and interpreted student comments and reactions to their teaching. The student perceptions were influential for the teachers, as they have been shown to be in other studies (Gatbonton, 2000; Nishino, 2012; Phipps & Borg, 2009).

The teachers adapted consistently in their beliefs about what was best for their students in terms of the context in which they were teaching (Kim, 2011). The developmental level of the students was a key factor in how all three teachers' beliefs about WL teaching and learning related to their practices. Calvin, Sarah and Evie each spoke extensively about the particular needs of elementary or early adolescent students in describing how they planned their teaching. Calvin shifted his teaching techniques to adapt to the different ages of his students, focusing on creating drawings and acting out plays for his younger students, while allowing older students to work more independently. Sarah prioritized building relationships with students, offering multiple paths to learning and making sure that they felt valued throughout their time together, a need that she knew was key to her early adolescent students. Evie loved middle/junior high school students and how funny they were, and she worked hard to keep class activities varied and exciting so that the students would stay engaged. It was easy to see in all three classrooms how the students and their needs as younger learners influenced how the teachers chose to teach. Engagement was high in the classrooms as the students worked with the teachers as they learned. As such, the dialectic between teacher learning and student learning identified by other researchers is observable (Johnson & Golombek, 2020).

For the rest of the book, I move into an exploration of secondary classrooms across a variety of schools and languages. These classrooms might share more structurally than the three cases in this chapter do, but they will offer unique insights to teacher beliefs and practices and how they relate to the learners and their contexts.

Questions for Discussion and Reflection

(1) Reflect on the information in Chapter 1 about the prevalence of and challenges to elementary level WL education in the US. How do these three cases support or refute those national data?
(2) If you learned a world language in a formal (school or class) setting at a young age, which teacher's practices most resemble the practices that your teacher(s) used? How?
(3) How did each of the three teachers take into account the developmental level of their students as they planned their instruction?
(4) What are some new ideas for world language instruction that you got from reading about these three cases? How could you use them in your own classroom?
(5) How did the three teachers approach the instruction of culture along with language? How did they talk about it, and how did that relate to what they did in the classroom?

4 The Singleton World Language Teaching Life

The size of school districts across the state of Iowa varies widely, with some districts numbering in the tens of thousands of students and others with fewer than 500 students total across grades K–12. The four Spanish teachers featured in this chapter all worked in small, rural districts. In these districts, there was just one high school, one middle/junior high school (sometimes combined with the high school) and one elementary school, often in connected or adjoining buildings. The graduating senior classes numbered around 50 students in total. Unsurprisingly, these small districts each only had one world language teacher (the 'singleton'), who teaches all levels of Spanish in the high school, as well as, in some cases, some middle/junior high exploratory language classes. Their experiences take center stage here.

Case One: Lydia

School context

Lydia was an experienced teacher who had taught Spanish in a variety of districts across Iowa and the Midwest. A white, US-born, native speaker of English, she had had a few experiences traveling abroad and yearned to travel more. Lydia's small, rural district contained about 600 students total across all grade levels, with about half of those students attending the 7–12 junior/senior high school where she worked. As with all four teachers featured in this chapter, Lydia's district had about one-third of its students receiving free or reduced-price lunches, no English learners and 96% white students. The population in Lydia's district was also made up of 2% Hispanic, 1% Native American and 2% multiracial students. Her district had an 81% graduation rate, which was slightly lower than the other three districts in this chapter. Lydia explained that many students in her classes intended to become farmers without attending a four-year institution after they graduated from high school. Lydia's school was a 1:1 school, where every student had a school-provided laptop.

In this section, I present data from two full days of class observations, one formal interview with Lydia and several informal conversations that we conducted during my observations.

Teaching environment

Lydia taught seven 43-minute class periods per day, with one period for preparation. This included two sections of Spanish 1, two sections of Spanish 2, one section of Spanish 3, one section of Spanish 4 and one exploratory Spanish class for 8th graders. Additionally, there was one 'Success Period' of 30 minutes when students could seek out additional help with teachers. Her class sizes were small, between five and 15 students. This schedule was the same every day for Lydia and her students.

Lydia's classroom was wide, with windows along one wall that looked out into the countryside. Through those windows, seven wind turbines were easily visible. There was a whiteboard in front of the class, with reminders written in English primarily about school events. The room had white tile floors, and students sat in student desks with attached tables arranged in rows and facing the front of the classroom with the whiteboard. The walls were covered with calendars, schedules, grammar posters, pictures of the target culture(s) and posters featuring silly phrases in Spanish.

Classroom activities

The instructional activities planned and carried out by Lydia primarily centered on targeted grammar structures that fit with her goals for that class. She said that she had a teacher-led teaching style: 'It's more like I'm teaching, they're following, I ask, they repeat'. She identified learning targets that focused on grammar skills, for instance, 'I can use and identify indirect object pronouns in Spanish and can use them when answering a question'. She then would review them in Spanish and English. She often used careful diagrams, tables and explanations written on the whiteboard in English to outline the grammar structures being targeted. She clarified complex concepts in English when students struggled in their grammar work.

One of Lydia's common practices in reviewing grammar rules was to call on students in English while referring them to where she had written the grammar structures on the board. She would then use prompts and questions, with some variation, to check their knowledge. Sometimes, she would have the students finish her sentences or respond to her questions to complete the rule. For instance, when reviewing a visual representation of verb conjugations in Spanish, she said, 'It only happens . . .' followed by a pause, and then the students responded, 'In the boot!' (referring to where in the diagram the verb was conjugated in a different way). She would ask questions like, 'When would you use this verb?' and then encourage students to respond in English. Her focus on grammar rules included the regular teaching and rehearsal of mnemonic devices and abbreviations to help students to remember rules in grammar and pronunciation.

Once the targeted grammar structures had been introduced to the students through the techniques above, Lydia would have them practice the structures through pair conversation work or answering her questions in Spanish. Some of these activities were more formal, with instructions projected on the overhead, while others were a part of more informal practice and repetition. During these exchanges, Lydia would correct the students if they made errors in the targeted structures.

Assessments and assignments often focused on grammar structures, and students were frequently reminded of the need to master the structures in order to be prepared for upcoming tests. Lydia assigned worksheets or worksheet packets for homework centered on the targeted structures that were then reviewed together in class. Part of the grammar instruction also included students taking notes. As every student had a laptop, Lydia encouraged them to take notes on their computers as they learned and practiced new concepts. A common assessment was quizzes on the targeted structures, and Lydia frequently reminded students of that impending evaluation. During one observation, she told her students, 'You might want to write this down – it might be on your test'. Lydia also encouraged students to use their computers and online resources for some activities during class.

Lydia varied some instructional techniques according to the proficiency level and age of the students. For her least proficient 8th grade students in her beginning classes, she used songs to teach basics like the alphabet. She also used Total Physical Response, having students physically respond to her Spanish commands, when the content was appropriate. One example was when she was teaching classroom objects and had students gesture to the object when she said the object's name. In her upper-level classes, Lydia explained to me that she often did projects like skits and cooking, and she led some groups of students in her Spanish 3 class to tutor elementary students once a week. She also described the arts projects that she did with them, like making sugar skulls and paper flowers related to the Day of the Dead. With the upper-level classes, Lydia also encouraged the use of Spanish more conversationally, for instance, in large-group exchanges about things like favorite foods. She used leveled readers with students in the large group, having them read out in turns and translating from Spanish to English to ensure understanding.

Themes and patterns in teaching and connection to beliefs

The importance of teaching grammar: 'I was in your boots once; you just have to memorize'

Lydia's beliefs about teaching grammar were reflected in her emphasis on grammar instruction in the classroom. She clearly prioritized grammar in her understanding of what language teaching was all about, stating,

'I love teaching about these grammar concepts, and the culture, and everything'. For instance, when talking about her need for professional development in studying abroad in a Spanish-speaking country, Lydia stated:

> I'm hoping to actually improve my Spanish by going there because classes will focus on grammar and vocabulary from what I understand. So, it'll help me when it comes to like the subjunctive tense, because I do not feel confident at all teaching about the subjunctive tense.

Clearly, in her goals for her own learning, Lydia closely connected grammar learning with language learning, demonstrating a belief that those two concepts were linked.

Her belief that teaching grammar was central to teaching language could be seen throughout her class in how she interacted with her students. She explained in her interview that it was important to explain the target language, especially with freshmen and sophomores 'especially if they don't understand the English concept of it'. The English teachers, she lamented, 'aren't teaching the grammar', so students sometimes needed her explanation in Spanish to understand grammar in general. She thought it important to teach grammar, and to teach it in an engaging way that went beyond what she called 'drill and kill'. To students, she explained, 'I was in your boots once, you just have to memorize'. Lydia's interactions with students in the classroom primarily consisted of discussions of grammar and rules, with a focus on details about spelling and accents, for example, when a hyphen might be used in a word versus a space.

Lydia expressed other beliefs about language learning that stood in contrast with her beliefs about language teaching. She stated that prioritizing conversation was important at the upper levels, but it was often a struggle for students, saying, 'They can read it, and they can understand it, it's just the speaking portion that completely gets them'. Lydia posited that students learn best through hands-on activities like role plays and manipulatives like plastic food, and that they demonstrate knowledge of the language by understanding, for example, movies in Spanish. These beliefs did not completely reflect her other beliefs, and indeed her classroom practices, about teaching grammar in the classroom.

Student management and student inspiration: 'I'm just trying to find a way to make it interesting to them'

Lydia articulated consistently during the interview and the classroom observations that part of being a Spanish teacher involved addressing student struggles or resistance while trying to connect with them. Teaching, as she said, involves classroom management, 'trying to get the students to stay focused and on task and not annoy each other'. As mentioned above, she considered it important to interact with students, to walk around and listen to them, and to help them if they had a concern or with their pronunciation. The focus in connecting with students was on getting them to understand the material. The best students, Lydia said, are 'willing to make mistakes. . . . They will come in and get help if they don't understand something'. She clearly considered mastery of the grammar and vocabulary concepts to be key to success in the language classroom. Getting students to 'love learning' meant getting them to love learning about grammar and vocabulary. Classroom observations supported this, in that Lydia primarily interacted with students about the lesson and concepts being taught at that time, usually grammar or vocabulary. I did not observe interactions that involved personal conversations about students' lives or other types of informal check-ins; Lydia was focused on the grammar lessons at hand in interacting with students.

Lydia also expressed that it was important to find ways to make what they were learning be relevant to students. As she said, 'I'm just trying to find a way to make it interesting to them, and to make it relevant to them, and some of them are like, "Well, I don't use it in English, how do I expect to use it in my second language?"'. This statement echoes Lydia's previous comments of disappointment that English teachers in her school did not focus enough on grammar. It was clear that Lydia's main focus in trying to engage students was to engage them with the grammar learning.

Lydia also clearly wanted students to connect with the broader goals of language study as a way to inspire them and engage them with the work. In the formal interview, she said that activities like cooking or the arts can inspire her students, even if they were only using the language a little bit. She stated that being a language teacher involves:

> Trying to take my opinions, and not force them on the kids, but you know, like share them with the kids in hopes of . . . creating a better world, or like at least they can know my little bit of the world a little bit better.

She stated that knowing another language can make you a better person, 'because [you] can see where other people are coming from'. Lydia shared that she believed that learning language could open more job opportunities for students. Again, this statement shows the competing beliefs in Lydia's conceptualization of her job as a language teacher. She focused on grammar teaching and connecting with students via helping them master the grammar and vocabulary structures being focused on in class, and yet the loftier goals of building a better world governed her thinking about being a language teacher as well.

Factors influencing beliefs and practices

Lydia's beliefs about the importance of grammar and vocabulary teaching were closely aligned with her teaching practices. She made the decisions about what to teach and how to teach it based on her beliefs. As she was a singleton in her school and district, she did not have colleagues to influence her instructional practices. When Lydia was observed for her job, it was by someone who was not a specialist in language education. As a result of this observation, she explained, she was told to get different students to participate and check for understanding more. More specific instructions from her institution about how or what to teach in Spanish class were not given.

More frequently, Lydia talked about her desire to get training and support that would connect her with people, concepts and opportunities specific to world language education. She had to navigate district initiatives like adopting field-specific standards without any support, remarking that she was often given directives that were difficult for her to follow alone. She needed to collaborate with other language teachers in the state to get the support that she needed. Sometimes, those opportunities for collaboration were hard for her to access. As she said:

> So I would really like to get into other things, you know, like comprehensible input, or . . . TPRS, or you know, some of those other things. I just never have been exposed to them fully. So I'm not sure how to include them into my teaching.

She sought out opportunities such as doing a summer immersion experience as a way to find new techniques to incorporate into her classroom.

The thoughts that she expressed about her students were primarily focused, as shown above, on imparting her knowledge to them rather than seeking their input on how they learned or how they wanted her to teach. She knew that she needed to change if her students 'all give me blank looks on their faces or . . . they don't do well on an assessment' or, alternately, if she was bored teaching it. As with other teachers in this book, Lydia said, 'If I'm bored teaching it, the kids are going to be bored listening to it'. She said that she made changes based on how long something took her, or how she felt it worked effectively with her students. Her students thus did factor in to how her beliefs related to her practices, in a way that was filtered through her own observations and experiences in the class rather than from direct input from her students through a survey or another way of getting feedback.

Case Two: Bryanna

School context

Bryanna, a white, US-born, native speaker of English, had grown up in the area where her school was located, and she attended school in that district throughout her K–12 education. She decided to return there to teach after getting her formal teacher training elsewhere in the state. Her former Spanish teacher was her instructional coach in the school, although that individual was no longer teaching Spanish. Bryanna's district was located in a rural, picturesque area of Iowa. Her district had around 750 students, and the 9–12 high school had around 200 students. Of these students, 31% received free or reduced-price lunches, indicating a comparatively high poverty rate in the area. The student body was predominantly white, with 95% of the students reported as white and 4% as Hispanic. No other racial or ethnic group comprised more than 1% of the school population. There were no ELs documented in the district. The graduation rate for the district was reported in 2018 as 100%.

I obtained the same data about Bryanna as I did about Lydia: two full days of class observations, one formal interview with Bryanna and several informal conversations that we conducted during my observations.

Teaching environment

As the only WL teacher in her school, Bryanna was responsible for all Spanish classes being taught. Bryanna taught two sections of Spanish 1, two sections of Spanish 2, two sections of Spanish 3 and one section of Spanish 4. Each class was 45 minutes long. This schedule, in an eight-period day, meant that Bryanna taught four different classes over seven periods, with one period to prepare her lessons and materials and to assess her students' work. Interestingly, when I expressed to Bryanna that I thought that she had a demanding schedule as a teacher, she was very surprised. There were between six and 20 students in each class, with most classes numbering around 12 students.

Bryanna's classroom was clean, bright and carefully decorated with a lot of materials hanging on the walls. She was proud of her decorations, and she encouraged me enthusiastically to take pictures as I looked around the room. The Spanish alphabet and colorful posters of different Spanish-speaking countries flanked one of the whiteboards. The daily lesson overview in Spanish was posted on a whiteboard for all four classes. Items were labeled in Spanish all over the room, and phrases like 'Espacio de Senora' ['Teacher's Space'] demarcated different areas. The only English-language display was devoted to helping students to self-identify their proficiency levels in areas like Vocabulary ('What language do I use?'), Function and Structure ('How do I use language?'), Comprehensibility ('How well am I understood doing the task?') and Comprehension ('How well do I understand?'). The desks were positioned in pairs, with each partner face-to-face with the other, in two long rows the length of the room. An aisle ran down the middle of the room, separating the two rows of pairs. Although students sometimes took the face-to-face desk positions to kick one another beneath the desks, the set-up generally seemed very comfortable and conducive to learning.

Classroom activities

Bryanna's classroom was busy and active, with students shifting regularly between activities or, in some cases, closely engaged with longer-term tasks. Bryanna organized the classes in 'chapter adventures', which she described as '[projects] where they can apply their new learning, so vocab and grammar combined. . . . And I try to keep those creative and project-based'. The lower-level classes followed the patterns of practicing all together on a grammar concept, to small-group activities or working in partners where they processed the information, to sharing things out. During large-group grammar instruction, especially in the lower levels, Bryanna often taught acronyms and other mnemonic devices designed to help students memorize and recall grammar rules, with an additional focus on written translation and error correction in service of teaching grammar. During one class, students did peer editing in pairs to look for grammar errors. Directions for small-group activities were projected on the board or provided in worksheet packets. She included assessments, including tests and smaller assessments such as quizzes, as a regular part of class.

To prepare for those tests and quizzes, Bryanna regularly, formatively assessed how well students were reaching her language and content objectives for the classes. She used the 'popsicle stick' technique, where each student's name was written on a popsicle stick and placed in a jar. Then, to call on a student, she selected one popsicle stick at random and called on the student whose name was on the popsicle stick. She also checked in with students to see if they were following along by talking individually with them and circulating consistently around the class and looking over their shoulders as the students worked. Her main assignments were listening and writing activities, often in the form of worksheet packets where the students had to complete certain pages individually, in small groups, or as a part of a whole-class activity. In addition to activities, these packets included strategy instruction about approaches like reading around difficult words. She was able to easily check up on how the students were learning the material as she circulated around. When her interactions with her students determined that they might need help ('I could see like the steam coming out of your ears' she said to one class), she checked in with them, once genially saying, 'Do we have to go back to our techniques from the beginning of the year, so we don't all freak out?'. In another example, when she saw that students in one class were struggling with a listening activity, Bryanna repeatedly encouraged them to listen for keywords, and she played the listening piece several times to help them.

The use of English and the target language in the classroom varied notably at the different levels of classes. Bryanna used more English at the lower levels (Spanish 1 and Spanish 2), especially when explaining grammar. She still included commands and simple words throughout the classes, however. She used many different ways to prompt students in recalling the correct Spanish vocabulary during vocabulary activities, including gestures and word equivalencies. She used Spanish more frequently in upper-level classes. Students used Spanish in a way that was generally structured around class activities and structured practice. In the upper levels, Bryanna arranged more small-group conversations on a pre-designated topic, in the form of a 'Café Conversation'. She used translation at those upper levels in games and activities, with the clear goal of encouraging the students' independence and creativity with the language. English was still present in those upper levels, primarily in terms of encouragement ('I wanted you to think through it before I spoon-fed you'; 'See, you guys don't even need me!').

Bryanna also used varied teaching techniques in a fast-paced class. She taught with games to review concepts like vocabulary and grammar, including online games as well as bingo and other memory matching games. She stated:

> The games . . . are a big part of my world, and I . . . I want to keep them that way. I think they really help students learn and they keep my world exciting. And different from other classrooms.

She constantly kept things moving in her class from activity to activity, as she said, 'like go-go-go'. During the observations, most activities lasted about 10–15 minutes, with some exceptions when students were doing individual work on their worksheet packets. Most classes included more than five distinct activities in the course of the 45-minute class. Students were constantly doing activities and working, with little down-time. She described it thusly:

> Just to give you an example, like the verb 'tener' ['to have'], when I teach the verb 'tener', we learn it on a Monday, we practice it on a Tuesday and a Wednesday, we might play a game with 'tener' on Thursday, and they're going to have a quiz on Friday on 'tener'.

Students in the observations were consistently engaged, even when struggling with exercises. They expressed frustration, but Bryanna's encouragement kept them involved and focused for the most part. Her directions and infrequent behavior corrections were always put in terms that the students could understand, with clear explanations of her expectations and why they needed to meet them.

Themes and patterns in teaching and connection to beliefs

Accountability: '[I need to] hold them accountable . . . for their learning.'

Given the focus on formative assessment in Bryanna's classroom, it is not surprising that one of her primary stated beliefs was about holding students accountable for their learning. She wanted her classroom to be active, fast-paced and varied, and to allow students to have opportunities to be creative and to show their knowledge in different ways. She explained to her students that language learning was meant to be challenging. One exchange between Bryanna and her students went as follows:

Bryanna: How many years does it take to become fluent?
Students: Sixteen years.
Bryanna: How many years have you been studying?
Students: One and a half.

Keeping the students realistic about how long it would take for their work to pay off was a part of keeping them accountable; they needed to stay engaged in order to meet their goals and to understand that the goals would not necessarily be easily attained simply because they put in the work.

Bryanna also expressed the belief that vocabulary and grammar were well-suited for activities that focused on memorization, especially if the activities were conducted in a fun manner and in a fun environment. She clearly felt that grammar learning was an important and potentially fun aspect of learning a language, stating, 'I just get so excited about grammar!'. Echoing her classroom practices, Bryanna also expressed that she felt that a focus on grammar and vocabulary was needed at the lower levels (1 and 2), and in the upper levels (3 and 4), concepts could be taught at a slower rate, with more listening and conversation built into the chapters. Her awareness of other forms of teaching language, such as the focus on comprehensible input more popular in Iowa, could be characterized as skeptical interest.

Relationships with students and the community: 'These people are my family'

Bryanna's warmth in interacting with her students was visible throughout the classroom observations, and naturally, she characterized her relationships with students as first and foremost in her classes. She called her students 'amigos' ['friends'] in one class, encouraging them by saying, 'Thank you for working *so* hard today amigos – en serio, buen trabajo [friends – seriously, good work]'. She had a comfortable, friendly relationship with students. In addition to saying 'These people are my family', she explained:

The relationship, though, is more than anything. I think after years and years of teaching, sometimes that's what the focus comes back to, like kids, of course you want them to remember every Spanish word you teach them, but . . . students are going to remember how you made them feel, not necessarily everything that you taught them.

The creation and maintenance of relationships with students, Bryanna argued, led directly to more substantive learning for them both within the classroom and in the future. Interacting and participating students, she believed, tended to be the best language students.

Furthermore, to encourage and engage her students in language study, Bryanna tailored her teaching and curriculum to the idea of inspiring her students and creating and maintaining relationships with them. As she said:

And I want to build and foster a love for the language and the culture, and I don't want to scare [my students]. I feel like, if I can foster and build that love for the language in the classroom, and whatnot, then I hope that follows them after here, and then they can have more of those immersion experiences as they advance.

She made choices in her classroom that explicitly aimed to foster their interest and engagement, for instance, planning activities for her Spanish 4 class, such as watching videos about government issues and policy. She explained to me that it fit better with that class than some of her more customary topics.

Factors influencing beliefs and practices

In both belief and practice, Bryanna valued the possibility of offering varied, personalized activities to her students that would engage them, so naturally seeking out new opportunities was key to her work. Bryanna articulated a consistent impulse to develop and change in her teaching practice, 'always updating and improving'. She added, 'I just don't ever feel like I have it right. There's never been one year where I can do the exact same things the next year'. She asked herself, 'Was that good enough? Am I making the right choices for my students, in the long run, to be successful?'. Even on a class level, Bryanna stated, 'Every single class is different every single day . . . I have no idea how my day is going to go'. She added that it depended on 'my mood, your mood . . . what happened in your life, what happened in my life, things that just come up in class, things that make you laugh, make you giggle'. Echoing her reliance on regular formative assessment of students, Bryanna also said that she regularly got feedback from her students to see what might need to be changed, and that her changes were 'in the best interests of students'. This motivation to change and grow led Bryanna, for example, to bring in the Café Conversation exercise as well as new units on Don Quixote and travel projects in recent years.

Bryanna also stated that she got ideas from online sources, those both behind paywalls and free, such as Pinterest, TeachersPayTeachers, blogs and Instagram, while also attending conferences on different teaching techniques, such as using more comprehensible input as a cornerstone of her class. Although she lamented her lack of a strong support group to go to for ideas when she was stuck, she said that she constantly reached out to her instructional coach in her school to reflect on her teaching. One realization she had was that she needed to be more flexible with her routine with the students.

Ultimately, Bryanna's own desire to constantly improve and explore new options led her to be connected closely with her students, her colleagues in nearby schools and her school supports like her instructional coach. These different influences did factor in to how her beliefs changed or stayed constant and how she enacted her beliefs in her classroom.

Case Three: Wade

School context

Wade, like Lydia and Bryanna, was a white, US-born, native speaker of English. After he had the opportunity to teach in Mexico during study abroad in college, he made the decision to become a Spanish teacher. Wade had been working at his high school for a few years, having taken the job after a longtime and beloved teacher in the district had retired. Wade's school district, located in a rural area of the state, was almost identical in size to Bryanna's district and just a bit larger than Lydia's district. There were about 800 students in the district, with about 200 attending the 9–12 school where Wade worked at the time of data collection. Of the students, 43% received free and reduced-price lunches, one marker of poverty in the area. The student population was 96% white, with 1% Hispanic, 2% multiracial and less than 1% Black students. There were no recorded English learners in the district. Overall, the district reported a 94% graduation rate. Thus, the district was predominantly white and rural, with a level of poverty that was high compared to most of the districts in the state. The classroom building for Wade's 9–12 high school was a large, sprawling building with many corridors and staircases, giving the impression of several disparate additions and updates over years of use.

The data consulted in this summary include two full-day observations of Wade and his students as well as a formal interview with Wade before the observations and several informal conversations during the observation days. I also interviewed three of Wade's high school students. During the member check procedure, Wade returned my analysis back to me with several comments, clarifying his practices and beliefs based on what I had written. None of these comments substantively changed my original analysis, and he stated that overall, it was a great summary.

Teaching environment

As the only Spanish teacher in the school, Wade taught six periods of Spanish classes during the semester when data were collected. He had two Spanish 1 classes, two Spanish 2 classes, one Spanish 3 class and one Spanish 4 class. There were between 12 and 20 students in each class, with the exception of the Spanish 4 class, which had five students. Wade had one period without teaching responsibilities when he prepared for his classes, and he had one shortened period at the end of the day designated as a study period for all students. The classes lasted 49 minutes.

Wade's classroom had hardwood floors, large radiators and windows along one side of the classroom. Whiteboards were at the front and the back of the classroom, and Wade could project his computer in the front of the room for videos and website sharing. Students in the room sat in student desks in rows, with one large aisle down the middle of the room. During the first observation, these desks were in rows facing the center aisle. About two weeks later, during the second observation, the desks had shifted to all be facing the front of the room, still with the aisle down the center of the room. Besides the windows and whiteboards, the walls were decorated with Spanish words, questions, rejoinders, posters and silly class drawings. There were also English posters with classroom rules ('Avoid English'; 'Respond to statements and questions'; 'Let me know if I am confusing you'; 'Body language'; 'Be kind'; 'No side convos') and inspirational ideas ('This is where we all come to use real Spanish with real people to communicate about real (and unreal) stuff. I'm very happy you're here') as well as key definitions of language learning words, such as 'fluency' and 'proficiency'.

Classroom activities

Wade's classes focused on creating a rich language environment in Spanish from the moment that students entered the class. Indeed, he began the class by standing at the door, providing the students with a target phrase in Spanish as a form of greeting when they entered. He then would incorporate that phrase into the class to question students and remind them of its meaning. The start to his class otherwise often varied quite a bit, sometimes including Spanish-language music and analysis of the music, sometimes an acknowledgement of a student birthday and a request to sing and sometimes simply asking questions to students as they settled in. Wade often introduced new vocabulary and had students review vocabulary through Total Physical Response, where the class paired physical actions with Spanish words, avoiding the use of English. In some cases, Wade used a gesture to prompt and remind students about a word; one student remarked in the interview that this was a technique that helped them; they said that Wade called it 'the power of the gestures'. He asked students to indicate 'cierto' ['true'] or 'falso' ['false'] with an open or closed hand when questioning them.

Students frequently remarked on the extensive use of Spanish in Wade's classroom, saying, 'We try to stick in Spanish like almost the time', and 'We're trying to stay in Spanish . . . [teacher] will try to keep everyone on there, he does a great job of that'. Both of these students used 'we' to indicate that they felt they were a part of the work on staying in Spanish, not that it was externally imposed on them. Even the type of Spanish used in the classroom was helpful to students, with one extolling the fact that 'we got to use language that we'd use in everyday conversation' during some activities. Another said that they were assessed not on 'perfect Spanish', but rather, the closer that a student was to being 'coherent in Spanish . . . the higher your grade'. In my observations, I remarked that, in the upper-level classes, students would sometimes respond in Spanish even if Wade asked them a question in English.

A common activity was to create a character with the students in Spanish by asking questions about family, location, wants and more. During this activity, Wade repeated and reviewed the dialogue with many questions, and students answered both individually and as a group. This activity was a particular favorite of one interviewee, who said that, during that activity, 'everyone was laughing because they're having a good time . . . we were learning new words along the way, we're all speaking Spanish'. Similarly, Wade allowed students to lead the class in telling stories, and then had students write the details. When students performed well or responded well to one of his questions, he had the class give an 'aplauso' ['applause'] in the form of a single clap. Students in his class usually showed 100% engagement with what he was doing, sometimes slightly less.

Other common class activities varied quite a bit. For example, Wade would sometimes provide a text (video about current events, novel, notes from a previous class discussion) and then review the text with the students by asking questions in Spanish. Wade stated that he assessed students through looking at their engagement and writing, through interviewing and talking with them about the topics that had been addressed in class. He had more formal quizzes on the fiction and non-fiction texts described above. He sometimes asked students to define words in texts as a part of these assessments. Another activity was what students called 'game day', when they reviewed vocabulary through simple games that were already familiar to the students, such as Bingo or Hangman. Wade also had

'English days', where the students watched videos in English about topics that were relevant to their Spanish learning. Wade also regularly included 10–15 minutes of reading time in class, where students selected their own texts and read them individually as a class. The classroom was filled with many resources for reading, including racks of books.

Beyond his general focus on the use of Spanish, Wade did regularly coach students on developing their reading and listening skills during his lessons via statements such as, 'Were you actively trying to make a movie in your head?' as the students read, or encouraging them to complete activities as he recommended, 'And that's how we're gonna get better'. He displayed rules prominently in the classroom as well as his thoughts about the processes of second language acquisition (SLA). Students were well aware of this type of coaching, and those that I spoke with often mentioned it during our interviews. One student recognized that Wade used 'the most efficient way' of learning language, after he had done research on 'how Spanish speakers and other language speakers learn the language'. Another interviewee mentioned concepts in language learning like the interpersonal and interpretive communication modes. Another student similarly explained:

> I swear, almost once a month, literally, every so often he would go on quotes and stuff up on the walls. And he'd be, 'Okay, wait, we're learning it this way, just because, the other way I was taught, I don't, I didn't learn anything from it'.

Wade was thus very clear on the messages to his students about how they are learning, as a matter of regular course throughout his classes.

As I have already mentioned, Wade's classroom featured a high percentage of time spent in Spanish, at all levels, but English was used strategically as a way for him to check on students' comprehension at many moments in the class. In a lower-level class, Wade frequently stated, 'How's my Spanish? Comprehensible?' when challenging them with new words or language structures. When reading to them in a Spanish book, he checked in frequently about his speed when reading aloud: 'How's my speed so far?' and, when he had determined that students were following along, said, 'I'm gonna speed it up, see if you can handle it'. Students noted the comprehension checks, saying, 'He'll ask us questions later to make sure that we were paying attention, and could comprehend the class discussion'. Another student stated:

> He does a really, really good job of making sure we all know. Like he will ask us if we are following along, and he will, like he'll go slower, and he'll just, he knows when we don't know a word, so he'll explain it, and he'll use circumlocution, and it just helps a lot.

When Wade checked on comprehension, sometimes students offered incorrect responses, which was met with equanimity and encouragement on Wade's part, with statements like, 'I'm glad you noticed it and took a guess!' before offering the correct response.

Translation between English and Spanish also featured prominently in a variety of ways in Wade's classes. While speaking in Spanish, if he used a word that he knew that the students did not know, Wade would translate the word or form into English on the whiteboard as they were introduced. At other times, he would ask students to translate a phrase to one another. With his upper-level students, he encouraged them to reflect on synonyms, asking questions such as, 'Another word for "empezar" ["start"]?'. He had them do both simple translation exercises ('"Como se dice" ["how do you say"] we saw?') and more complex vocabulary-focused activities, including writing sentences about vocabulary in specific verb tenses and tracing the precise meaning of complex Spanish phrases while using English. In some cases, he would allow students to write answers in Spanish or English. Importantly, Wade almost never corrected students' usage or provided Spanish translations when the students were presenting or leading class activities.

Themes and patterns in teaching and connection to beliefs

Engagement as key: 'Keep asking questions'

Wade actively encouraged participation from all students by both calling on them individually and getting volunteers, sometimes encouraging, 'I'd like to hear from someone I haven't heard from yet'. Wade identified what he sought in students' engagement thusly:

> [Students should be] paying attention to what they're hearing, and seeing, and watching stuff, tracking things with their eyes, um. Answering questions in whatever way they feel comfortable, whether it's with their face, or with their head, or their words, um, with their hands, whatever way, just responding to my questions, reacting to my statements, and my comments, bringing out their own comments when they feel comfortable.

Thus, he saw demonstrations of engagement as key to his classroom, and closely intertwined with a detailed system of verbal and nonverbal formative assessment. Students interviewed agreed that you had to 'pay attention' and not be afraid to 'ask questions' to be successful in his class. One advised, 'Keep asking questions when you're confused so you don't fall behind'. This type of interaction and engagement was thus clearly understood by Wade's students to be a vital part of succeeding as a student, too.

SLA theories guiding practice: 'I'm adhering better to principles.'

One strong belief held by Wade was the importance of using theories of second language acquisition to guide his practice. With the goal of getting proficient or fluent students in the language, he expressed clear ideas of the theories which guided his practice: 'We need to comprehend messages to acquire more language'; and, the most impact on language acquisition occurs through 'content that is so compelling that . . . they don't even know it's in another language'. As mentioned above, he often did not plan or target specific vocabulary or structures, instead teaching Spanish through 'stories and conversation that students understand' via what he called the comprehensible input approach.

One important part of Wade's personal story as a teacher was his decision to teach in a different way, a way that adhered 'better' to the principles of SLA than his previous ways of teaching. He did this when he began in his job at his school, about five years prior to data collection for this study, although it was a challenging time for him. He confessed that he often struggled with stretching and doing new things, as he did not like to 'appear like I don't know what I'm talking about or appear wrong'. Nonetheless, this offers further evidence of the importance of his beliefs to Wade – even though it was difficult to change his teaching to focus more on providing comprehensible input, he considered it vital to his overall work as a teacher.

Wade's adherence to principles of SLA could also be seen in his consideration of the importance of student engagement and language usage in the classroom. He believed that, to learn or acquire language, students needed to pay attention in class to messages in Spanish, and teachers had to enforce that expectation of attention. Although his beliefs focused on providing comprehensible input to students, he also knew that there was a tension between the overall focus on the interpretive mode and the push to find a way to assess students, often through asking them to respond to his questions. As he stated in the interview, he encouraged but did not expect 100% Spanish from students (and himself) throughout all levels, often preferring to refer to the 90% recommended by ACTFL (2010b). He explained his choices to make exceptions to Spanish in the classroom by saying that it was primarily when there was a lack of understanding. He did not 'make it extreme', in his words.

Planning in detail is not always necessary: 'In terms of planning, I'm totally a minimalist'

Finally, Wade believed that deciding what to teach and when did not necessarily always need to be planned out ahead of time. He felt that improvising instruction was ok to an extent and under the right circumstances, 'if you feel comfortable with what you're doing and if students are comprehending what you're saying'. He appreciated the flexibility and liberty that his job afforded him, and his ability to change his plans as needed as he taught. Some of this liberty could be certainly linked to Wade's status as a singleton with no colleagues in his school. As Wade told me, he often changed the plan for the class, sometimes during the class, to best encourage proficiency. One student observed, 'I'm learning in multiple ways . . . more than one'. Students remarked on the lack of a set plan or guiding text, noting that Wade did not use a textbook, and that often his activities did not focus on only one structure.

His ideas about flexibility and freedom in planning were also linked to his appreciation of variety in the classroom. Although he espoused 'everything in moderation', because telling stories every day would 'wear off the shine a little bit', he also wistfully stated that it would be 'an explosion of acquisition if it was just stories, stories, stories, stories all the time'. Wade's working situation as a singleton afforded him the ability to explore his interests and variety in the classroom, but it had its limits.

Relatedly, Wade found that seeing students develop language and attain success in class was very rewarding. He appreciated students who were risk-takers, who spoke willingly in class and who offered ideas and contributions in class, finding them easier to teach. He linked students' engagement in class with easier classroom management, stating, 'When [kids are] happy, then they're listening and when they're happily listening, the problems and the attitude just seem to disappear'. Wade's belief that engagement led to better classroom management fit with the patterns that were observed in his teaching, where most students were engaged and connected with his learning opportunities throughout the observed classes.

Factors influencing beliefs and practices

Wade clearly thought a great deal about how his students were experiencing his teaching. Although he generally seemed to trust his own perspectives on his students at this point of his career, he also sometimes expressed doubts that he was truly capturing their experiences, stating, 'I don't know if this is just my teacher mind projecting what students are thinking'. His decisions to make changes were based on what he called his 'perceptions of the students' perceptions'. When he began to feel less satisfied with those perceptions, he felt that it was 'inevitable' to make a change. Interestingly, Wade's students picked up on his observational habits, with one stating, 'I feel like he knows when you don't understand'. This was a function of his frequent and pervasive formative assessment techniques, but the overall image was that he depended on his perceptions, and many of his classroom activities were oriented around giving him the best information possible on which to base those perceptions.

Like Bryanna, Wade spoke at length about what he was able to learn from people outside of his school and his district. He stated that he was often challenged by the fact that he had primarily worked in small schools where he was the only teacher. By necessity, he had to collaborate and learn from others outside of his school. The students were aware of this shift, with one explaining that 'he told us that in previous schools, he used to teach a different way . . . and he talked with other Spanish teachers, and he got advice from them'. Facebook pages and social media groups related to comprehensible input were also 'big influences' on his work. He stated that he was always reading articles and Facebook posts about other teachers' experiences. As he explained, 'That's how I feel I grew the most, having constant, rigorous, back-and-forth with like-minded colleagues for half a decade and, at the same time, feeling motivated to want to create myself as well'. Wade's work in finding inspiration and community was not only about being a consumer but also about interacting and sharing ideas actively with others. Unsurprisingly, he found inspiration in face-to-face conferences with colleagues, where he could 'stay in the same room' with other teachers and 'talk as much as we can in that amount of time'. Unlike Bryanna and Lydia, Wade did not seem to struggle with finding ways to connect and seek out other teachers, and he relished the opportunities when they did come up.

However, Wade emphasized during our conversations that he preferred to work out problems himself, in his classroom. As he stated, 'I just know myself too well . . . I always have to be driving the car'. The ultimate impression of Wade, therefore, was as someone who sought out others for inspiration and debate, but who appreciated and enjoyed his independence as a singleton.

Case Four: Abbie

School context

Abbie's background was remarkably similar to that of Lydia, Bryanna and Wade – she had decided in college that she wanted to be a Spanish teacher after an influential trip abroad, and she was a white, US-born, native speaker of English. Abbie's district was the smallest district included in this project, with 450 students total in the district at the time that data were collected. The district was located in a rural part of the state, not far from several other teachers in the study or major urban areas. There were about 250 students in the 6–12 school where Abbie taught. The whole district was housed in one building in the town. The district was made up of 89% white, 7% multiracial and 2% Hispanic students, with no other ethnicities reported. There were no ELs reported in the district at the time of data collection. The district, as with the other three districts in this chapter, had about one-third of its students qualifying for free and reduced-price lunches based on household income. The district had a 94% graduation rate.

Data from two full days of observation, one formal interview with Abbie, and several informal conversations during the observations are the data sources for this section. Additionally, Abbie authored a blog about being a Spanish teacher that sometimes explained her lessons, teaching techniques and beliefs; although this did not serve as a major data source, I did consult it from time to time during the analysis procedures, and it was brought up in some of our discussions.

Teaching environment

Abbie taught six out of seven academic periods of the school day, as the only Spanish teacher in the junior high and high school. She taught one exploratory 8th-grade Spanish class, two sections of Spanish 1, two sections of Spanish 2 and one section of Spanish 3. The exploratory class had new students every quarter and was intended to introduce students to Spanish. In addition to those classes, Abbie also led an advisory period during a part of the day set aside for advisory only. Her classes lasted 50 minutes, and she had between 10 and 20 students in each of her classes. Abbie had been identified as a model teacher in the district in the year when data were collected, meaning that she invited other teachers into her room to observe her teaching.

Abbie's classroom was meticulously labeled, neat, updated, seasonal, colorful and bright. For instance, at the time that I observed her, she had one bulletin board at the back of the classroom devoted to a project where she recorded students' votes on their favorite Spanish-language songs in a music bracket competition. Other decorations included both information for students about the Spanish language, like verb lists and conjugations, and more metalinguistic information, like a description of the proficiency levels. Whiteboards and small bulletin boards in the front and at the sides of class were full of useful information. This included announcements that were posted in the front of class, with the agenda for different classes listed to one side in the classroom. Some English-language posters featured advice like 'PREPARE! PREPARE yourself to listen to understand!' and 'ENHANCE, INITIATE, & CREATE in Spanish'.

The tile-floored room included student chairs organized in a half-circle. Abbie had a deskless classroom, so students sat in those chairs and only worked at tables infrequently during the classes. When needed, they wrote in notebooks on their laps, gathered on the floor, or sat at the tables around the sides of the classroom. Tables and reading corners with comfortable chairs, area rugs and libraries of Spanish readers lined the walls of the room. Some books were organized in bins where they were sorted by topic and labeled clearly.

Classroom activities

Abbie's classes did not follow a set pattern, but rather included a wide variety of activities focusing on providing students with comprehensible input in the language and then assessing their comprehension of that input. Select activities were more focused on interpersonal communication between teacher and students or student-to-student. Abbie confessed that she felt she did a great job with starting classes, but she felt she struggled more with ending them. She started classes with engaging videos, individual reading time or, in lower-level classes, interpersonal teacher-led questioning with a simple question like 'Te gusta comida?' ['Do you like food?'] with single-word or yes/no choices. After those introductory activities, Abbie often moved into group or individual activities focused on texts or encouraging students to interact with one another in Spanish.

Abbie, like Wade, focused on providing her students with comprehensible input in Spanish during most of the activities that occurred in her classroom. Unlike Wade, she prioritized variation in her activities quite a bit, stating:

> I feel I do a lot more than [just tell stories] because I would get bored if I just did. Some people like . . . to do just stories. Story after story after story and so I like to incorporate other things and mix it up.

Novels written for Spanish learners were an important part of her class, and she assigned individual reading time in nearly every class observed. She coached her students through prereadings to prepare them for reading activities with the books, then she debriefed with them about how their reading went after the activities. Abbie also read books out loud to students, especially at the lower levels, often acting out parts, making silly noises, making gestures and stopping frequently to ask questions about content. For another input-focused activity, Abbie showed students movie clips while narrating and asking questions in Spanish. She used Spanish-language music in the classroom in the form of songs written for popular play, not songs meant for language learners *per se*. She and her students used both Spanish and English, with some emphasis on Spanish usage. Directions and redirecting students often took place in English. Although Abbie deemphasized the importance of translation in her classes during our conversations, her materials often directed students to translate sentences to show their understanding of the content.

Abbie's teaching showed a great deal of attentiveness to students and student needs. She was constantly smiling in her classes, she never seemed frustrated and she always paid close attention to what students were doing. She differentiated instruction with novels and activities as needed, often in response to direct student requests. One example of this was her approach to teaching grammar. She focused on teaching grammar that needed to be taught based on the text (book, video, readings) that they were considering, interjecting a quick grammar lesson in what she called a 'pop up'. Another example of this attentiveness could be observed in how Abbie taught different sections of the same class. I was able to observe how she often varied the pace in different groups of students while she was still teaching the same thing. For instance, one of her Spanish 1 classes seemed much less compliant and cooperative, so she kept her focus on the class while they were doing group tasks; in the more cooperative Spanish 1 class, she allowed herself to focus on individual groups rather than constantly monitoring the whole room.

Abbie's planning could be detected during the observations in all her classes. She clearly sequenced activities thoughtfully when it came to writing due to her classroom set-up. As she stated, once she decided to have a deskless classroom, 'a lot of it for me was figuring out how to order activities or deciding if it was worth it to write'. She spoke in our interview about grouping writing tasks or eliminating the writing component of her teaching in some cases. This could be complex, as she changed her activities about every 10–15 minutes, rarely doing anything lasting longer than 15 minutes with her students. She used projections and directions written on the whiteboards to guide students through her planned activities, including in some cases a projected timer so they knew how long they had left in an activity. Her agenda was written clearly on a whiteboard for each class, and she often edited the agenda when needed so that students knew what was happening.

Abbie assessed based on all four modes of communication, including presentational, interpretive reading, interpretive listening and interpersonal communication, so she worked hard to be sure that she addressed all of them during her classes. Quizzes often focused on comprehension quizzes based on the texts consulted during class, for example a 'Quien le dijó' ['Who said it?'] quiz about a TV episode that they had just watched in Spanish. Students sometimes had to translate or order sentences or even draw their interpretations of the readings. Other assessments included students' completion of online modules associated with the website Señor Wooly, which provided skits and songs in Spanish that then had short comprehension-focused modules. All assessment was classroom-based, as Abbie did not spend time on homework, checking homework or assigning homework, as she stated that it was not part of the school culture and was not common. She prepared and supported students and informally assessed them throughout activities in addition to these more formal instances. She consistently and continually checked for comprehension.

Themes and patterns in teaching and connection to beliefs

Supporting students where they are: 'Everyone is engaged and accountable'

When I asked Abbie what she would want an observer to see in her classroom, she stated:

> [That] it's entertaining and that the kids are having fun. That they're getting a lot of input in the language and hopefully, maybe using the language depending on the level . . . and that they're engaged. It's the goal.

Keeping students engaged and learning language was vital to Abbie's instructional approach in the classroom. Abbie believed strongly in making sure that every student was engaged at the right level, and that they were supported whenever needed. As she stated, the same curriculum in classes could be paced differently either because of the characteristics of the student group, or because she had learned how better to support students in the first class. For instance, in our conversations, Abbie identified a class that was 'high energy' and 'involved', so she planned for that when she was looking ahead to what to do with them. In the observations, it was easy to see that Abbie planned for student needs.

Many of the ways that Abbie supported students had to do with structured ways that they could participate in and navigate class. Abbie explained how she used surveys to help students tell her if they preferred to work independently, collaboratively or with her for extra support on a specific project, and then she created working groups based on those preferences. In other contexts, she talked about giving them 'specific jobs they need to do that everyone is engaged and accountable for being a part of the team and bringing back the information'. Her work in planning and incorporating student feedback helped her to get the support that students needed.

Comprehensible input and communication: 'Our goal is to acquire the language'

Abbie self-identified as a 'comprehensible input' teacher, stating that her goal for the student was to 'acquire the language', which to her meant that 'we do things naturally through reading and listening and watching things'. She felt that she was on solid footing with this belief and her accompanying approach, stating, 'Honestly, I haven't really had any pushback from it, and so I haven't really had to defend it very much . . . the students enjoy the class, they seem to be learning the language'. As a singleton, Abbie was independent in selecting her approach, and she felt comfortable doing so according to her beliefs. Although she had no other WL teachers to consult in this decision, she looked to her students, their families and non-WL colleagues to affirm her choice, which they did through their lack of objection.

Abbie stated that 'presentational, interpretive reading, interpretive listening and interpersonal' communication modes were her 'essential standards, [her] big things'. Abbie did not prioritize these four types of communication equally, however. She stated multiple times that input should be a primary focus in her classroom. For instance, when I asked her what helped students learn language the most, she said, 'Anything that gets them to use the language later, like outside of class', clarifying that she meant students who listened to Spanish music outside of class or watched online streaming TV shows in Spanish. Abbie thus defined 'using the language' as accessing input in the language. Abbie argued that output in the form of the presentational mode was not as important to emphasize in the classroom. Formal presentations in particular were rarely if ever included in her classes. Less systematic or substantive output, what she called 'sprinklings of output', were seen by Abbie to be acceptable, especially to build student confidence and to allow them to 'see that they know more than they think they do'.

Independence and materials: 'I was up front like, "I don't want to use your textbook"'

As the only language teacher in her district, Abbie had a great deal of freedom in her classroom and in her curriculum. She embraced and enjoyed this independence. She based her curricular decisions completely locally, within her classroom, without influence from the school or district. This unusual circumstance gave her the opportunity, in her first years of teaching, to move from having her curriculum governed by textbooks to finding her own resources online and selecting them based on what appealed to her personally. She described this process, stating:

> When I moved [to my current district], I was up front like, 'I don't want to use your textbook', and they were cool with that and . . . it was my year to get curriculum and they were open to use that money for whatever you want. So I got tons of class sets of books and teacher's guides.

Thus, having a certain amount of experience helped Abbie to advocate for her independence, and she was supported in that by her district.

Abbie described her process of creating new learning opportunities and sequencing learning for her students as 'jumping into it all at once' and 'mixing it up'. She worked hard to research the materials that she wanted to use in her classes, explaining how she 'spent the summer reading all of the [graded reader] books' when her school said she could pick one book per level. She graded in a way that was streamlined and deemphasized in favor of focusing on building students' language proficiency. Assessments did not need to be formal or frequent for students to learn effectively. As shown above, Abbie planned her teaching meticulously, and she did so through leveraging her knowledge as an experienced teacher and her consultation with curricula and sources that she sought out herself.

Factors influencing beliefs and practices

It was clear that Abbie's engagement with her students played a large part in how she organized and planned her classes. She worked hard to differentiate her instruction for the students and to meet their needs as learners. Although learner influence on her instructional decision-making was perhaps less direct than in some other cases discussed thus far, such as Sarah in Chapter 3 or Bryanna earlier in this chapter, Abbie certainly took her learners into account in how she constructed her beliefs and her practices.

Abbie's beliefs were socially constructed, like some of the other singleton teachers like Wade and Bryanna, via the communities of like-minded language teachers in other schools, which she accessed regularly for ideas and community. One such community was online. She said that she learned a lot from connecting with other teachers on X (formerly known as Twitter), via the hashtag chat #langchat, which took place normally on Thursday nights. She stated:

> [Online] is how I feel I learned a lot of new things and shared . . . participating in #langchat, learning about different things that I've never tried before. It kind of gives the push to go: 'Ok, I can try that out, and see if it works, and if not, well, I'll try something else!'

Thus, Abbie gained many ideas from the online community, and then tested them through careful consideration of her own students. Both her colleagues and her students shaped her practices as she tried new things as a teacher.

Abbie also participated in a group of teachers from neighboring small districts. Although she stated that these teachers all 'do very different things', she benefited from the time that they spent together sharing their activities, asking for advice with activities that 'flopped', and consulting on grading practices. As she said with a laugh, 'Other Spanish teachers help me out with whatever I need'. In both the online community and the community of neighboring teachers, it was clear that Abbie considered the advice and interactions carefully, and that she applied them to her own classroom only when she found that they matched her beliefs and her goals in teaching.

Indeed, Abbie recognized the complexity of changing her practices and how they might affect her class in general. One example was changing from desks to the deskless classroom. She got that idea online and aligned it with her belief in creating a space where she could provide comprehensible input. Making this change also forced her to be patient with her students as they got used to it, to assess if it was really the right change for her classroom and to sequence her activities so that the students did not have to take out writing materials and then put them away again repeatedly.

Abbie saw new changes on the horizon, too, and was energized by them. One example was moving toward standards-based grading, which was about to be imposed by her administration. She anticipated working with other language teachers who already used standards-based grading for advice. Although she was rarely influenced by institutional factors in how she ran her classes, it was clear that it might be changing for her in the future.

Looking across the Four Cases

When considering only the size and the demographics of their schools, these four singleton Spanish teachers were very similar. All four of the high schools had a student population of between 200 and 300 students. None of the schools reported having any ELs, and all had between 30% and 45% of students receiving free and reduced lunches. The racial and ethnic background in all four schools was overwhelmingly (between 89% and 96%) white. The four teachers all had very similar cultural and linguistic backgrounds as well as teaching responsibilities, teaching two sections of Spanish 1 and Spanish 2, one or two sections of Spanish 3, and then additional classes at the 8th-grade exploratory level (Lydia, Bryanna, Abbie) and/or Spanish 4 (Lydia, Bryanna, Wade). All four teachers had one period per day when they were not teaching and were able to prepare, grade and reflect.

Because of these very similar institutional contexts, the four teachers shared a great deal. All four had great freedom to determine how they wanted to teach. They were able to select and implement their teaching materials with little oversight, a factor that has been shown in some research to suggest that teachers would be more capable of teaching according to their beliefs (Assen *et al.*, 2016; Borg, 2017; Farrell & Guz, 2019; Farrell & Lim, 2005; Farrell & Yang, 2015; Rahman *et al.*, 2018). They also had no world language teaching colleagues with whom to collaborate or interact. They were, for instance, able to easily determine the alignment and articulation of their Spanish program both horizontally (making sure every Spanish 1 class was taught the same material) and vertically (making sure that the expectations of students starting a new level matched what they had been taught at the previous level). On the other hand, these teachers all had very little planning time given the number of different classes that they were expected to teach, so their planning and reflection time was seriously curtailed.

I found that, despite these nearly identical institutional contexts, the four singleton teachers in this study were quite different in their beliefs and practices in their classrooms. Two of the teachers held core beliefs about the centrality of teaching grammar in their classrooms (Lydia, Bryanna), while the two others believed that deemphasizing direct grammar instruction in favor of providing comprehensible input to students was key (Wade, Abbie). This debate, and research on it continues, so it is not surprising that it exists within classrooms and among teachers as well (*cf.* Vyn *et al.*, 2019). Wade and Abbie differed quite markedly in terms of how much they believed in the importance of planning in their classrooms. The four teachers held different, complex beliefs about their role in encouraging student engagement in their classes, with Abbie prioritizing differentiation and consulting students, Bryanna focusing on building relationships with students to encourage them to follow her curriculum, Wade constantly altering his plans to always ensure 100% student engagement and Lydia addressing student resistance and classroom management to keep them on task. Where Abbie and Bryanna consulted students directly about their reactions to classes, Wade and Lydia focused on their interpretations of student reactions to their lessons to guide their instructional decision making. The ways that learners and learner beliefs mediated the relationship between the singletons' beliefs and practices thus varied considerably; there was not one consistent way to identify this relationship due to the varied nature of the teacher beliefs about learners and their role. Recall here that the scholarship, similarly, does not make a conclusion about how learner beliefs and behaviors affect teachers, and thus this complexity and chaos in this relationship follows prior scholars' work (Breen *et al.*, 2001; Burns *et al.*, 2015; Farrell & Guz, 2019).

One other interesting contrast in how these teachers navigated their beliefs and practices was in terms of their engagement with professional development. All four teachers wished to continue to develop as educators, and they all sought out opportunities. Bryanna and Lydia both depended on resources in their schools, including instructional coaches and supervisors. These two teachers also expressed that they found engaging with communities of educators outside of their schools as a difficult process. Wade and Abbie both described their community of educators as existing outside of their schools or even their local areas, focusing on connecting via social media and with the larger state community. Both integrated easily into that larger community. The *ad hoc* nature of professional development for in-service world language teachers, especially those teachers working alone in their schools, was brought into relief with this contrast.

Questions for Discussion and Reflection

(1) Out of the four teachers featured in this chapter, which one most resembles how you teach or hope to teach in the future?

(2) Imagine yourself as a student in each classroom. How would you respond to the teaching practices and techniques used by each teacher?

(3) Select one teacher as a focus. If that teacher were to take a position in a larger school with more students, how do you think that they would adapt?

(4) Wade had a number of students' voices in his data. How did those students support or contradict some of his belief statements?

(5) Despite the similar demographics of these four schools, these teachers expressed very different beliefs about many aspects of their teaching. Why do you think that this is the case?

5 Experiences in Small to Mid-Sized World Language Programs

In this chapter, I examine the world of three Spanish teachers in small to mid-sized world language programs. These teachers faced similar structures and challenges to the teachers in the previous chapter, although they were not the only teachers in their districts or schools. They all had one or two Spanish-teaching colleagues. Caitlyn taught in a smaller, rural district, and both Veronica and Marlene taught in the same larger district on the outskirts of an urban area that was undergoing growth. These three teachers' contexts, thus, included colleagues and perhaps more institutional scrutiny than the singletons featured in Chapter 3.

Case One: Caitlyn

School context

Caitlyn had wanted her whole life to be a teacher and decided in college to become a Spanish teacher. Although white, US-born, and a native speaker of English, Caitlyn was married to a native speaker of Spanish from a Latin American country and was raising a bilingual, biracial child. Caitlyn taught in a middle school and a high school in a district that was just slightly larger than some of the schools featured in the previous chapter about singletons. Caitlyn's high school, containing about 200 students in grades 9–12, and her middle school, containing about 200 students grades 6–8, were housed in the same low, one-story building that housed the elementary school in a district with about 850 students total. A generally calm and quiet atmosphere pervaded, and the hallways, often peopled by teachers standing outside of their rooms, did not seem crowded or busy. The hallways in the school were decorated with posters encouraging their sports teams on the walls and the lockers, with the name of the school prominently displayed and cases full of trophies. In Caitlyn's district, about 10% of the students qualified to receive free or reduced-price lunch in the district, suggesting a low rate of poverty in comparison with the other communities featured in this book. The district was recorded as being 99% white, with less than 1% ELs recorded.

The district also reported a 98% graduation rate. Caitlyn's school had two Spanish teachers who shared the responsibilities for the program.

As with other participants in this study, the data sources for my analysis of Caitlyn's experiences and beliefs include a formal interview with her, two full days of observation, informal interviews during those two days and classroom documentation. Additionally, one of Caitlyn's students consented to be interviewed.

Teaching environment

Caitlyn taught one class of 7th-grade Spanish and one class of 8th-grade Spanish. She also taught four periods of Spanish 1 and one period of Spanish 4. All these classes took place in the same classroom, as the middle and high schools were connected in her building. In the 8th-period academic day, she had one period for preparing her classes and then one additional advisory period at the end of the day. The classes were 43 minutes long, and her class sizes ranged from seven to 22 students, with several of the classes containing about 15 students.

Caitlyn's classroom was deskless, and she organized her chairs in a large U-shape for most classes. In one of the observed classes, she had students gather around and sit at a small desk to do a group activity. The room was decorated with words and phrases in Spanish, promotional photographs of school sports teams and posters for a local university mascot. During my days of observation, there were few images or maps reflecting the target culture or countries on display. The carpeted room was homey and cozy, with twinkle lights in the front of the room, lamps around the room, a fruity smell in the air from scented oils, and a ceiling fan turning slowly. During one of the observation days, a scented oil dispenser filled the room with fragrance.

Classroom activities

Caitlyn often began her classes while chatting with students in Spanish about their weekends or their days, asking questions appropriate for their language levels. From the first moments of her class, she exhibited a positive attitude with her students, constantly smiling and avoiding any defensiveness or authoritarian posturing, making for a feeling of camaraderie in the class. Sometimes, she gave time for the students to read quietly from leveled readers as they settled into the class. Other times, she conducted 'Special Person' interviews, where one student was asked a series of standard questions in Spanish about their lives by the other students in the class. After introductory activities like these, she then began the main part of the class. Usually, this consisted of activities that were a combination of large-group discussions, individual work or worksheets based on that large-group instruction or discussion, and tasks where students had to communicate with one another in Spanish or read in Spanish. Her students remarked on the consistency of the schedule and activities in Caitlyn's classes.

Individual worksheets were often handed out during class, and students completed them during class and then handed them back in as they left the room. Her Spanish 1 student explained the activity that they remembered the best in their class, where Caitlyn would play a Spanish video with English subtitles 'in case we don't understand all of it', then asking the students to complete different worksheets in Spanish either during or after the video to identify 'how much of it we got'. Caitlyn's use of worksheets gave her a chance to direct students' attention and provide a way for her to assess them formatively as they were interacting with the texts. This student had also been taking classes with Caitlyn for several years, and they remarked that the types of worksheets had changed from 'colors and things' to worksheets where 'she gives us . . . more time to try to understand things a little bit more . . . I feel like this year it's been more of discussion of what we don't understand'.

Relatedly, Caitlyn used the target language regularly in the class. Using the target language was clearly the default and was actively sought in class, even though English could be heard from the teacher and the students frequently, particularly during explanations and instruction at the lower levels. In the example from the student above, where English subtitles were used with a Spanish video, the student explained that 'it actually helps me, cause sometimes I don't understand some of the things they're saying, and so I can look at that'. Her use of Spanish, her Spanish 1 student explained, often created a situation where the students had to actively engage with Spanish in order to complete class activities. The students had to 'read through it and try and see if we know most of it . . . and then, we can always ask her questions'. Caitlyn told me during one class that she tried to stay 90% in the target language as recommended by ACTFL (2010b), although that was not always what I observed at the lower levels, where coaching and directions were often given in English, while questions about the content were in Spanish. Students were regularly asked to interact with one another and with her in the target language. Caitlyn communicated almost entirely in Spanish with her students in the upper-level classes and in the lower levels whenever she was able to use simple language and instructions.

Caitlyn did not focus on teaching grammar, although she included some grammar explanations in the class as needed. She selected specific target phrases and words at different times of her class. She would remind the students metalinguistically of their focus as needed, saying things like, 'Remember "busca" ["search"] is one of our targets!' and 'Can anyone guess why I used "comica" ["funny", feminine form] and not "comico" ["funny", masculine form]?'. She clearly knew how to ask questions about texts and how to use translations in her classes. She also chose carefully when to correct students and when to let them repeat errors. For instance, in one observation of the 8th-grade class, which was incidentally their first class session ever, she allowed them to make a simple error repeatedly.

Although she followed similar patterns and practices from day to day to maintain consistency, Caitlyn also programmed variation in her days. One technique that she used to achieve this was to have different activities scheduled for different days of the week, for instance, Friday was 'dancing to target language songs' and Thursday was 'ja ja jueves' ['ha ha Thursday'], when a joke was told. She assigned, discussed and shifted specific roles and duties to students in the classes, for instance, having one student act as 'librarian' who made sure that the shelves of class books were in order. Her student said that they liked this practice, as it encouraged students 'who don't say anything or do much in the class' to 'do a little bit more that way'. Caitlyn used 'brain bursts' and 'brain breaks' when students seemed to stop paying attention or engaging during the class; as she said in one class, 'It's time to relax our brains'. One popular brain break was to play a Spanish song, sometimes with the accompanying video; the students sang along and responded to the songs such that it was clear that they knew them well. Her student liked those activities, in order to 'learn some different things in Spanish' and to 'keep those in my mind a little bit'.

Caitlyn did sometimes struggle with student engagement, with down to 40–60% of student engagement during some classes. Her student noticed that sometimes attention waned in her classes, saying, 'Some days we just, our class didn't really . . . pay attention all that well, and then it was kind of confusing the next day when we were supposed to do things'. Interestingly, this varied considerably across the four Spanish 1 classes, which all had the same curriculum and instructional tasks. Caitlyn encouraged student attention by having them clap for one another with 'un aplauso' ['one clap'] for specific students, or to have them 'give your neighbor two snaps and a woot woot'. She drew her students' attention by using regular, practiced call-and-response phrases in Spanish. She also adjusted her instruction, eliminating activities that required attenuated student attention in the less focused class, increasing the amount of Spanish that she used in more cooperative classes. Her student noted that her teaching was also structured that students were held accountable for their learning and therefore needed to be caught up if they missed it.

Caitlyn monitored the students' learning using a variety of assessments and tasks. Students were rarely working on their own for long without her checking in with them. She stated, 'Formative tasks guide my instruction', suggesting that assessments were used throughout her classes and as a way of helping her to make instructional decisions. Homework was generally not assigned in her classes. Participation in class was organized with techniques like drawing popsicle sticks randomly with students' names; students all seemed to be aware that they might be asked to respond, and they behaved accordingly. When she used a more free-form way of calling on students, she sometimes encouraged quieter students to participate with statements such as, 'Let's hear from some people we haven't heard from yet at all'. In another case, to encourage students to work independently in their responses, she said, 'I'd like for you to see if you can answer [question] three silently'. During one Spanish 1 class, I observed Caitlyn saying, 'Give me a thumbs up if you understand!' and one student responded, 'Can we go over it?'. Caitlyn then reviewed the material once more. She also focused on giving students tools for clarification, like teaching them the question, 'Como se dice?' ['How do you say?'].

Although Caitlyn did include videos, songs and readings that reflected cultural phenomena, most of her course objectives and targets were focused on language. For instance, her approach to using songs from the target culture(s) and readings about cultural facts or phenomena often focused on language, asking students to do things like count how many times they heard a specific word. Her student identified the 'daily target of the day' as being simple language things like 'I can introduce myself in Spanish' and then growing more complex in language as they proceeded.

Themes and patterns in teaching and connection to beliefs

Positivity and realism: 'I really work hard to provide a lot of energy'

Caitlyn provided a lot of evidence that her beliefs, and her behaviors in class stemming from those beliefs, were grounded in connection with her students. She wanted to provide them with 'novel and fun' instruction and activities so that the 'language learning is enjoyable' for them. She prioritized her ability to give a lot of energy and to create a positive environment for her students. This effort was something that she knew that they needed, but she also admitted that she herself needed it too, stating, 'When the students come in excited, I think it makes it a lot easier for me to teach'. She described a give-and-take relationship between what she believed was important for students to have ('a lot of student autonomy in the classroom') and what she wanted to see the most ('seeing them create with the language'). Thus, her beliefs, when enacted in the classroom, gave her the positive feedback and support that she needed as a teacher.

This belief in positivity in the classroom was tempered by a realism to Caitlyn's relationship with her students. Specifically, she valued being realistic about the challenges involved in learning a language. Part of her positive classroom was the space for students to 'feel safe to speak the target language and to make mistakes'. With this, she also tried to share stories with her students about how long it took to learn a language and the patience required to learn language. I observed a conversation between her and a Spanish 4 student where she told them her story of learning Spanish for eight years. She also built closer relationships with them, explaining, 'And I also show them that, like sometimes I fail, too. And I think being transparent and vulnerable before them allows them to feel that they can make mistakes, too'. Caitlyn believed that a positive classroom was important, but that it was also vital to be realistic with her students and to connect with them over some of the struggles or challenges that they might have in learning languages, too.

Intentionally based in research: 'The research says that you remember better in blue'

Caitlyn repeatedly shared her core belief that research, including both research about second language acquisition and research about learning processes in general, was the most important basis for all teaching decisions. She spoke about the importance of research in our conversations as well as in her messages and advice to her students during class.

Caitlyn firmly believed that students would acquire language and be ready to produce output eventually, in a similar pattern to first language learners. She explained that she wanted her students to learn language just like her small toddler son was learning language. This belief, echoed by many teachers who, like Caitlyn, considered themselves to be focused on comprehensible input in the classroom (see Wesely *et al.*, 2021), was connected directly to Caitlyn's classroom practices. When she stayed in the target language 90% of the time as she hoped, the amount of comprehensible input students was receiving would result in acquisition. As she explained:

> And so I think organically as it comes . . . I try not to force it, but I think that the speaking is just part of what we're doing in the classroom, and it kind of comes. And a lot of the students have said this year: 'I know these things and . . . I haven't really had to study this'. It's kind of been acquired.

For Caitlyn, language acquisition was not about studying language, it was about exposure to language via input, a belief grounded in research and nested in her core belief of the importance of research to guide her classroom practice.

Although this might seem to suggest that Caitlyn's core belief was in the importance of comprehensible input and input-before-output, she also argued for a varied approach to language teaching, as long as it was based in the research. Although 'a light bulb went on when [she] found CI [comprehensible input]', she believed that any approach shown in the research to be effective was worth implementing in her classroom. Other similar research-based beliefs included Caitlyn's contention that lessons needed to be planned with 'prime time lesson planning' in mind, that focused on what the brain was ready for and when it needed a break. She told students research facts, such as, 'The research says that you remember better in blue', and 'It's proven that you learn more vocabulary from what you read'. She told me that she felt that the teaching technique that helped students the most was giving appropriate feedback at the right time. Even moving around during class, she argued, was shown by the research to be important, one reason why she no longer used desks in her classroom.

Factors influencing beliefs and practices

Caitlyn's instructional practice and thinking about her practice was influenced by many different people that surrounded her. She connected with other teachers in the state and locally, regionally, nationally, and internationally, often via social media. She talked about how she watched one online language educational celebrity's videos online. She connected both in getting ideas and in sharing her ideas with others. This professional development practice was very important to her vision of how she would continue to learn about teaching. She did sometimes collaborate with the one other Spanish teacher down the hall, although she said that she found it difficult to connect with the other teacher. They often had to communicate via email and Google Docs, since they had to synchronize their work about Spanish 4. During our conversations, Caitlyn mentioned her desire to connect more with the state organization for language teachers.

Caitlyn also looked to her students to help her to continue to grow as a teacher. She gave them a survey at the end of the quarter and the semester that asked them questions like, 'What can your teacher do better?' and 'Do you feel your teacher believes in you as a language learner?'. She also included regular check-ins with students as a part of formative assessments throughout her classes. Her goals for the year were centered around student engagement, 'making sure that the students are with [her] and that [her] language is comprehensible'. She used regular self-evaluations using tools like the TELL Project (Teacher Effectiveness for Language Learning Project, n.d.), a teacher evaluation tool for language teaching contexts. She further explained:

> I feel like this year, if I could title it, I think I would title it 'My Year of Growth'. Last year was like, trouble-shooting and problem-solving, tearing it all apart and re-doing it, kind of, and this year is my year to expand.

This expansion was centered on her students. She saw part of her responsibility as pushing herself to move 'outside of [her] comfort zone', focusing on meeting the needs of diverse learners. In her largely homogeneous white district, she also reflected on the lack of diversity and potential for racism that she saw in her students.

This overall concept of growth was important to Caitlyn as she considered her path forward as a teacher. She had both 'tried-and-true things' that worked for her, but she was also willing to 'scrap it in the middle' if something was not working. She identified technology as a great place for innovation and change in her practice, explaining that incorporating new technologies with different capabilities could change the nature of an activity. She explained:

> That's something that I really enjoy about this, is all those puzzle pieces and making them work together and kind of problem-solving what can I fix and what went well last year and what can I use from last year and make this year better.

Caitlyn was energized to do well for her students, and she found inspiration in them, in her fellow teachers and in a general desire to continue to improve that permeated her work.

Case Two: Veronica

School context

Veronica had been teaching Spanish for approximately five years in a few districts before I interviewed her. A white, US-born, native speaker of English, Veronica had learned Spanish in junior high and high school and chose to become a Spanish teacher while in college after realizing that another possible career would be too unstable. Both Veronica and the next teacher in this chapter, Marlene, taught at White Mountain High School, located in a community on the outskirts of a large metro area in the state. The area around the school felt like a large sports complex, with prominent sports fields on the approach to the school. The school itself was a low, broad building with a busy parking lot. It had a clean and new feeling, with some decorations on the walls and narrow, short halls. The main entrance was in a low, clean area that opened quickly into a large cafeteria with hanging lights. The school had a courtyard that opened to the outdoors within its walls and with windows looking into it along the hallways.

The 9–12 high school building where Veronica and Marlene taught had about 450 students during the time of data collection, with about 1600 students total in the district. One-quarter of the students in the district received free or reduced-price lunches. Ninety percent of the students in the district were white, with 6% Hispanic, 2% multiracial and 1% or less Native American, Asian, Black or Pacific Islander students. Students receiving EL services comprised 2.1% of the district, and overall the district had a 98% graduation rate.

In my discussion of Veronica's classes, I draw from my formal phone interview with her, as well as several informal discussions before, during, and after her school days. I had a long-standing professional relationship with Veronica due to our work together on various professional development opportunities in the state, so these conversations were comfortable and familiar. Additionally, I observed two full days of Veronica in her classroom. I was not able to arrange interviews with any of her students.

Teaching environment

Veronica taught three classes of Spanish 1 and two classes of Spanish 2. She taught part-time in the year that I was observing her, teaching five out of eight periods of the school day. She had a free period at the start of the day and had one lunch period. She was able to leave early each day due to her part-time status. Her classes lasted for 42 minutes, and she had between eight and 20 students in each class. There were three Spanish teachers in Veronica's school, including Marlene.

Veronica's classroom had a tile floor, with windows on part of one side of the room. There were shelves around the classroom. Overall, the room had a generally warm and cozy feeling. Veronica's students did not use desks, and the chairs were set up almost arena-style in rows about three chairs deep. The walls of Veronica's classroom had a number of charts with verb conjugations featured on them. A large whiteboard was at the front of the room, where she often wrote vocabulary words and other language items for students to reference as they completed class activities. She would use the laser pointer during class to highlight these words and phrases on her walls. Other decorations in the room were maps and pictures of students.

Classroom activities

Veronica's classes frequently started with warm-up activities that featured a different grammar focus every week. In these large-group, teacher-centered warm-up lessons, Veronica explained grammar through explicitly connecting rules with English and doing focused practice on a given concept through examples and review of the rules. I observed a high level of student engagement during these grammar warm-ups, where students were all writing down notes and copying from the board. Using these targeted forms, as Veronica explained to me, was a slight modification from her focus on providing comprehensible input, but she then used the targeted form throughout the rest of the class. For instance, she would ask questions to her students in Spanish during class such as, 'Are you special?' to get them to practice the targeted form.

After starting the class in a large, teacher-centered activity, Veronica frequently divided her students into small reading or activity groups, often where they were focused on reading a novel. She used the flexibility of her deskless classroom to have students move around from place to place in her room for groups and activities. One reading-focused grouping was done by level; for instance, the advanced group read individually and had to create a quiz based on the reading; the intermediate group read in a group and did an activity where they put sentences in order; and the low-proficiency group read with Veronica and responded to questions as she read. They were allowed to decide on their own groups, but she sometimes advised them if she felt like it was not working. In some cases, she assigned packets for students to complete based on the readings in the classes, where the packets included a variety of activities for students to do to demonstrate comprehension. Often, the students were allowed to choose which activity they wanted to do, and they did not have to do all of them.

During this small-group time, when possible, Veronica circulated to make sure that students were all on task. I observed her check on one group and see that the students had made very simple choices of writing and communicating in basic sentences that did not meet her standards. She corrected their actions so that the students in that group instead engaged in a real language interaction. At the end of the small-group time, especially when the students were focused on a group reading activity, Veronica followed the group with a large-group discussion to review the 'eventos' ['events'] in the book.

Veronica used both English and Spanish to explain content or clarify meaning. During large-group discussions, as she spoke, she wrote translations and definitions of Spanish words on the board throughout the lessons. She focused on using spoken Spanish for most conversational interaction. She described another way that she helped students with understanding her Spanish, stating:

> [I teach] with a lot of gesturing and a lot of stories to help students remember vocabulary better, and we really focus on really giving them a lot of input at the beginning . . . so that they can become better speakers and writers.

During the small-group activities when students focused on their differentiated activities with books, Veronica communicated almost always in Spanish, with English sometimes just to clarify. Students spoke in English with one another but responded in Spanish when asked. Veronica, during this time, often reminded students about responding in Spanish to one another in their groups.

Veronica's activities in all parts of class were often complex, involving many different skills including listening, speaking, reading and writing. She explained that she graded on the four skills and culture and learner outcomes according to the demands of the school, using standards-based grading. She did not grade on interpersonal communication.

Veronica rarely corrected spoken language errors unless they reflected a lack of understanding of the targeted grammar concept explained at the start of the class period; my only observation of her correcting a student was in such a case. She would say things like, 'We really want to focus on asking correctly', in order to prompt students to focus on some level of accuracy, but that rarely meant that she asked them to restart or revisit something in correct that they had said. For example, in one activity, students came up and gave examples of what they had done in small groups. Several students made numerous mistakes but still stayed in Spanish and were comprehensible, and she did not correct their mistakes. This error-correction approach did not mean that Veronica did not help students when they were confused. I observed her several times helping students who expressed confusion about one of the tasks in the class, with a great deal of warmth and support.

Veronica often communicated warmly and personally with students during the transitions and activities in her class. She engaged frequently in joking conversations with them. She shared opinions and thoughts about herself and her life freely with them, and I observed that she fed off the students in the class and their energy. When a student was distracted and off-task in her class, she said his name, and then 'mi amor' ['my love'] to get him back on task. She encouraged students to build on and personally connect with the novels that they read, and they often did so through creating class jokes and hypotheses about the readings. She used silly, attention-getting examples to illustrate grammar issues, like asking her students the importance of the difference between the phrases, 'Do you want to smell my farts?' and 'Do you want to smell your farts?'.

She worked to maintain control and authority in the classroom, too, often reminding students to stay in Spanish and to put their phones away. She called on students seemingly randomly to answer when there were large-group discussions. This combination of building relationships and maintaining control resulted in generally quite high student engagement during Veronica's classes. The lowest engagement I observed was sometimes in small groups when 70% of the students were engaged when Veronica was not directly supervising them. At the end of class, I observed that students were sometimes doing other activities, and Veronica shared with me during the interview that she did not care if students did other things after finishing work assigned in class.

Themes and patterns in teaching and connection to beliefs

Balancing grammar and input: 'Kids need to be able to do these things at some level'

Veronica had been a leader in the state in the community of teachers who focused on comprehensible input in the classroom, like some of the other teachers in this book, including Wade, Calvin, Abbie and Marlene (in the next section). However, unlike most of those teachers, Veronica stated that she felt that teaching grammar explicitly was important. As she argued:

I feel we're doing a severe injustice to the kids who go on to college. And so many in the comprehensible input world will say, 'Well colleges are just doing it wrong!'. And it's like, but unfortunately this is our reality. And kids need to be able to do these things at some level, you know.

In this, Veronica was a pragmatist about teaching grammar. Since her college-bound students would need to know it for their further studies, she incorporated it into her classes and her instruction. She enacted this belief in her focus on grammar instruction at the start of each class, as well as when she incorporated target structures throughout the class.

Veronica stated that she believed that students displayed knowledge of the language when they were able to produce rejoinders in the target language like, 'I'm afraid!' or 'Yes, I am smart', in a way that was accurate and natural for them. She explained that both accuracy, or what she called 'refining' of the language, and fluency, or the ability to communicate, were important to her. This sometimes came at the expense of other components of the language classroom. She explained that she had made the decision to change from a focus on culture to one on 'the I/he/she/you forms of words, because our kids don't know them and it drives me bonkers'. Thus, she felt that prioritizing grammar and mastering forms was one of the most vital projects in her classroom. She was sometimes challenged by this project and this belief. She repeated a comment to me several times on one of my observation days: 'I don't understand why they make some of the mistakes that they make'. She continued to try to align what she did in the classroom to meet her students' needs in this respect.

Getting kids moving and thinking and demonstrating: 'Paint a picture in their head'

Veronica believed that engagement was key to student language learning, and she felt that the most effective ways to encourage and cultivate engagement involved movement and activity in the classroom. As she explained, 'Tons of visual engagement is what I think really helps them . . . you know like moving around, sound effects, things like that, trying to get them to . . . paint a picture in their head'. She further explained that she thought that classic Total Physical Response (TPR), where students respond with gestures, was an ideal activity. She explained that it gets the students moving, there are a lot of variations, and students really listen. Activities where students could incorporate a lot of different skills, like running dictation where students had to write down a paragraph by running back and forth between papers to recall it, could be effective as well. Veronica was encouraged in enacting this belief into practice by her principal, who noticed her lack of desks in the room and investigated her practices. Veronica already knew that her students benefited from moving around and being deskless, and the encouragement from her institution via the principal reinforced this belief. She knew that student engagement was a vital part of every class, and this was how she identified the best way to encourage it.

Importantly, engaging students in this way also allowed Veronica to identify if they were learning. She connected this type of active engagement with seeing evidence of student learning, stating that students demonstrate learning by producing the language. She stated, talking about how she asked students to repeat or respond back to her in Spanish, 'I guess I'm looking to see if the kids linguistically . . . can do it back'. Having students be consistently engaged through active activities helped her to navigate some of this confusion or lack of clarity for her about what students knew.

Factors affecting beliefs and practices

As mentioned above, Veronica's beliefs and practices were influenced by the knowledge that many of her students were college-bound. As she articulated, '[I am] trying to kind of balance previous experience with what I think my kids need and what I'm expected to teach'. In this way, Veronica's core beliefs about teaching, generated from what she had learned and experienced in the past, were literally, in her mind, being 'balanced' with her understanding of her learners' needs and the institutional expectations. Other things that she mentioned as influencing her practice included other aspects of her learners' lives, including individual student mental health and social issues.

Veronica had changed in her approach to things such as grammar because she saw the needs that the students had. As she had changed districts and students, she shifted her practice accordingly. One example, as mentioned above, was her change from focusing on culture, which she thought she did very well and had prioritized in her previous job, to focusing on verbs and grammar, because she saw that the students in her current district did not know them as well as they needed to in order to perform at the appropriate level. Another example was her need to adapt her assessment to standards-based grading, which was required in her district. Although she said that she didn't think that she 'changed the way [she] taught', she did have to grade differently, and in a way that made 'a lot more sense for [her] kids for the way [she teaches]'.

Veronica's exposure to different ways of teaching or new materials and new resources from the larger language teaching community also altered her beliefs and corresponding practices. She explained:

> My first year teaching, I was really, really traditional . . . so my textbook had a supplementary whatever [about TPRS] and so I did one of the stories, and it had nothing to do with the unit it said it was supposed to go with. But I tried it out, and it was the only words that my kids remembered on their end of year test.

As she saw it, when she was a new teacher, she was open to trying new things in her classroom, and she was still in the process of forming and shaping her beliefs about what the best ways to teach might be.

She later explained that she often now changed her practice when she found new activities or selected new novels to have her students read, stating, 'I'm willing to try anything once'. She elaborated, 'I feel like, if it's new for me, it keeps it exciting and I'm more interested and I'm more apt to try new things within that realm'. However, Veronica also explained that 'it's hard to really find that much new stuff all the time . . . I'm just not quite [excited by learning] in the actual act of teaching right now'. As a teacher several years into her teaching practice, she was sometimes challenged by finding new materials. In this way, the nature of Veronica's beliefs about language teaching and learning allowed her to explore new things, suggesting that one core belief was also the belief that there was not just one right way to do things. However, as she gained experience, she also struggled with staying engaged as a teacher/learner.

Case Three: Marlene

School context

Marlene was an experienced teacher of more than 20 years, with experience teaching in a few different districts in Iowa. She was white, US-born, and a native speaker of English. Marlene taught in the same school and district as Veronica, as one of three Spanish teachers in the school. In this section, I draw on a formal interview with Marlene, two days of observation, informal conversations during my observation days, digital classroom documents supplied to me by Marlene and interviews with two of Marlene's students. One of the students had just completed Spanish 2, and the other had just completed Spanish 4. One of the two days that I observed was cut short due to an early release due to weather, so I did not observe the last period of that day or the last meeting of that day.

Teaching environment

Marlene taught six Spanish classes every day out of the eight-period day, including one class of Spanish 2, three classes of Spanish 3, and two classes of Spanish 4. She had one period to prepare her classes, one project-based class called 'Launch' that included Spanish and other content and was not formally counted as a Spanish class, and one shorter 'seminar' meeting at the end of the day that served as a study hall and a time to meet with students. Her standard classes were 42 minutes long, and her class sizes varied from eight to 30 students, with most classes numbering between 16 and 20 students.

Marlene had a clean classroom that was crowded with student desks. The desks were arranged, like Veronica's, arena-style in two rows with a big space in the front of the classroom near the whiteboard, where Marlene spent most of her time when actively teaching. Cabinets and shelves lined some walls, and the teacher's desk was in the back of the room. The floor was made of tile, and there was a large window to the outside on the opposite side of the classroom from the door into the hallway. Marlene's classroom walls were covered in posters, signs in English and Spanish and flags. Pictures were on the walls and bulletin boards. The student designated as the 'Estudiante del mes' ['Student of the Month'] had a large picture prominently displayed in front of the class.

Classroom activities

Marlene started every class with simple questions such as 'Qué tal clase?' ['What's up, class?'] and 'Qué pása?' ['What's going on?'] and 'Anuncios' ['Announcements']. She had students explain what was going on at the school or in their lives in Spanish. She knew the students well, and she built on her knowledge of them to have conversations in Spanish and to question them on what they had been doing. One of her students described this as a time when 'you can just raise your hand and share anything good you have going on, or something like you did last night'. The student also thought that this effort tied into a school-wide initiative called 'capturing kids' hearts' which was intended to build connections and relationships between teachers and students; Marlene did not mention this school initiative in our discussions. The student also explained that throughout the class, Marlene would ask her students about their lives, and 'make [them] feel like she was genuinely interested in what [they] were doing'. The student said that they would talk with her both as a teacher and a friend, and that she would observe when they looked tired or seemed like they were not doing okay. The Spanish 2 student recognized the positive environment that Marlene tried to encourage, saying that 'that's obviously something that she had to like consciously create, too'. These announcements at the start of the class set the stage for this type of sharing and relationship-building.

During this time and the rest of her classes, Marlene spoke gently, in a friendly way, and with a positive demeanor with her students throughout her classes. Her students showed high levels of engagement with her lessons throughout my two observed days, even the first day when the weather turned bad partway through the day. The Spanish 2 student described her class as a 'brain break' where 'you can just talk and that counts as your class'. Marlene regularly used positive reinforcement for class actions and behavior. For instance, she awarded her students with 'chicletas' ['gum'], which were actually stickers that looked like gumballs collecting in a poster in her room. Eventually, students could collect enough of the gumballs to win a prize. She also encouraged her students to praise one another with 'aplauso' ['applause']. At the end of her classes, she had a call-and-response with her students where she said, 'Gracias por aprender' ['Thank you for learning'], and the students replied, 'Gracias por enseñarme' ['Thank you for teaching me'].

Stories and narratives constituted a big part of Marlene's instructional activities. During the time when Marlene spoke with students individually in formative assessments, the other students in the class were quiet and most were reading diligently, with books from the *Magic School Bus* in Spanish to Spanish-language children's books to more advanced books. If they finished, she directed them to 'share with someone else if you read a book you liked so they can find it'. When the class read a text together, Marlene asked questions to review sections, then had students retell the story in partners. She would ask, 'How are we stuck?' and 'Uno para cinco ["one to five"], how are we doing?' to check up on their progress. After these readings, she would often have the students do a writing task, where they talked through the comprehension questions in pairs, then in the large group, then with longer, varied comprehension questions on an online quiz site. A simpler writing task was to rewrite the story in Spanish in 100 words in five minutes. The Spanish 2 student explained that these 'quick writes' sometimes surprised them, 'because I'll understand what's going on in the book, but I'm always surprised that I can write that much about it'.

Beyond assessing students' mastery of stories, Marlene formatively assessed her students with minor activities throughout her classes. She had students prepare skits to demonstrate their knowledge of concepts. I observed her assessing oral proficiency via having students tell her stories individually based on pictures. She asked questions and gave feedback on pronunciation and vocabulary. The Spanish 2 student also described being informally assessed in small groups when they had to discuss a topic completely in Spanish. The student added:

> One of the rules is if you're confused, you stop her . . . [I am not] afraid to say, 'I don't understand something, you lost me'. And she will totally go back and explain it. So, I would say, as long as you try and pay attention, you would be totally fine.

The Spanish 4 student described 'talking days' where they were assessed on participation and use of Spanish that they maintained throughout the class period. On those days, the student explained, 'We were graded, but . . . as long as you spoke in Spanish and made a good effort the whole time', you would be fine.

Marlene communicated with her students primarily in Spanish in her classes, with a few exceptions. Her classes were often centered on specific language structures or vocabulary words that she had selected to focus on.

In Spanish, she discussed targeted vocabulary with her students through a variety of techniques, including asking repeated personal questions; projecting a question for discussion that elicited a specific grammar or verb structure for the group to practice (for example, 'What do you want to study?'); repeating a target phrase up to 75 times in one class period and creating a story through pulling images of students off of their social media and inserting them into other pictures. Her use of Spanish created a 'comfortable environment' from the beginning, as the Spanish 4 student said, which allowed the students to easily transition into staying only in Spanish in the upper-level class.

Marlene did use English for select classroom activities. She translated phrases directly and allowed students to use translation, although she did not allow the use of Google Translate, instead encouraging her students: 'You have very strong language skills so use them, don't use Google'. She coached students in English in a way that encouraged the development of their metalinguistic knowledge, making statements like, 'Really get that mental image, that mental movie going on there'. One of her classes was working on a portfolio assignment where they had to give evidence and commentary about what they had achieved; she coached them in completing this assignment in English. Finally, she would also use English to correct student behavior: '[Student name], make sure that you're reading!'.

I observed several activities in Marlene's classroom where students connected with authentic voices and diverse perspectives from the target culture(s). With her upper-level students, she had them work with authentic texts, like texts about Spanish idioms, then led a discussion in Spanish about the connection between language and culture. She tried to create opportunities for students to connect with native speakers of the language, like people she had met in other countries. Marlene also used videos and songs regularly in class with her lower-level students. She often had them process the information in a way that was reflective of their language level. One activity that I observed in such an instance was when she played the video and students had to write down the vocabulary that they heard in the song, then she went around the room to see who heard the highest number of different words. Thus, an authentic task was paired with a fairly simple vocabulary exercise.

In addition to the different activities mentioned above, Marlene taught using several activities that required students to work cooperatively and independently from her guidance while communicating in Spanish together, including running dictation (also used as a technique by Caitlyn), breakout games where they had to solve a series of mysteries or puzzles together and even games that mimicked traveling across Spanish-speaking countries while completing tasks. These games required students to use Spanish in addressing the content questions that Marlene had prepared. During these activities, she watched them carefully, but did not help as they worked. She had some classes at the upper levels create portfolios that 'reflected their learning process'. On these projects, she offered a lot of coaching in the content but not a lot of feedback except for the summative grade.

Themes and patterns in teaching and connection to beliefs

The importance of good language acquisition: 'It's all about communication'

Marlene had a very clear belief that that good language acquisition was more important than producing 'perfect Spanish'. As she explained:

> A lot of times I will forego structure and grammar and vocabulary just a certain way as long as they can get their point across . . . very much founded in communication. Because that is one thing, that when I started traveling and interacting with native speakers, I was so set on doing it exactly right and having the perfect grammar, and in the end, it's all about communication.

As evidenced by her strategic use of English in the classroom, Marlene found it important to make the Spanish language – and communication in the Spanish language – as accessible to her students as possible. She identified herself as a 'CI teacher' who did 'a lot of stories in class', focusing on providing comprehensible input and not demanding perfect output from students. This belief fit with her broader, core belief that people learn language best by going to the country and immersing themselves, that getting students outside of the classroom in an authentic way is important.

Some of these beliefs tied into the larger idea that language acquisition was both unrelated to and superior to memorization of language. Marlene suggested that when things got stressful, students automatically relied on what they had 'acquired' rather than just 'memorized'. She said, 'We are a very communicative-based class, that is focused on acquiring language rather than on memorizing lists of vocabulary that may or may not stick with them in the future'. This concept of 'sticking with' students was, for Marlene, the goal of language teaching. As mentioned above, she also said, 'That's how we build language in the classroom . . . they need that repetition, they need to hear it hundreds of times, and eventually they will start to produce it at will'.

The students understood what Marlene wanted them to do in her classroom. Her Spanish 4 student knew that Marlene's 'ultimate goal' wasn't for them to get an A or to do the homework (a more traditional version of language learning and assessment), but rather to 'learn language' and 'grasp the knowledge' (a more acquisition-focused approach). Both interviewees recognized why Marlene did what she did, as she explicitly shared some of her goals about developing their interpersonal communication, but they primarily understood her approach through observing her actions and her focus in class.

Connecting with students: 'Surprise and delight'

For Marlene, a big part of the joy of teaching was getting to know and work closely with students. As she said, 'Just helping them through the struggles of those teenage years, but at the same time, celebrating those small successes that they have, and just letting them share things'. She called upon the idea of 'surprise and delight' – a way to help students who are stressed or agitated. This principle could be achieved by doing something out of the ordinary, Marlene explained, like having a snowball fight. Her technique described above of pulling her students' pictures off of social media was another way to connect with and surprise them in the classroom. She recognized that students could be very energetic, but as long as they were learning, she said that it was ok.

Marlene's belief in the importance of connecting with students and supporting them could also be seen in how she described the students that she found to be most fun to teach. She appreciated when students had a growth mindset, when they were 'not afraid to struggle with things, they easily help each other out . . . and they stay in the target language as much as possible'. She wanted to push them, to have them take risks because that led to the best learning, she believed. She wanted also to expose them to as much culture as possible and to help them see that other people lived in a different way than she did and with many fewer privileges.

Factors affecting beliefs and practices

With some probing, it was clear that Marlene formulated these beliefs around what she had observed in her students. As already noted, Marlene believed that students relied on what they had acquired rather than just memorized, especially when they were stressed. This belief came in part from her work with teaching comprehensible input novels. Once she started using them, she could see that 'kids are able to do things that I have never been able to get them to do with traditional teaching'. In this sense, Marlene's beliefs and practices are evident in a dynamic relationship that involved her students, with her beliefs influenced by how she was able to observe her students interacting successfully with a new practice. She stated that she often created 'new material' every year instead of just 'recycling', because 'different groups of kids have very different needs from one year to the next'. Marlene also sometimes asked students directly what they needed in the classroom, sending them surveys and questioning them during class. In some ways, student feedback was incorporated into all of her classes through her use of formative assessment. The portfolio assignment in her most advanced class similarly asked students to provide evidence of what they knew about Spanish culture and language, giving her other insights into what students felt that they had learned in her classes.

This is not to say that the relationship between Marlene's beliefs and practices were mediated only by her observations of her students. Marlene relied on her own instincts and experiences as a teacher in how she determined when to change her practice. As she explained, 'I may want to change [my teaching] just for my own sanity, because what I've been doing has been too routine . . . I figure, if I'm getting bored, they're probably getting bored'. In this sense, Marlene was still keeping her students in mind, but she was focusing on her own experience and instincts. She brought in other feedback on her teaching, including inviting visitors to her class and asking them for feedback. She used her private network of teacher collaborators, usually accessed on social media, to help her improve, including some people that she described might not know that they are mentors. She explained how she brought in new ideas even from a 'two-line tweet', which would inspire her to 'figure out how that will fit my classroom, my teaching style, my students . . . and just go from there'. Again, here is a return to her consideration of her students in how she formed her practice, in a combination of influence of her teacher collaborators and her students.

There is also a relative absence of the influence of Marlene's administration or even her collaborators in her school. She described herself as having a 'growth mindset' and having 'high expectations for herself' – 'push myself to improve and get better and learn more and do more'. 'All of the brain research makes me giddy!' As mentioned above, some of Marlene's ways of making connections with students might have been indirectly affected by the school's initiatives about 'capturing kids' hearts', but no explicit connection was made by Marlene in our conversations. Her school, she described, had a great deal of tech support and was very social-media savvy. The teachers were allowed to create their own standards and curriculum, so Marlene did not find herself to be influenced so much by school requirements. Ultimately, Marlene felt that she set her own goals and operated independently, in part because, as she said, 'I'm an elective so I'm fighting for kids anyways'.

Looking across the Three Cases

Caitlyn, Veronica and Marlene have offered three perspectives on teaching in smaller schools (Caitlyn's high school and junior high with about 400 students altogether, and Veronica and Marlene's high school with 450 students). Their teaching loads were comparable, with full days of teaching and no more than one preparation period per day, and they only taught some of the levels of Spanish across the Spanish program. Their three classrooms looked very different both physically and instructionally, with different emphases put on the skills required of students, the assessments and the overall structure and pedagogy of the classes.

The beliefs articulated by these three teachers all included strong thoughts about relating to students and balancing a focus on communication with grammar instruction. Although they all articulated core beliefs, those beliefs were by their nature flexible, for instance, Caitlyn's belief that instructional decisions should be research-based, Veronica's belief that students should be thinking and engaging with the language and Marlene's belief that connecting with students was the most important thing. These expressions of core beliefs echoed Phipps and Borg's (2009) characterization of core beliefs as more general than peripheral beliefs. All three teachers spoke about their close consideration of the students in the classrooms, either through directly surveying them about the instructional effectiveness (Caitlyn, Marlene), or in simply identifying the students' needs based on their knowledge of language learning and child development (Veronica, Marlene). They all spoke about the affective and emotional needs of their students, as well. In all three cases, it seemed as if Caitlyn, Veronica and Marlene were cultivating a class ecosystem that did not focus only on one approach or one way of considering students, which was consistent with their shared belief that they needed to be responsive to student needs. In this, their examples echoed other studies where beliefs and practices were aligned (e.g. Farrell & Ives, 2015; Farrell & Yang, 2019).

One of the main components that set these three teachers apart from the singleton Spanish teachers in Chapter 4 was that they had fellow Spanish teachers in the school with whom they could collaborate, share materials and coplan. However, none of these teachers mentioned their school colleagues as major factors in helping them to make decisions about their instructional practices.

The social construction of their beliefs (Borg, 2017), therefore, was not grounded in their school or teaching context. They shared this characteristic with the singleton teachers. Instead, it involved their students and the teachers from outside of their schools, their community and sometimes even their state. They sought language teaching community beyond their school even though they had the option to look within their own buildings as well.

All three of these teachers spoke at length about reflecting and evaluating their own work while sustaining a growth mindset as a teacher. Recall here that research has shown that teachers who regularly reflect on their own practice demonstrate greater alignment between their beliefs and their practices (Farrell & Ives, 2015; Farrell & Yang, 2019; Watson, 2015b). Given that no significant discrepancies between their stated beliefs and their practices were observed, the data from these cases appears to support the findings in the other studies. Additionally, as noted above, the teachers shared sophisticated core beliefs that allowed for flexibility and adaptability in their practice, which also could be traced to their habituated reflective practice.

Questions for Discussion and Reflection

(1) Out of the three teachers featured in this chapter, which one most resembles how you teach or hope to teach?

(2) Imagine yourself as a student in each classroom. How would you respond to the teaching practices and techniques used by each teacher?

(3) These teachers all looked outside of their schools for inspiration and community with language teachers. What are the advantages and disadvantages of looking for that kind of community outside of the classroom?

(4) The relationship between the beliefs and practices of these participants seemed to be well-aligned. What techniques did they use that you thought helped them in that?

(5) If you were the supervisor of one of these teachers, what type of support would you seek to give them to help them to reach their goals of continuous improvement?

6 Large World Language High School Programs: The Spanish Teachers

This chapter explores the experiences of two Spanish teachers in large high school programs, Diana and Gabriel. They taught in schools that offered more than one world language, although the Spanish programs in both schools had the largest number of students. Both Diana and Gabriel taught a combination of Spanish heritage learners (HLs) and non-HLs. Similar to Chapter 5's teachers, they did not teach all levels of Spanish because of the large size of their programs and the number of Spanish teachers that they worked with. Their experiences can elucidate how working in larger schools with more resources and more students might influence how teachers navigate the relationship between their beliefs and practices.

Case One: Diana

School context

Like Sarah (Chapter 3), Diana came to teaching Spanish after another career, earning her licensure through an alternative program. She said that she knew she always wanted to be a teacher, but she did not realize Spanish would be the topic. A white, US-born, native speaker of English, Diana was married to a native speaker of Spanish and had traveled and lived extensively in Spanish-speaking countries in her adulthood. Diana taught in a large high school in a district of about 14,500 students. This school, with about 1700 students, included grades 9–12. The school was more racially diverse than most schools featured earlier in this book, with about half of the students identifying as white, about 20% as Black, about 20% as Hispanic, about 5% as Asian and 5% as multiracial. The racial diversity of the school was different from its linguistic diversity, as only about 10% of the students received EL services. About half of the overall student population qualified for free or reduced-price lunches. The school had a 94% graduation rate.

Located on a large campus in a residential neighborhood, the high school building was surrounded by green lawns, which in turn were surrounded by parking lots and sports fields. The large, attached brick buildings that made up the high school sat somewhat up on a hill, giving an imposing appearance. At the start of the day, students approached the building from all angles, some from the busy parking lots where they had parked their cars, others from a city bus dropping them off and yet others from the neighborhood on foot. The main school entrance had a high ceiling and led into a wide staircase featuring a mosaic of the school's encouraging motto. The hallways were wide and lined with lockers and, above the lockers, signs, awards and screens with images highlighting school announcements and achievements. Students traveled calmly on their way to class.

I present findings from two full days of classroom observation, a formal interview, many informal conversations during the observations and one student interview. I did know the teacher ahead of time both from personal contacts and professional contacts, so our conversations were familiar and easy.

Teaching environment

As a member of a large department, Diana benefited from being able to share the teaching duties with a large number of Spanish teachers. Although there were many students to teach, there were many teachers to teach them. Therefore, Diana taught two different classes: Spanish 2 Honors (three periods) and Spanish 4/Advanced Placement (also called Spanish 4/AP; two periods). Diana's full-time load was to teach five out of seven periods, thus giving her two free periods for her planning per day. Her class periods lasted for 50 minutes each. Her day also included a short advisory or tutoring period, which allowed her to meet with students to make up work if needed. Diana's classes all had 20–25 students.

Diana's classroom was filled with student desks grouped into groups of three or four. There were about eight of these groups in the room. The desk and chair legs had cut tennis balls on them to prevent them from scraping the floor. Her room had hardwood floors, high ceilings and a wall of big windows along one side of the room overlooking the lawns. Most of her walls had culturally appropriate posters and maps, with nothing hanging from the ceiling. There was a whiteboard where Diana could project her computer screen at the front of the room.

Classroom activities

After greeting students at the door in Spanish or English, Diana often began class by explaining a grammar or content concept, with students following along. After the short lesson was completed, she had students follow up with a variety of activities on the topic that she had addressed. Sometimes, she would put a question on the board in front of the room that built on the targeted grammar form for the students to complete or discuss at their desks. For instance, she asked students in one class to ask each other, 'Hablaste con tu familia anoche?' ['Did you talk with your family last night?'] to evoke the past tense. Sometimes she would ask students to determine if a sentence was 'lógico o no lógico?' ['logical or not logical?']. In other cases, she would have students write on the board to fill in sentences designed to get them to practice the targeted form. In reviewing that work with her class, she would explain, often through translating into English, what the sentences meant. If the activity involved students working independently, she often would circulate in the class to check the students' homework (which the interviewee described as, '10, 15 minutes of work, but it was like every night . . . so you always practiced a little bit outside of school').

Diana was able to answer many types of complex questions asked by the students. She gave positive feedback and engaged students with the learning process by asking for clarification. For example, she asked, 'What process did you go through?' when a student answered a hard question correctly. In interacting with them, she demonstrated her pedagogical content knowledge, identifying common mistakes that might trick them ('"llegar" ["arrive"] always has an "a"') while still encouraging them as they developed their understanding of the language. She talked in a gentle, quiet voice and did not correct or change anything that students shared when speaking up in the large group. She stayed in the front of the room during these exchanges, only going to the back to gather materials.

She spoke primarily in Spanish during both the Spanish 2 Honors class and the more advanced Spanish 4/AP class. She explained the differences between Spanish and English ('We don't have "ago" in Spanish') and rule exceptions ('Your Spanish brain would tell you to . . .') in English as needed. Although she clearly prioritized speaking Spanish, she also knew that English was important. As she said, 'I need to give explicit examples and identify patterns and talk about structure and formation'. As her classes contained a number of HLs, she called on them to help with questions when there were times of confusion in class. Her non-HL Spanish 2 Honors student stated that she saw the main difference between Spanish 2 Honors and Spanish 1 was that there was 'a lot more Spanish speaking happening in the class'.

After those first warm-up activities, the classroom activities were varied, as Diana explained, with a focus on everything from 'pop music to a grammar lesson to reading about a famous person from a Spanish-speaking country'. Diana's classes did not have a rigid structure, but she did have a plan for each class. Sometimes these activities built further on the homework such as worksheets or projects that students had begun outside of class. One example of an activity in the upper-level class was a listening exercise with an authentic text. Diana gave the Spanish 4/AP students directions in Spanish, then played the recording, and the students listened and read their worksheet with comprehension questions. Students did not ask questions during this time. They answered questions on their papers as they listened then Diana reviewed the responses. Diana assessed these projects and worksheets, along with student participation and small quizzes that she gave during class. The student remembered the review games for the quizzes well, which included both computer-based review and drill games, and board games, 'where to move to a certain spot, on the board game, you had to conjugate a verb correctly'.

Diana's class was characterized by regular small-group work, as she directed students in talking with one another and sharing information as they worked. She often had students work in their desk groups, having conversations primarily in Spanish with some translating into English. As the student interviewee said, 'I feel like we have a lot of small group conversations. 'Cause like all the desks are scattered in groups of like three or four. So you talk a lot with those people'. The student explained one memorable activity with this structure:

> We would watch a video in Spanish and have to answer questions about that. And we would discuss those in our small group . . . when we had prompts for homework, when everyone wrote their own thing, we would share those in small groups, to be able to hear Spanish from other people, like how they pronounce stuff.

During these small-group activities, Diana gave the students rules that she wrote on the board that they could refer to during these lessons. She would circulate around class during this time to answer their questions, consult with them and check their work. During one observation, I saw her focusing her help on one group of students who were struggling. First, she went by to clarify the directions, then returned later to define a word for them, then went by a third time and looked at their notes and encouraged them. When talking about what she wanted an observer to see, Diana said, 'That I . . . move around the classroom, and that . . . I'm aware of what's happening with every student'.

When appropriate, the small groups had to report out about what they had been doing in Spanish to the big group or share their projects by circulating around the classroom to other groups. During the large-group reports, Diana did not correct or change anything, instead giving positive feedback, asking for clarification or expanding on what they were saying. She sometimes would finish a sentence or thought for a speaker who was struggling. This type of reporting-out seemed more common in the Spanish 4/AP class than in the lower-proficiency Spanish 2 Honors class, where students more commonly were asked to share their work in smaller groups. One such example was during a 'museum' activity where students had to answer questions on a worksheet about nine other students through asking them questions about their projects. The students then returned to their desks and completed the worksheets while Diana went around and checked their work.

During Diana's classes, I observed that the students were extraordinarily engaged with their learning. I had trouble identifying any students who did not appear to be focused on Spanish learning at any time, often noting 100% engagement for every activity. The student interviewee noted this, stating:

> There was a lot of like, active engagement in the class, and not that much taking notes on stuff. 'Cause you had to like, talk to other people, and do activities. I think, I've had two Spanish teachers, and both of them did a good job of having a lot of like, activities and games to help you remember the vocab.

At one point during the observation, a student asked Diana if they could make up some work during class, and Diana's response was that they were doing activities during class that the student could not miss. Indeed, the classes felt very much this way during the observations: activities in class were integral to her teaching and could not be missed. Some of this dynamic could be attributed to the fact that all of the classes taught by Diana were tracked classes, either Honors or Advanced Placement classes, and so ostensibly included students who were already interested in or skilled at Spanish study.

Diana gave feedback in a number of different ways. She formatively assessed students regularly via online quizzing and drilling websites. She had students respond to questions by writing their answers on little whiteboards; this gave them the opportunity to show mastery of vocabulary and grammar. Sometimes she would ask the class to share language elements in a brainstorm-like activity, and then she would write their suggestions on the board for all students to see. In the event that a student made a language mistake, she would correct it as she wrote. She explained to me that she appreciated resources available through technology, especially interactive reading supports and things that allowed for innovative feedback structures.

Some more formal assessments were also a part of Diana's classes. One of the more formal formative assessments that I observed was a current events quiz in Spanish with multiple-choice items. Diana followed up the quiz by explaining in English some of the culture associated with the items. Indeed, the student interviewee highlighted both the cultural assessments when students had to 'read a passage and have to answer questions to it', and the type of quiz that was 'vocab and grammar', where students would have to write an answer with 'proper grammar'. Diana assessed students on both of these components of her classroom.

Themes and patterns in teaching and connection to beliefs

Content themes, communication, and grammar:
'The way that I want to teach'

Diana had a number of different, sometimes competing, beliefs about what her students needed in her classes. She told me that she believed that communication should be the goal in her classes, but that students did need grammar instruction. As she explained:

> I struggle with incorporating [grammar] with the way that I want to teach with always staying in the language. . . . not focusing too much on the grammar, keeping communication as our goal. But giving students the tools and structures that they need, to communicate at more and more . . . advanced ways.

Even in this short statement, Diana illustrated how she shifted between communication and grammar, between form and function in how she defined and thought through her role in creating learning activities for her students. This shifting thinking could be observed in her teaching practices, where she often explained grammar in the midst of other lessons or as a jumping-off point for a more communication-based activity. As she explained, it was sometimes necessary to switch over to a grammar explanation, 'to give explicit examples and identify patterns and talk about structure and formation'. Sometimes this also meant that she would have to switch over to English, as that worked best with the high school student mind, she explained.

When Diana focused on communication, she often aimed to surround her students with as much language as possible, using texts and activities around texts. She believed that making those texts relevant and interesting to students were the most important things that would help them to develop proficiency. Along with that belief, she argued that students needed the space to talk and work together in Spanish, especially at the upper levels.

In selecting her themes for the instructional materials and activities, Diana thought through not only the language that the materials presented but also the themes, ideas and politics that were introduced and explored, especially at the upper level. She explained:

> I think that the themes that we talk about in the AP Spanish class are . . . I work to choose things that will keep students engaged and will be provocative but not divisive. You know you have to be careful and try to walk that line between things that could get too much into politics, or bring about just too challenging of things. But yet [we must discuss themes that are] based in the real world and be issues we need to talk about and we need to learn about.

Diana's reflection on the nature of the materials that she used revealed an important belief that went beyond relevance for the sake of keeping students engaged. It was clear that she also felt that some themes were vital for students to process. She argued that cultural comparisons needed to be a main component of the class.

Connecting with all students: 'Something bigger than the class was happening here'

Diana believed that it was important to know what was going on with every student, and to be responsive to them. She felt that assessment would ideally be done through having conversations with her students and talking with them about what they are doing well and what they could continue to develop. Communication and connection with her students were paramount in Diana's priorities, and where she felt some tension between teaching grammar, communication and content, no such conflict could be seen in how she wanted to interact with her students. To illustrate this, one activity that I observed involved baby pictures of the students. Diana explained that she enjoyed that activity because it allowed her to 'glimpse their life beyond school', giving them a window into their lives outside of her classroom. She heard the students talk about their lives when they were younger and their old friendships and family. This type of activity gave her the insights and connections with her students that she appreciated.

Diana's classes included both HLs whose home language was Spanish and non-HLs whose home language was English or another language. She was very aware of this issue, and she stated that when there were HLs in class, it was the responsibility of the teacher to teach to both groups effectively. Although she stated that helping HLs to feel more comfortable in her class was never an explicit goal of hers, she cultivated that community as a natural outgrowth of the type of teaching that she did. I observed her asking HLs in her classes some questions about spelling. As she explained:

> [I realized] that that was happening through group work, through the nature of the class, through helping [the HL] feel comfortable enough to talk to others, um, that was a really good feeling and really rewarding, that something bigger than the class was happening there. Before this class, he was nervous and kind of afraid to talk with American students. And that now, because of things that we did in this class, he felt comfortable talking with American teenagers.

Diana thus saw her class as a place not only where she could get to know her students, but where they could get to know one another. The point of her teaching was not just familiarizing students with the Spanish language, cultures or other content, but also to help them create connections both with her and with one another.

Factors influencing beliefs and practices

Diana was influenced significantly by feedback from her students. She saw student feedback as key to her process of improvement as a teacher. One example of this was her change in practice regarding sharing her class goals with her students. She had noticed from student feedback that her students felt she was 'unorganized in what [she] expected from them. I guess unclear student expectations'. So she began 'starting each day saying what our goals are, what our plan is, communicating that verbally on the board, on the blog'. Although Diana did not have to report on her goals for her school and district, she nonetheless used some of ACTFL's Proficiency Guidelines (ACTFL, 2012) as the basis for the goals and outcomes for each of her units. She explained that this was intended to be there for her students 'from the beginning', and so that students 'know that their ultimate evaluation, assessment for each unit will be based on those goals'. Indeed, Diana's student remarked on this practice in the interview, stating that they recognized that Diana worked to share the class objectives, and they always knew what they were learning about and why.

More generally, Diana explained that she changed things when something was not going well, or if she received a lot of questions or emails from students. She had a plan but not a 'rigid structure' to her teaching, but she was willing to change that plan 'if the conversation goes another way or if students are struggling'. Sometimes this change involved slowing down or just doing things differently. She stated:

> I think that's where you need to be flexible and realize if you had a quiz scheduled on Friday, maybe you need to push that back, because if your goal is success and you want to check mastery of a concept, then you know, best to slow down and do that well rather than just stick to a calendar.

Diana thus was consistently influenced in her behavior by her students and their needs, sometimes in the form of their direct questions, or sometimes when she observed that students needed more support or time to understand a concept.

Diana also talked about how she was influenced by other teachers. In situations like the one detailed above, she said that she would often ask other teachers what they would do. In working in a large district, Diana had a number of teachers in the district at the same level. She also had a teacher in another district who taught AP classes as she did. She described this connection and interaction thusly:

> So [the three teachers who teach Spanish 2] just touch base every week. Every week, just to kind of monitor how we are, how a certain topic is going, any things we might want to change from our shared folders from

last year about how we did something . . . I really depend on that for pacing. I think if anything pacing is something that can get away from me

Even though she was able to attend these meetings, Diana also expressed that she missed 'really talking with other teachers'. She talked about how she wanted to listen to what other teachers did or what activities they carried out with their students. She wanted to have people observe her and wanted to observe other teachers. She wanted to be able to ask another teacher, 'How do you teach this? Because my students are struggling'.

Ultimately, Diana said that her beliefs changed easily, often depending on her context, based on the different jobs that she had had as a Spanish teacher over the years. This varied prior experience was important in how she viewed herself as a teacher. As she stated, 'Have my ideas changed? Yes . . . because my groups, my places have changed'. She was interested in trying new things based on what she heard about, trying to be 'really open' even to ideas about new ways of doing what she had always been doing.

Case Two: Gabriel

School context

Gabriel was born in Mexico City and came to the United States about 15 years prior to the data collection for the study. A native Spanish speaker, Gabriel spent several years studying English and studying abroad in locations such as Spain and Norway. After gaining his teaching credential, he taught Spanish in Iowa for a few years, then took a job teaching in Spanish in the Middle East. After that, he returned to Iowa, where he accepted the position at the high school where I collected data. Gabriel taught at a large high school in a very large district. The 9–12 high school contained about 1100 students, and the district served about 34,000 students. From the outside, the school was a large building similar to many other urban US schools on a large lot in a busy, densely populated area. His school had the highest percentage of students receiving free or reduced-price lunches among the schools featured in this study, with over 75% of the families in the school qualifying. The student population in the school was roughly 25% Hispanic, 25% white, 25% Black and 25% Asian. Just over 20% of the students received EL services, and the school had a 90% graduation rate. The school visibly celebrated the diversity in its student population; on one of my visits, it was 'Global Gala Week', with decorations and music being played to reflect a different ethnicity each day. The school was decorated with many plaques and visual celebrations of alumni, indicating the age of the school and its long presence in the large city where it was situated. Teachers stood at the main door of the building when I entered to greet the students, and one student who checked in at the main office at the same time as me was quickly identified by office staff as a new student in the school. Thus, I got the distinct impression from the short amount of time that I spent in the halls that despite the size of the school, the educators made an effort to know the students in the community well.

I observed Gabriel for two full days, interviewed him formally once and had several informal conversations with him. Additionally, I was able to interview one of his students to give some insight into their experiences in his class.

Teaching environment

Gabriel taught with block scheduling, so he saw each class every other day for a 90-minute class period. Every day, he taught two Spanish 2 classes and one Spanish 3 class, with one free period, one advisory period and lunch. So, Gabriel taught six out of eight classes spread over two days. He had 13–25 students per class, with most classes numbering about 20 students. His classes had HLs and non-HLs together. Gabriel himself spoke Spanish as his first language, coming from Mexico and thus sharing a background with many of his HLs.

His classroom was a large, light, rectangular room with a door on one side and a window on the other, with a long wall in front with a whiteboard on it where things were projected. The floor was linoleum. The desks were triangle-shaped and pushed into groups of two or four, with a few desks alone in the room. They were arranged in columns facing the front of the room. The brown-and-white walls were decorated with maps, cultural posters, inspirational quotes in Spanish, useful words (numbers, vocabulary and colors) in Spanish and English, questions about going to the bathroom and information in English about language acquisition. Given the size of the room, the wall decorations did not cover all parts of the walls.

Classroom activities

Gabriel's curriculum and planning were founded in 'three worlds', as he called them: the International Baccalaureate program in Spanish 1 and 2; the district's requirements in Spanish 3; and in Spanish 4, it was the themes suggested by the Advanced Placement (AP) test. For both IB and AP classes, the district agreed that the curriculum should be organized by units suggested by those assessments, so there wasn't, as he said, 'a specific curriculum for that' in the district. For instance, he did not use a textbook in Spanish 2 but rather used the IB units. He explained that the IB required him to focus on four skills while the district expanded that to six skills that are similar. He posted and shared the goals of each day and the agenda for the day with his students in Spanish 1 and 2, a requirement of the IB curriculum. His student interviewee recognized that this was a practice of Gabriel's, saying that they saw the learning targets posted on the wall and that they recognized that it was a part of the grading system. The student saw 'how each activity is going to help us achieve our learning goals'.

Gabriel worked to structure his classes in a way that would work with the long periods of block scheduling, as well as the focus on thematic units. He explained, 'I try to do different activities in the [class], because we have an hour and a half . . . so students keep engaged most of the time'. He did not have bell ringers to start class or exit slips to dismiss students, rather working with a more flexible plan that never looked the same twice. To achieve this and to conform to the IB and AP theme structures, Gabriel organized student work around little projects, as he described them, 'little things that they enjoy doing, like the readings are new, relevant, of what are their interests'. He put a lot of effort into explaining these projects, including going through guide worksheets, writing information on the board and explaining things verbally. With the type of extensive and detailed projects that he was assigning, this seemed necessary. Additionally, during the students' worktime, he would circulate, coach, answer questions and keep students on task as they did individual or small-group work. One example that I observed was a project where students had to answer questions about how different societies and countries were addressing environmental issues; additionally, his student described a project where they had to create a book. I saw Gabriel supplement this independent work with videos about the topics addressed in the projects, often discussing them in English.

Gabriel also addressed grammar as a concept as well as specific grammar structures as a routine part of his teaching. Sometimes this grammar teaching was embedded in the projects described above in the form of helping students to strategically develop their metalinguistic awareness. For instance, he coached students in writing, including appropriate use of dictionaries and Google Translate. He drew attention to specific forms in the supplemental readings. His student explained that in one reading, 'you would read it, and then you'd look at the verbs'. I observed similar practices and patterns in Gabriel's teaching, when he regularly drew students' attention or answered students' questions regarding language structures and forms. When students had to write, he coached them, often explaining confusing grammar concepts in English and answering students' questions in English, using English-language grammar terminology like verb tense names. Some examples included, '"Are we burning?" You have to use the present progressive'; and 'Preterite is going to be used when you use the word "did" – imperfect is "was"'. When students handed in smaller assignments, he would often correct them publicly and highlight common errors by writing them on the board and explaining them.

Gabriel also played grammar games with his students, especially his Spanish 1 and Spanish 2 students, regularly in the classroom, telling me that they were one of his favorite things to do with students. I observed him leading the competitive game of Battleship to review and drill grammar like verb conjugations. His student also described a dice game that they often played to review verb conjugations. Some of the signs posted on his walls helped his students to participate; I often observed them examining his walls to check their responses. At one point during a game, he said, 'Guys, please turn around you have to use those endings!' and gestured to the back of the room where different verb endings were posted. Gabriel really got animated as he coached students through games, often getting very loud, yelling, 'Listos!' ['Done!'], teaching the students how to say 'ganador' ['winner'], counting down until the game time was up, and more. The students seemed very engaged during the games that I observed. When there was extra time in his upper-level class, he assigned review activities for students to complete individually, like completing online quizzes or a word find. He used Duolingo as a back-up activity when a website went down during a class project with his Spanish 3 students. I saw few examples of students filling out worksheets or doing other more traditional grammar assignments, but his student interviewee did say that they had completed those assignments before.

Gabriel used both English and Spanish throughout his classes at all levels. Some of this was simply to clarify meaning. For instance, in his lower-level classes, he coached them through activities primarily in English with some phrases or words said in Spanish ('Get a "lápiz" ["pen"] and "un cuaderno" ["a notebook"].'). One Spanish 2 activity took the IB text and then they all translated it together, with Gabriel using drawing on the board to illustrate words like 'niveles' ['levels']. At the upper levels, he had students collaboratively translate more complex Spanish texts as a large group in class. When students struggled with understanding or writing something, Gabriel asked them to translate. At another point, when helping his students with ideas about things to write about in Spanish, he listed multiple ideas for them in English, for them to presumably translate into and write about in Spanish.

In some ways, Gabriel's differential use of Spanish and English, and the separation of Spanish and English in his classes, traced along the linguistic backgrounds of his students. I observed one Spanish 3 class activity where students were working independently on a task where they had to answer questions in Spanish about a Spanish source text; during this time, Gabriel tended to use English to coach the non-HLs and Spanish to coach the HLs. When students were sitting in his classes, the HLs were often speaking with one another in Spanish, while the non-HLs were talking with one another in English. Gabriel highlighted the similarities and differences between English and Spanish in his classroom in a way that seemed designed to engage all students. For instance, he often indicated some of the unexpected connections or contradictions that he had observed between and within the languages. In welcoming the students to class one day, he mused on the expressions in English that 'don't make sense', like 'stand up' versus 'sit down' or 'write it down'. Students engaged with him on these topics, and these spontaneous conversations often included many linguistic comparisons from all students.

Assessments in Gabriel's class were conducted in Spanish. One that I observed was an oral test designed to address a topic and to elicit specific vocabulary and grammar structures. For instance, in the environmental project described above, Gabriel asked students to talk about the environment in the past, present and future, or he had them compare different environmental concerns. Students were allowed to prepare ahead for these assessments. The student interviewee highlighted the several different types of tests in describing the class, also talking about writing ('you'd have to write an email or a letter to someone for some reason'), listening ('you had to listen to a recording and answer questions about the recording') and reading tests ('you'd have to read a paper and then answer questions on it'). The student also explained that with some speaking tests, the teacher would ask questions and 'you'd have to be able to answer confidently in Spanish'. From both Gabriel's explanation, IB guidelines, and the student's explanation, it was clear that his assessments focused on the four skills. Interestingly, the student was very aware of that structure.

Finally, Gabriel's interactions with students during his classes were encouraging and positive. Sometimes, he had a silly teasing manner with them. As he explained, 'I am always screaming or yelling and jumping . . . teenagers don't get how I'm extremely energetic at that [early] hour'. He spoke honestly and directly with students when they did not behave, or he quieted them with a 'shush' sound. His student offered several thoughts on Gabriel's demeanor and personality with them, calling him 'eccentric, and positive about learning, and positive about us learning, and . . . cares a lot about how we do in our classes'. He was 'bright. Cheery, very happy . . . [he's] doing like really fun things and over-exaggerating things and like [he's] just making it interesting'. The student explained that they didn't want to disappoint Gabriel because he's a nice teacher.

Themes and patterns in teaching and connection to beliefs

Giving tools to succeed: 'They have to have those inquiry questions'

Gabriel made strong statements of belief about his teaching. He explained that he expected students to 'figure out themselves' in a way that was student-centered, not teacher-centered. He saw himself as a 'guide' or a 'support', and students had to have the 'inquiry questions . . . on their own, more than the teacher'. Gabriel thus saw his process of bringing in games and projects to his classroom as a way of decentering himself as the teacher. As mentioned above, he also expressed trust in the curricula (IB, etc.) that he followed at every level. Gabriel's use of metalinguistic coaching and translation also helped students to take charge of their own learning. He said he liked having students think of where verbs came from when they were trying to figure something out, because then it allowed them to work more independently and think through things on their own. He believed that students learned vocabulary by thinking of similar words and comparing across languages. His student recognized Gabriel's approach and said that he often told them, '[There are] some things that I want to let you guys figure out, and if you need help, come get me'.

As described above, Gabriel included a great deal of grammar instruction in his classes, and he considered this to be an important part of his job. Gabriel characterized his approach to grammar by stating, 'I tend to make the grammar as easy as possible, and not as seriously, probably, as other teachers'. Thus, although grammar was an area of focus in his class, he saw the way that he addressed it as 'easy' and 'not as serious' as other ways of teaching grammar. He further explained that grammar was easy for him to teach because of his linguistic background. Gabriel thus connected his instruction of grammar to his use of translation and his creation of connections across languages, features of his teaching that were easily observable in all of his classes. He also said that his own background as an English learner helped him to understand 'where [his] students will struggle the most'. Grammar was another area where Gabriel sought to empower his students to learn the language. His student said that learning how to conjugate words helps them 'know how to frame our things, and as we go along . . . we need words to be able to make sentences', echoing the importance of learning grammar and word forms as well as Gabriel's idea that they were responsible for their own learning and their own mastery of the language.

Teaching culture: 'I take those experiences back to my classroom'

Many of Gabriel's beliefs about connecting with students and teaching about culture in his classroom were rooted in his identity as a Mexican and a native speaker of Spanish. This could be seen in how he connected personally with his HLs. He explained that he often will share things like, 'Hey, you know, last night I ate tacos with mole', and the students say, 'Wait, do you eat, you eat that?'. He explained that this gave them something in common, and that helped students to 'open up even more'. He also said that he felt that all of his students trusted native-speaking teachers because 'they have that confidence of, "Hey, you know, he knows the language right" so they can learn more'. As such, Gabriel expressed his self-efficacy in his ability to teach Spanish well because of his own linguistic background. As above, he used his experiences learning English to 'try to transfer that to [his] students, so that it's easy for them'.

This confidence and belief in his own abilities was not just about language, but culture, too. He explained that he thought that being a teacher was not just about teaching the language for him, but also the culture, 'what I have experienced, all the countries I have been visiting'. He worked to share his experiences traveling to different countries, even with the goal of taking his students abroad to places like Costa Rica and Peru. His personal experiences were a vital area for him to draw from in his effectiveness as a teacher to all students, including but not limited to his HLs.

Managing and management: 'Level of maturity'

Gabriel had strong beliefs about how to manage his students, although he did struggle with some of the internal contradictions of that process. For instance, he shared that it was important to give students a second chance to hand things in, but he had to be careful about being fair to all students and giving them all equal opportunities. He stated that two things were important to an effective class: (1) maintaining classroom management and (2) helping the students understand what they were learning that day.

It was easy to observe that Gabriel prioritized classroom management through his consistent interactions with students as they worked on projects and his energy and focus during the class. I did observe some students actively resisting the activities and lessons that he was asking them to work on, sometimes looking on their phones or otherwise not paying attention. He recognized that, and he explained that sometimes students did not like repeating activities, and he often had to deal with them having negative attitudes. He said that these struggles were important to acknowledge especially when working with student teachers. Gabriel thus believed that classroom management was a very important part of his classroom, but it was not necessarily an easy part, and it was something that he constantly worked toward.

The second part of his stated priorities was for students to understand what they are doing every day. Research shows that student awareness of goals contributes to higher levels of motivation (Moeller *et al.*, 2012), and it was clear both from observations and from his student statements that this was something that connected Gabriel's beliefs and practices. He saw this in his students, explaining that they often looked for his goal or agenda of the day, telling him, 'Hey, I think you're missing the questions of the day or the goal for the day'. I saw him often coaching students on understanding why they were doing certain things in his classroom, explaining and previewing multiple days at a time with statements like, 'My expectation is that we can get as much as we can done today and Thursday'. He communicated consistently and clearly with his students, fitting well with his belief.

Factors influencing beliefs and practices

Gabriel was clearly strongly influenced by students at all stages of his teaching. When he made changes in his curriculum or instructional practices, he got feedback from students to find out if the changes were worth it. He described to me that they would tell him, 'Hey, you know what? This didn't work', or 'We didn't understand it this way'. He felt that those comments helped him learn how to improve, to 'keep doing the things that I'm doing or to quit the things I'm not doing well'. Sometimes students indicated their reactions through nonverbal expressions, such as having their heads down during an activity. He would change his class from one period to the next, meaning if something did not work in his first period Spanish 1 class, he would change it for the next period's Spanish 1 class. Gabriel thus used student feedback both to reinforce his decisions and to inspire him to make changes as necessary.

Additionally, Gabriel made changes according to the linguistic background of the students in his classes, particularly in terms of the inclusion of HLs in his classes. From year to year, he had differing numbers of HLs in his class, and he acknowledged that his teaching style shifted based on the composition of the class. He stated that having HLs affected his teaching style, insofar as he tried not to be 'the one explaining things', but rather that students had to figure things out themselves based on their prior knowledge of the language. Again, he felt especially qualified to teach grammar because of his own background as a language learner and his own deep awareness of the language connections as a full Spanish-English bilingual.

Gabriel also called on his prior experience in putting his beliefs into practice. His experience as a student in Mexico, he explained, was much more discipline-focused. The systems in the US, he said, seemed permissive to him, including allowing students to be late to class and not have uniforms. However, it was clear that he had adapted his practice to fit his teaching context.

Another factor that influenced how Gabriel was able to enact his beliefs in his practices was the availability of materials for him in his classroom. The IB units sometimes did not have accompanying class materials. Gabriel thus struggled with having a lack of resources in his classroom. He explained that he often repeated activities and assessments from year to year to help with this demand on his time, which, as he mentioned above, sometimes caused students to grow frustrated. He identified this constraint on his time and resources as the 'hard part of his job', stating that 'there's nothing out there yet that can help us' do the projects. He reluctantly acknowledged that he sometimes wished he had a textbook to guide him. Additionally, he sometimes felt pulled in two directions, one by the IB curriculum and the other by the district. In this sense, this factor in his teaching was both institutional and personal; the way that his job was structured required him to create his own materials, but he felt that he did not have clear guidance as to how to create those materials to satisfy all of the curricular demands of his job.

Finally, Gabriel worked with other Spanish teachers in his school for a collaboration group, where they met every other day for 40 minutes. They talked about 'what we do about our classes, we share activities . . . we do collaborate, we have PD and we try to teach it together'. This work with other teachers was the primary way that he was influenced by his institutional context, beyond the general curricular guidelines. He did have to submit his unit plans to his administrator, but by his own admission, he was rarely observed ('I don't get observed as much as other teachers. And I think it's just because they . . . they know what I'm doing in class, so they don't have to worry too much.'), and he rarely got feedback from them on what he had submitted. He was required to be accountable for his unit plans, but he was not regularly assessed on them.

Looking across the Two Cases

Diana and Gabriel taught in schools of similar sizes and in classrooms with a similar profile of HL and non-HL students in their classes. There were notable differences between their contexts, however. Diana taught the same standard schedule every day, and Gabriel taught with block scheduling so that his classes were longer and met every other day. Gabriel had significant constraints on his teaching, notably imposed by his district as well as the guidelines provided by the IB and AP programs. Although Diana, too, was preparing her students for the AP exam, she spoke of the constraints of the curriculum very differently and did not calculate it in as a major factor in her decision making. In terms of their identities, Diana and Gabriel did not share a linguistic or cultural background, with Diana being a native English speaker born and raised in the US and Gabriel a native Spanish speaker from Mexico.

Indeed, identities were a major component of how both Diana and Gabriel framed their beliefs, similar to Calvin and Sarah, two other teachers who either were native speakers or taught HLs (Barcelos, 2015; Barcelos & Ruohotie-Lyhty, 2018; Kubanyiova & Crookes, 2016). Diana discussed identity insofar as she related to her students who were a mixture of HL and non-HLs, explaining that she wanted to support them and recognize that their needs were different in her classroom. Her selection of materials, designed to get students to engage with content that went beyond a focus on language into current events or other political or societal questions, were designed to engage all of her students. Gabriel's relationship with his HLs related to his own identity as a native speaker of the Spanish language, using it as Calvin did as a source of strength and authority, echoing the native speaker ideology prevalent among the language teaching community (Llurda & Calvet-Terré, 2022). Both teachers framed their language classes as places where everyone could learn about language, regardless of their language background, yet they also brought their own identities and students' identities into how they framed their beliefs about teaching.

Another shared factor in how Diana and Gabriel connected their beliefs and practices was in their access to classroom materials. As in Borg and Sanchez's 2020 study, these two teachers used their materials to align their beliefs and their practices, although creating those materials was a challenge for Gabriel. They both used content-based instruction and focused on themes for their units that aligned with institutional constraint like the AP or IB themes. Within those constraints, they found ways to teach both grammar and content in a way that fit with their beliefs about the important things to teach (Borg, 2017). Additionally, Diana and Gabriel spoke openly about teaching culture and could be observed doing so in their classrooms; this was not the case for most teachers in this study.

Finally, in contrast with other teachers in this book, these two teachers worked in programs that included a large number of teachers who were teaching the same language, sometimes the same level, and who created a broad team of support and collaboration. Both Gabriel and Diana spoke about their collaboration with their in-school and in-district colleagues. In fact, they both connected with those colleagues more than teachers outside of their schools, in contrast with Caitlyn, Veronica and Marlene in the previous chapter.

Questions for Discussion and Reflection

(1) Out of the two teachers featured in this chapter, which one most resembles how you teach and/or world language teachers that you have had in the past?

(2) If you were a student teacher, how would you approach working with each of these teachers? What would you prioritize learning from them?

(3) Diana and Gabriel both drew explicitly on their own identities and their students' identities when teaching. How did that focus on identity relate to their beliefs about language teaching?

(4) How would Diana or Gabriel have to change their practice if they were teaching in a small district as a singleton teacher? Do you believe that their beliefs would change as well?

(5) How do you think Gabriel or Diana would change their teaching practice if they taught one class of HLs and one class of non-HLs, similar to Sarah in Chapter 4?

7 Large World Language High School Programs: Languages Other Than Spanish

As shown in Chapter 1, Spanish was by far the most commonly taught language in the state of Iowa. It was also the language taught by 11 of the 15 participants in this study. This chapter will explore the stories of the four teachers who taught languages other than Spanish. All four of these teachers taught in large high school programs, which was necessary in Iowa to sustain the teaching of multiple languages. Through the stories and experiences of these two teachers of French, one of Chinese and one of German, it will be clear how teaching languages other than Spanish caused them to relate in unique ways with their students. Their isolation in some ways mirrored that of their singleton colleagues investigated in Chapter 4. Therefore, the ways that they sought inspiration and motivation, and how they developed as teachers, mirrored some of the experiences of those teachers.

Case One: Evie

School context

Evie the French teacher first appeared in Chapter 3 through her work at the junior high in her district, specifically in terms of how she connected with younger students in a more exploratory context for language teaching. As I mentioned there, Evie shared her time between a junior high school and a high school in the same urban district. In this part of the book, I discuss the part of Evie's day that she spent with her high school students, where she taught three French 2 classes. The focus of this section will again be on her teaching techniques, but at upper levels.

Evie's high school had about 1100 students in grades 10, 11 and 12. The school had a slightly lower percentage of students needing free or reduced-price lunches, with about 15% compared to the junior high's 25%. The racial/ethnic composition of the student body was about the same, with just over 80% white, about 5% Asian, 5% Black and 5% multiracial students in the school, with a slightly smaller percentage of

Hispanic students. Like the junior high, the high school had about 5% of the students identified as ELs. The high school had a 96% graduation rate.

In this chapter, I review my two observations of Evie's three high school classes, my interview with her in which she discussed both her junior high and high school teaching and four interviews with her high school students.

Teaching environment

Evie's three high school language classes were all the same level – French 2 – and were taught in the same classroom in the large high school building. Her classes contained between 12 and 20 students, and the periods lasted 50 minutes. During her time at the high school, Evie also had one period of lunch that was combined with a period when students could come in for work and tutoring. She also had one prep period. This meant that overall she taught five classes (two junior high, three high school) with one prep period, one transit period and one tutoring/lunch period.

After traveling by car from her junior high building in her allotted one period for transit, Evie went to her classroom that she shared with the Spanish teacher. The high school where Evie worked was a large, peaceful building in a heavily populated area of the town. The size of the school gave a feeling of a large, busy, diverse community; I was not greeted by anyone, and I almost felt as if no one noticed me as being an outsider to their school. Evie's classroom featured colorful realia and vocabulary in both Spanish and French throughout the room and on the teacher desks. The classroom did not have the themed bulletin boards that some other teachers in this study had. The student desks in the room all faced the front in rows. The room was an interior room in the building, with no windows, flanked on three sides by high-ceilinged hallways and with three doors leading to those hallways.

Classroom activities

Many aspects of Evie's teaching in her junior high classes could be seen in her high school classes as well. She had a kind, easy and friendly manner with students in class, smiling a great deal. She often laughed and clapped when something struck her as funny or surprising during the class. Students seemed happy and comfortable as they interacted with her. As with her younger students, Evie clearly capitalized on her familiarity with them and her young age to make connections. All her students responded to the French names that Evie assigned to them in the class.

Evie's patterns of instruction were also very similar in her junior high and high school classes. Like in her French 1 class, she started her high school classes with a question of the day in French (for instance, 'Quel est le meilleur film, d'après toi?' ['What is the best film, in your opinion?']), asking each student to respond in French and offering feedback on each response. The feedback was sometimes focused on the content of what they said, asking students to expand or elaborate, and sometimes the feedback was focused on the grammar usage, particularly in cases where there was a targeted structure being used. One student said that this was the most helpful and favorite part of class 'because I learned some more casual speaking', but it also 'really stressed [them] out'.

Evie then focused most lessons on grammar, often asking students what they remembered or knew from studying a specific grammar rule or concept before ('What do you know about the "imparfait" ["imperfect tense"] so far?' or 'Turn to your partner and describe how we do comparatives.'). She would then present or review the grammar rule or concept, often using textbook pages projected in front of the class. She would read through the rules in English and offer examples in French. Evie followed the themes and grammar points in her textbook, even when it was not interesting to her ('like speaking activities, "Who washes the dishes in your house?" Oh God I don't care!'). Nonetheless, the textbook served as her guide throughout her curriculum. As she presented each concept, the students were asked to take notes for consultation later ('Il faut écrire ça' ['You have to write this']). During the instruction, Evie emphasized details relating to pronunciation and unusual spellings that were exceptions to the rules that she was teaching. She often explained why those exceptions existed ('It's just for pronunciation!') as she emphasized them in class. Her students identified this as 'textbook style' learning, which some found to be less preferable to 'speaking with people and picking up on informal speech things', but some appreciated the attention to the 'tiny rules', stating, 'It really matters if you understand what the word means, and you could probably say it correctly'.

After this detailed presentation of the rules, Evie would then ask students to complete translations or other activities, using their notes, that helped them to practice the grammar rule or concept. They were often instructed and reminded to work in partners, which required Evie to remind them from time to time to stay on topic and engage. Some of these review activities involved listening. In that case, Evie offered scaffolded help, doing things like playing the tape first, then reading it herself, then having students compare answers, then having them translate, then writing the answers on the board for them. She encouraged them by admitting that it was hard to complete the activity, saying things in both English and French like, 'It's hard, it's the first time, "c'est difficile mais ça va" ["it's difficult, but it's ok"]' and 'It's really hard to hear the difference so don't stress about it'. She allowed students to consult their notes as needed for some of these activities and small assessments.

Evie frequently used an online drill game that put students into teams and then gave each team a series of translation questions. The interviewees all mentioned this as a technique that they enjoyed in that they could review and practice on their own. For instance, one of the observation days included review games about numbers and counting, which Evie explained was always important and shouldn't be forgotten. Other activities similarly focused on formatively assessing students' mastery of grammar and vocabulary. Assessment, in fact, was an important part of Evie's planning with students. As she explained, she was transitioning between different ways of assessing her students, but it included assignments, tests and quizzes. Her students explained that their tests included listening, writing, and then comprehension questions.

Evie still taught culture with these older students, but with less focus on 'hooking' the students as was featured with the younger ages. Evie did a music activity every Friday to engage students in a different way with vocabulary and culture, and students often noticed when it was not used. She also used resources on a French TV channel website for cloze activities and related comprehension-focused exercises. These activities were well-liked by the students who were interviewed. One student praised Evie's references to how language was used in France, saying that she would often say, 'These sentences might be used in a French country, so you should be familiar with how they sound and how they look'. One student said that they thought that Evie looked at 'seeing different cultures and kind of just traveling places' as the reason why she was a teacher. They also identified this as a reason why they were learning the language, to become 'more immersed into the culture'. Thus, although grammar and vocabulary were certainly the organizing principles of the class, it seemed that both teacher and students knew that culture was both a motivating component of the class and a lens through which to view the studies.

Evie worked hard to keep her students engaged throughout her classes. Recall here from Chapter 3 that her general mantra was, 'If I'm bored, probably the students are bored with it, too!'. The longer grammar lessons did sometimes result in her losing students' attention; I observed anywhere between 50% and 100% engagement in her class at different times. Students usually paid strong attention during the review games and individual activities, losing attention when the class was taking notes or listening to grammar explanations. Sometimes the students said that class activities could become repetitive, including the translation and drill games, even though it helped them the most to learn and their 'competitiveness' could be engaging, too.

In the interviews with students, they were sometimes ambivalent or unclear about the messages Evie was giving them about what was important to know in French. One student said, 'She hasn't really set the guidelines for [the class goals], like, compared to my other classes . . . I think it would be better just to know what we're going to be studying'. Another said that they knew that she 'wants us to learn about French . . . 'cause I know that she really likes it, and she really appreciates the language as well'. Indeed, Evie expressed that she cared about their struggles in her class, and she tried to be responsive whenever she could. Some of this came out in her statements of her beliefs about teaching.

Themes and patterns in teaching and connection to beliefs

Boundaries and feedback: 'They know what to expect'

Evie believed that it was important to set boundaries in her high school class and to allow students freedom within those boundaries. She stated:

> I manage my classroom well, and they know what to expect, and I post every day about the schedule and what we're doing, so they know that. But I set my boundaries, and they have to meet those, but they have a lot of freedom within the class, which is good.

She understood the need at the high school level to be clear with students and create an inclusive environment where they could understand the expectations. Evie was a planner. One of her students expressed content-ment with these boundaries and directions, as that student said that they liked being told, 'This is what you need to do', so that they could 'plan out everything a lot better'. However, recall here the student quoted earlier in this section who stated that they did not know the guidelines of class; in this, we can see that this was a belief that sometimes was not fully enacted for the students.

Evie also worked hard at the high school level to incorporate new resources, especially music, and she saw that students were really inter-ested in that. Her Friday music days were an area of her teaching that she really enjoyed developing, even going so far as to call it 'transform-ative': 'I think that's been really kind of transformative in my teaching, because um it's something they look forward to, and I think that I enjoy it as well'. Seeking out that kind of enjoyment in her teaching, particularly as a teacher who was still discovering what she liked and did not like, was key to keeping her engaged and motivated in her classroom.

The students realized that Evie wanted to both challenge them ('push ourselves out of our comfort zone') but also support them as needed. One student, when asked what they would say to another student about to be in Evie's class, advised them to 'ask a lot of questions, because sometimes she doesn't repeat things'. So the students were working with Evie to make sure that their learning experiences in French were good, and they knew that she would help when she could.

Growing as a teacher: 'I was up to my eyebrows in "What was I doing?"'

Evie, as a relatively new teacher, was still discovering new things about the profession, and she was continuing to explore new ways of being the teacher that she wanted to be. Her beliefs were thus somewhat in flux, as evidenced by some of her statements about changes in her practice. She described her recent journey as a new teacher, saying:

> Because my first year, it was pretty traditional, especially French 2, because I was up to my eyebrows in 'What was I doing?'. [My teaching] was pretty traditional grammar and vocabulary, which they learned, but it wasn't best practice at all. So just really finding those um, those deeper activities with the form of the communication has been great.

As evidenced by the observation data, Evie was still incorporating the emphasis on communication into her classes, recognizing its importance and believing that it was the right change to make for her students. She also spoke about trying to focus more on vocabulary instruction and staying in the target language, recognizing that 'the goal is to be 90% in the target language'. She also believed that she needed to continue to coordinate what she called 'essential learnings' with what she was already doing in the class.

Evie's beliefs about the importance of communication in French had not yet permeated all of her teaching practices. Both observations and student interviews revealed that grammar drilling and translation was a very common focus in the class, and that Evie often spoke in English, as one student said, 'she doesn't have a lot of faith that we understand her, because . . . she'll say a command in French and then she'll translate into English'. Evie was still very much learning, and larger projects like moving to a new grading system in collaboration with her colleague were also on the horizon. Perhaps more than some of the more experienced teachers in this study, Evie was still figuring out her core and peripheral beliefs.

Factors influencing beliefs and practices

In Chapter 3, I addressed some of the key ways that Evie found inspiration, especially as she taught her younger students at the junior high level. She taught those classes according to institutional dictates that culture and language instruction be separated at the lower levels. She enjoyed having fun with those younger students, and in connecting with them as a younger teacher. At the high school level, institutional influences were less notable, but Evie spoke a great deal about how her students affected her practice.

Evie's students influenced both her planning and her motivation to change. Her desire to keep both herself and her students from boredom was key in her approach to and behavior in teaching ('It looks like they're engaged, but I can almost guarantee that most of the time they're not.'). Evie sought out student perspectives a great deal in her classes to help her make her instructional decisions. She explained, 'I love getting feedback about student engagement, because I think as teachers we're worried about what we're doing'. As a result, Evie often had students complete surveys of three questions – what did you like, what did you not like and what are your suggestions. Sometimes she was able to follow student suggestions, but sometimes she was not: 'I usually try to listen to them, but there are some things that I just can't [do]'. Other more informal feedback was gleaned through her observations of her students. She acknowledged that her students sometimes didn't seem to care that much about the work that she was putting in, but said, 'I hear about it if I don't have a song ready on Friday!'. Evie's students were aware of the effect that they had on her, stating that they thought that she did choose certain activities 'if we're struggling with it'. One student talked about some of the supports that Evie gave for the listening activities, and another time when she had them do an extra review and 'spent a lot of time' on a concept that they did badly during a review.

Evie did collaborate with the other teachers in her school to prepare for new initiatives and to develop her work. Regarding their work on developing their grading, she said, 'Not to say that we weren't doing it before, but we weren't holding ourselves accountable if we didn't'. Therefore, Evie felt that external influence of collaboration with other teachers to keep her on task and at work with her teaching. This factor in mediating her beliefs and practices was clearly still in development compared to the consistent influence of her students and their feedback, however.

Case Two: Molly

School context

Molly was a white, US-born, native speaker of English who was a French teacher. She had experience teaching French in a variety of locations in the United States before she settled in Iowa to get her master's degree in French and ESL teaching. She had been an EL teacher for several years before an opening for her French position opened in a medium-sized district in the state that was not a suburb of any major city but also was not a small rural area. Similar in size to Evie's district, there were about 5300 students total in the district, with about 1500 in the high school where she worked as the only French teacher. There was a high rate of poverty in the district, with just over half of the students receiving free or reduced-price lunch benefits. The district was 40% white and 50% Hispanic, with the rest of the students divided among Asian, Black and multiracial students. Twenty-five percent of the students were identified in the district as ELs. The district had a well-established Spanish dual immersion program option that enrolled many students, both HLs and non-HLs, in the school. Molly's students largely had not attended that program. However, Molly shared that in one of her classes, out of 21 students, 12 were not native

English speakers and the majority of those students were Spanish speakers. The school overall had an 85% graduation rate.

I observed two full days with Molly's students at her high school. I also interviewed her once more formally and then conducted informal interviews and conversations with her throughout my observation dates. I present data from those sources as I talk about Molly's case.

Teaching environment

As the French teacher in her high school, Molly taught three classes of French 1, two classes of French 2 and one class that combined both French 3 and French 4. Her classes were 45 minutes long. She had one combined preparation and lunch period that lasted 85 minutes, and one homeroom period during the day that lasted 25 minutes. During the homeroom period, Molly sometimes had to engage her students with specific activities; at other times, it was more of a study hall. Her classes had between 10 and 20 students, with most around 15 students. All students in Molly's classes had individual school-supplied Chromebooks.

Molly's school felt large, with a gym complex and a large entry atrium in the building. From some sides, the school had an institutional feel with big brick walls and small windows. It was two stories high, with a standard layout of long hallways and classrooms off the hallways. There was also a feeling of security to the building, including a lengthy check-in process for me as an outsider, and multiple signs warning about not parking in the wrong place in the parking lot. Molly's classroom was a square room with a tile floor and shelves and whiteboards along the walls. There was a small window on one side. The walls were light blue cinderblock, densely decorated with sheets of notes and vocabulary, divided by class, including a 'Mur des Mots' ['Wall of Words']. The desks in the room were two-tops placed facing one another to arrange students in groups of four, placed throughout the room so that some students' backs were sometimes to one whiteboard.

Classroom activities

Molly's classes were animated at the start by her high energy in welcoming students as they entered and moved throughout her room. As she said, 'I don't sit in my chair. Like, I am on my feet, I wear my Fitbit, I'm going through my room'. This constant monitoring of the room and circulating among the students occurred throughout the observations. Each class also had the class objectives written on the board, as required by Molly's administrative leadership in the district. She did not always review them with the students, but they were available for the students to see. On days when students were doing largely independent work, like if Molly was doing individual oral exams with students, she projected the directions of what they should do and in what order in French on one of the screens in the room.

Molly used a French textbook to guide her instruction and structure her classes. I observed her several times introducing lists of thematically grouped vocabulary words (e.g. nationalities) taken from the textbook. Molly would say the words and have students respond chorally. She would then give explanations often in English about origins of words in the lists, their cultural background and mnemonic devices. As explanation, she would write color-coded notes about each word on large sheets of paper posted around the room, and students would be expected to take notes. She often jumped up during her explanations to add additional notes. Some of her explanations of vocabulary involved connecting the words to other French words, some connecting them directly or obliquely with English words, and some with Spanish words, given the number of Spanish speakers in her class. She would call upon Spanish speakers to provide translations to Spanish, welcoming observations from students who said things like, 'It's kind of like Spanish'. In some cases, she would add in vocabulary that was not in the book but that she felt would be important for her student to know, like 'ouvrier' ['worker'], stating, 'I'm sure that some people from the class would need this'.

While having students become familiar with the vocabulary, Molly employed a variety of techniques that engaged students in multiple ways. Some activities included showing a video corresponding with the textbook and having students fill out a worksheet focused on the vocabulary and details in the video and conducting listening activities with recordings from the book that the students had to answer on their Chromebooks. Students could also review vocabulary through completing online homework and participating in online games designed to drill them in that vocabulary.

During these whole-class lessons, Molly used some different techniques to check in on her students' learning. She would ask questions such as, 'Facile ou difficile, mes amis?' ['Easy or hard, my friends?']. She would often say a question to the whole class and wait for a response. If no one volunteered to answer, she would provide an answer herself. Students did sometimes seem to stop paying attention during these vocabulary review lessons, with about 70% engagement with what she was doing. She told me how she took a different approach once to whole-class activities, asking students to cocreate a story with her about her cat, then having them draw it, illustrate it and send her pictures of themselves reading it to people at home.

Much of Molly's time in class was not spent on whole-class activities, however. She frequently had students working in small groups or individually on different projects. As she said in the interview, 'I've really come around to this idea of the student-centered learning environment'. This occurred not only in her multilevel French 3/French 4 class but also in her French 1 and French 2 classes. In the multilevel class, it was more likely that they were working on different projects, for instance, reading through a text or writing creatively in French. During that group time, she would circulate and monitor their work actively. After she did that once during my observation, she said, 'So that was my attempt to differentiate instruction'.

Sometimes, the students were all collaborating in teams on the same project. In those cases, Molly organized things in the class so that students were in charge of their own learning. During this time, she explained:

> They get in teams, and they discuss and work through their thinking, between English and French, to see if they all agree. And if they don't agree, it gets flagged and goes up on the board or circled and penned, and so they know to ask me, for like the whole class's sake.

I observed one class when students had to work together to correct their tests. Molly circulated during this time, often communicating with students in English as she circulated and coached them. The students connected with her in English and one another, though still were on-task. She would make comments about verb forms, and she would sometimes translate what they wrote to point out an error. Generally, when checking up on students' individual work, she would focus on grammar corrections. She would sometimes pretend not to understand something if it needed to be corrected. Molly also joked around with students quite a bit during this time.

Although the individual work did sometimes motivate students to stay on task, classroom management during these activities was sometimes challenging. Sometimes only about 60–80% of the students seemed to be on task, although during the test revision activity, the participation was almost 100%. Molly struggled with students who did not follow her directions. When she had them complete work on their Chromebooks, students sometimes got distracted and did other work. She expressed frustration that students were sometimes not working unless she was standing right over them. She would make statements such as, 'Les Français 3 – let's all do our jobs please!' and 'Eh mes amis! Je dois écouter' ['Hey my friends, I need to listen']. She monitored their technology use but incorporated it regularly in her class.

Formal assessments were a common occurrence in Molly's classroom. For the testing of speaking and listening, she had students converse with her individually while other students worked through a list of individual activities posted on the overhead, as mentioned above. During the oral tests, Molly was very positive and responsive to students, often nodding and smiling. When a student struggled, she asked them in English to explain the rule in order to give them some coaching. Students took paper and pencil textbook-created tests and quizzes, as well as performance assessments like writing short books. She would allow students in some cases to take and retake assessments as needed until they mastered a concept. As mentioned above, she had students work together to correct their tests, grouping the students strategically so that they could focus on the same errors. She would also assess students informally, reviewing a quiz and going through the answers to listening comprehension activities.

Finally, Molly spent some moments in her class coaching students explicitly with reading and test-taking strategies. She often pointed out and highlighted the different academic skills she was focusing on in a specific task or test.

Themes and patterns in teaching and connection to beliefs

Grit and resilience to learn language: 'You need to struggle a little bit'

Molly repeatedly expressed the belief that learning a language was work, and that sometimes that work was not fun. At different moments in our conversations, she called learning language 'a slog', 'a struggle' and a process that just requires 'to be immersed' and to put in 'time, skills, and practice'. Molly saw herself as pragmatic and realistic in her framing of language learning in this way. In general, she characterized teaching thusly:

> [Teaching is about] making students think, making students problem-solvers, able to be resilient and use grit, and come at it from a different perspective, a different approach. [Asking themselves,] 'If that didn't work, what else could work? What else haven't we tried?'

The idea that learning language was work could also be seen in some of the classroom practices described above, especially in Molly's focus on getting students to master lists of vocabulary, to correct errors and to take notes. Molly believed that, to reach these goals, she needed to engage her students and avoid boredom. She saw this as key to her success. She prioritized students being busy and active in class, saying, 'I would like [observers] to walk away saying, "Wow! Her kids were doing something"'.

Molly did not see learning language as only a rote memorization process, however. She also identified the mastery of more complex language forms as key to the process of learning. She saw '[learning] how to do vocab' and '[using] cultural stuff' as what a student might do to meet basic expectations. However, to really advance in learning language, she said that students needed to be able to provide correct verb forms, make adjectives agree in gender and number with the nouns they described and construct sentences. She described this at another point in describing what makes a good student in her class. She said that a good student can 'push it a little bit further' and 'they're able to play with the language, they're able to make things humorous, [they] have the basics . . . but then they can do one step further'. To get students to this point, Molly worked to include new ideas in her classes, as she termed it, 'things that are kind of out of the box . . . like a little bit different or unexpected'. She provided several examples of times that she had brought in new ideas to try with her students. Molly saw true success in learning a language as building on grit and resilience and adding in a personal element and effort.

Communicating, connecting, and compassion: 'We need to be ready'

Molly wanted to focus with her students not just on learning new vocabulary and forms, but also on the bigger goals of language learning. In this, she focused on two main beliefs about the purpose of language: to communicate and connect and to develop compassion. When she spoke about communicating and connecting, she termed it thusly: 'If you're motivated to communicate and transmit a message, or to read, or to write a contract, you're going to learn what you need to learn to do that'. To encourage her students in this goal, Molly tried to get them to work independently and to see the value in her activities. As she said, 'I want kids doing the work and they learn more by using and doing'. She struggled when students did not show this motivation to learn and communicate, as she saw that motivation as key, particularly in group activities.

Molly also believed that one major goal in learning language was to be able to connect better to the changing communities in Iowa and in their local community. The influx of immigrants from French-speaking countries in the school and the state, particularly from French-speaking West Africa, was an important reason for students to learn French. As she said, 'And we need to be ready, we need to be able to speak to these people'. Furthermore, Molly articulated that broader goals like 'building . . . compassion, empathy and cultural competency' leading to a support of multicultural Iowa were all vital components of what she was trying to do. Some of these aims could be seen in some parts of Molly's teaching, as it was clear that communication and connection were at the heart of what she did.

Factors influencing beliefs and practices

Like the singletons featured in Chapter 4, Molly did not have to coordinate with colleagues, since she was the only French teacher in her school. There were few if any institutional factors that figured into her instructional decision making in her classroom. She mentioned some of the professional development opportunities offered by her school, although they did not always align with what she wanted to do, and she felt free to disregard them in some cases. Many of the ways that she chose to change practice were rooted in her own identification of her weaknesses, stating that she needed to 'be willing to be uncomfortable myself, as an instructor, to get my kids to do better'. As the only French teacher, she focused on her self-selected professional needs in identifying her path forward for professional development.

As with many of the other teachers in this book, Molly was inspired and influenced greatly by attending conferences. She said that she went to a local conference specializing in teaching techniques centered on providing comprehensible input 'because I'm super-curious and a lifelong learner, and I just want to do better'. She focused our conversation a lot on her current efforts for learning on becoming more familiar with these techniques, even though she had not known much about it previously. She said that she went from not knowing much at the start of the academic year to implementing some of it to ordering more materials for it in the next year. She also knew that she was more flexible in this exploration because, again, she was the only French teacher.

Molly also talked about how she learned from student teachers who came from universities and brought new ideas. Molly did connect with French teachers outside of her school, as another source of information and inspiration. She communicated with them with Facebook pages, conferences when she was able, readings, listening to podcasts and reading teacher blogs. As she described:

> [I am] actively going on to teacher boards, . . . doing research projects, reading stuff, signing up for things, going to IWLA . . . I try to keep current with best practices. Just like we have to do relicensure credits, just like medical people have to go to conferences, just like any profession, you've got to kind of stay on top of it, little bit by little bit.

Clearly, Molly saw her responsibility as a teacher to keep herself current and open to changing what she was doing, and not to fall into complacency.

In many ways, Molly regulated a fairly strict alignment between her beliefs and practices. She identified few strong influences that caused her to enact instructional practices in the classroom that did not match her beliefs, although she seemed open to changing her beliefs and her practices if something that she discovered through her self-guided professional development caused her to change. She was not averse to change, and she controlled the process of change as she saw fit.

Case Three: Toby

School context

Toby had been teaching Chinese for a few years by the time I collected data. Our conversations were facilitated by our prior relationship and familiarity with one another, as Toby had been my former teacher education student and had received his MAT from the program where I taught.

Toby was a white, US-born, native speaker of English who was married to a native speaker of Chinese. He had started studying Chinese in college and had spent time in the military before deciding to return to school to become a Chinese teacher. Toby taught at the same large 9–12 high school as did Gabriel, featured in Chapter 6. The 9–12 high school contained about 1100 students, and the district served about 34,000 students. The school had a large number of students (75%) who qualified for free or reduced-price lunches and a diverse student body.

I observed Toby for two full days in his classroom. He and I spoke in a formal interview and then spoke at length during my observations. He often came by and explained what he was doing as he was teaching, and we had long conversations during his planning periods and even went out for lunch during one observation day. I present data from these conversations and observations in this section.

Teaching environment

Toby's school was organized in block scheduling, with four blocks of 90 minutes taught per day and a two-day rotation. Toby taught three of the four blocks, plus a 30-minute flex time when students could get tutoring or participate in guided and ungraded activities. On the days that I observed, I happened to observe the same day of the rotation, so they included the same three block classes. These included one block of Chinese 2 and two blocks of Chinese 3. On the rotation day that I did not observe, Toby taught two blocks of Chinese 1 and one more of Chinese 2. There were about 10 students per class in the observed classes, and Toby told me that there were more students in the Chinese 1 classes that I did not observe.

When approaching the Chinese classroom, it was easy to recognize with Chinese characters posted on the wall outside the classroom in cut-out red paper. Inside, the Chinese classroom was small but spacious, with white walls and no windows. The desks were grouped up in groups of four, with the students facing one another. The room was decorated with hanging lanterns, large dragon costumes, and other realia on shelves and in cabinets around the room. Low bookcases of books about China and in Chinese were against one wall. The walls were hung with many laminated posters with pictures of the zodiac and pictures of China. As the school was an International Baccalaureate (IB) school, the proficiency level guidance about different levels in the IB language assessments were also displayed in large posters. Toby had some wipe-off posters with class topics and objectives posted for each class, although some were not completed. One poster of a stoplight indicated if students could have their phones out with no oversight (green), or they could have their phones out for class activities only (yellow), or they could not have their phones out at all (red). By the door, he posted a long list of Chinese phrases with their English translations, using romanized language and not Chinese characters, that addressed common requests like, 'Can I go to the bathroom?' Students consulted this list regularly.

Classroom activities

Toby greeted students in the hallway in Chinese as they entered his room. After they were seated, he then greeted them again in Chinese with a formal welcome to the class, to which they responded in Chinese. After that point, the most spoken language in the classroom was English. He often started with a quick warm-up exercise on the board, for example, translating two sentences from English to Chinese. In the classes that I observed, Toby followed the warm-up with this sequence of activities: (1) he would explain a grammar structure in the large group; (2) he would refer students to resources in books; (3) he would have them work alone or, more frequently, with one another during small-group work time on written translation exercises, writing projects and games that gave them the scaffolding for writing. Recall here that Toby taught with block scheduling, in which students were with him for 90 minutes; this type of structure influenced how he taught, as he said, allowing more time for larger projects and chunks of time for students to work together.

Some examples of project work that I observed included collaborative writing of scripts for role plays, translating sentences reflecting a specific grammar point, preparing responses to questions determined by rolling dice and selecting vocabulary and writing stories. Toby's assessments were based on these project-type assignments, which were frequently scored on a simple rubric that assessed whether students met or exceeded the minimum requirements. He was able to give homework, but that homework was not allowed to be a part of the students' grades.

Toby' focus in his main activities was always on teaching grammar structures. He focused on translating things from Chinese to English to verify students' comprehension, asking questions like, 'What are some of the ways we could have translated this?'. He did incorporate some speaking activities that the students used with romanized Chinese characters (also called pinyin writing), but rarely did much with Chinese characters in his assignments or activities. In preparing and organizing these activities, Toby was required to connect his teaching to the IB charts which, as he explained, 'show what's the unit, what's it about, what's the main global connection', with 'factual, conceptual, debatable questions, and then assessments'. Supervisors would verify that Toby was meeting the four IB criteria for foreign language.

During his classes, Toby displayed his comfortable and familiar relationship with some students, even while managing his class through staying 'rigid with timekeeping and activities'. He seemed to get joy out of silly interactions with students, smiling a lot. He would make comments from 'Seems like you are making good progress' to 'What was it you could use your phone for today?' and 'What do you have done for Wednesday?' that guided the students and helped to encourage them to stay focused on the work. He posted his PowerPoint slides and other materials online for his students, used an app that reminded them of upcoming assignments and class requirements and directed them to use online sources and translation software to help them. At the same time, he suggested that students were very familiar with him, as he often taught them for multiple years in a row. As he stated, 'Students are like my nieces and nephews . . . maybe I've been with them too much?'. He warned me on one day that I observed that they might ask me personal questions. I observed a definite familiarity between Toby and his students, although their discussions were rarely personal, and were more focused on the work in the class. He circulated in class as they did individual and group work, keeping them on task and helping them when needed. He spoke with me about times in the past when he had also brought in outside speakers who could explain to the students about the utility of knowing Chinese.

Students during Toby' classes often stayed on task when he was questioning them or redirected them. When directed to individual work, some would work carefully together, talk and eat snacks, while Toby circulated to work with others. At other points, the students were not as engaged with their assigned activities. I observed some on their phones and completely ignoring their work, while others were talking with one another. It sometimes seemed like a power struggle with students taking their phones out when Toby turned his back after telling them to get to work. At a point when Toby left the room, the students all stopped working and spoke with one another.

Themes and patterns in teaching and connection to beliefs

Centrality of teaching grammar: 'Something finally clicks for them'

Toby clearly believed that teaching grammar structures was vital to teaching Chinese, the 'basics of activities'. He felt that students needed a foundation in Chinese that could be presented using methods like the audio-lingual method (where dialogues are memorized and repeated) or grammar-translation (where students focus on translating texts in written form from one language to another). As he explained, 'They have to be taken very clearly, step-by-step through'. This foundation, then, would give students the tools they needed to do other things with the language. Directions on the board were often literal grammar structures such as 'Double objects: S+V+O1+O2' indicating the exact order and sequences of different parts of speech. The important moment happened when, 'somehow through all the exercises and activities, and explanations, something finally clicks for them'. That understanding of grammar after working on it was important for how Toby envisioned his students learning. He also said that, even though it was not his favorite thing to do, he felt he was the most skilled as a teacher at 'clarifying . . . [and] getting people to understand Chinese grammar structures'.

Once the central need to teach grammar was satisfied, Toby believed that students needed to be guided through processing the lessons. The materials used in the class needed to include enough information without being overwhelming. Some of this could be difficult since the materials were often based on the IB framework. As he explained:

> [I need to] get them to think about things for the unit and how to get them to apply those principles both to what they're learning, and then also what they're supposed to be learning beyond simply just the grammar and text.

This mandate to move beyond just grammar was important for students to master the language as the IB program dictated, while not getting overwhelmed and while building on the foundation of Chinese that they had developed. Furthermore, the block scheduling could be a challenge, and it made Toby feel strongly that the 'basic structures' needed to be prioritized in the two or three days that he had with them per week.

The challenge of learning characters: 'There really is no magic'

Toby expressed the belief during the interview that the memorization of Chinese characters had the most impact on students' Chinese development. Chinese, unlike the other languages taught by the participants in this study, is a logographic language that does not share an alphabet with English. Chapter 1 discussed that Chinese has been rarely taught in the US (Wiley *et al.*, 2012), and that the expectations for attaining fluency in Chinese for English speakers have been lower than those of other languages. Chinese scores in reading, for instance, are often well below reading scores in other languages even when students have the same amount of time of instruction (Avant, 2017). Toby suggested that one of the reasons for this was because, even when pinyin romanization was used, the lack of 'cognates or equivalents' in Chinese in comparison with Spanish or French made it much more difficult for his students. In addition, Toby did not teach characters extensively in his classes, something that he acknowledged as a challenge for himself, saying, 'The thing I struggle with is getting students to be able to transition to the writing system unless they do it on their own'. During the observed classes, students in the more advanced Chinese 3 class were instructed to write their notes for an oral presentation in pinyin as well as in Chinese characters. They were allowed to use all resources to help them with this writing; memorization of the characters was not emphasized at that point.

Toby was still learning how best to teach characters to his students. He would explain to his students why they were reading a text without pinyin, saying that there is 'no magic to reading Chinese characters other than listening, reading, and getting familiar with them'. He wanted to give them a 'magical way', but he had realized that they just had to take it home and 'read it themselves'. This contrast between his belief of the importance of teaching the Chinese writing system, and his struggle to do so, was notable. Like many teachers in this study, Toby believed that this component of his instructional planning was very important to effective teaching, but he also recognized that he was still developing as a teacher in how to do it well.

Relating to students: 'The most important thing . . . is to develop relationships with students'

Toby expressed that it was important to him to enact a pedagogy that was responsive to keeping classroom control. Above all, he shared that he 'realized . . . that the most important thing for me in teaching language is to develop relationships with the students'. He found it more rewarding when students could do more work on their own, apply themselves and make connections on their own, when he did not have to constantly intervene and keep them on task. During the observations, he frequently encouraged the students by using stories from his own experiences learning Chinese, reassuring them that it was ok to make mistakes as a non-native speaker. He found that being a US-born Chinese teacher could give him opportunities to connect with US-born students and to model what might be possible for them. He explained:

> It's my job, in a sense, to convince them that [Chinese study] is important for them. It's helpful and useful. But more importantly, to convince them why, outside of this context, [knowing Chinese] benefits them. Why it may be good.

Toby thus saw building relationships with students as an important way to connect and convince them why their studies were important.

Factors influencing beliefs and practices

The importance that Toby assigned to creating and maintaining relationships with his students meant that those students often had a strong influence on his instructional practices. Toby said that he made changes to his curriculum when he observed his students struggling with understanding the material. He said that he would try new texts and other instructional materials and see how well they met the students' needs and the overall curriculum demands. He would then make changes, for example, adding more cultural information to his teaching, as he saw fit. Some of his instructional decisions were focused on meeting students' self-regulation and organizational needs. For instance, Toby helped students to organize themselves with reminder apps, stating, 'There are a lot of other issues that my students are dealing with, that, just providing them with a quick remind helps them . . . to be able to do the work'. Toby thus believed that he needed to be responsive to student needs as he perceived them and experienced them in the classroom, building off of his relationships with students to do so.

Toby was also influenced by his institution, whose procedures and rules were shared with him via his supervisor and his IB colleagues in his school. For example, his supervisor requested that Toby bring in more learning explanations and clarity for his students, including providing more information on the board about the day's agenda. Toby also added in more pacing activities and warm-ups based on supervisor feedback. He was learning to plan in more detail through these interactions, explaining:

> And so I've been trying to do that ahead of time when I do readings, or do activities, I try to figure out so what are some problems that this has. Then I go ahead and I get feedback from the IB coordinator cause they do a lot of . . . methodology and ideas that work well to fix things.

His faith in his supervisor served as his primary support and motivation to develop his teaching, and it was clear that he had a great deal of confidence that his supervisor was giving him good ideas and information to use in his teaching. Toby's instructional decisions thus were grounded in his own beliefs in their first version, but his supervisor and IB colleagues influenced the practices as he tried them out several times.

Unlike other participants in this study, Toby did not connect with other teachers for inspiration. This was in part because Toby was the only Chinese teacher in his school, and he did not have a common planning time with the Spanish teachers who were his colleagues in his school. He did have Chinese teacher colleagues in the area, but he rarely connected with them. He said that he 'can't really find time to collaborate with anybody. There's no time to sit down and really do that'. He expressed disagreement with the ways that some of the other Chinese teachers taught language, saying that the lack of attention to explicit grammar in his feeder classrooms was 'killing' him in his own classroom. He thus stayed consistent between his beliefs and practices, even when it did not conform to the practices of others in his professional environment.

He felt that sometimes at department meetings he was able to talk with his Spanish-teaching colleagues, but because they were busy and they did not always realize that he wanted to connect with them, it was hard to build those relationships. I ended our conversations with a feeling that Toby felt somewhat isolated, and that he did not often feel inspired or motivated in the same ways as other teachers that I was able to talk with.

However, it was clear that his interactions with students and his support by his IB supervisor had a strong influence on how he enacted his beliefs in his classroom instructional practices.

Case Four: Demi

School context

Demi was a white, US-born, native speaker of English who taught German. She gained her credentials to become a high school German teacher after she was a flight attendant when the 9/11 attack on the World Trade Center happened. She had been teaching in the same school for the past 10 years at the time of data collection. Located in a larger town on the state border, Demi taught in a district that was comparable in size to Evie's and Molly's districts, serving about 5200 students in total in the district. The 9–12 high school had about 1500 students in attendance and was the only high school in the district. About 40% of the district's students qualified for free or reduced-price lunches. Two-thirds of the district's students identified as white, with one-third identifying as Hispanic and between 1% and 5% identifying as Black, Asian or multiracial. Just under 10% of the district's students received EL services, which categorized the district, according to the US Department of Education, in the 'medium' category of the four possible categories (US Department of Education, n.d.a). The school had about an 80% graduation rate documented by the state's department of education. Multiple languages were taught in the school, including Spanish, French, German and Chinese. Demi was the only German teacher in the school.

Demi, like the other teachers in the study, spoke with me once in a formal interview and again several times informally as I observed her in her classes. I observed for two full days. I did not have the opportunity to interview any students in her classes. I also looked at class materials and websites during and after my observations.

Teaching environment

Demi taught four levels of German as the only German teacher in the school. Two classes were German 1, two were German 2, one class was German 3 and one was German 4, totaling teaching six periods out of the day. She had one planning period and one enrichment period that was combined with her lunch time. Demi was also serving as the department chair at the time of data collection for this study. Classes in her school were 49 minutes long. Demi's classes included between 12 and 26 students, with most classes in the 20s or high teens.

Demi taught in a sprawling school building near the edge of town. Inside the school, hallways were tiled or carpeted, with narrow staircases leading from floor to floor. Some areas were full of students while others were empty. There were few teachers in the hallways, and when I asked for directions to the German room, a few directed me in the wrong direction or did not know where to direct me. The language teachers all taught in roughly the same general area. Demi's classroom had two thin temporary walls, one purple cinderblock wall and one wall to the exterior in her classroom. Along the exterior wall, which was situated in the back of the classroom, there was a set of small, high windows above shelving filled with books. Demi arranged two-top tables in rows facing the front of the class with an aisle down the middle, with additional two-top tables in big columns facing in along the left and the right of the class. The room was decorated with German labels on objects and classroom features. One wall featured a large illustration of a proficiency continuum, with examples of what students would need to be able to do in order to reach different levels of proficiency. A whiteboard was in the front of the class.

Classroom activities

Demi greeted students with 'Guten Morgen, Clase' ['Good morning, class'] and they responded 'Guten Morgen, Frau' ['Good morning, teacher'] at the start of each class. Then, she guided them through a variety of activities that varied a great deal from class to class and day to day. Demi explained that she tried to 'lesson plan so that we do each week one reading, one writing, one speaking, [and] one listening . . . activity'. She prioritized having 'a variety of activities' and 'more than one . . . method of communication'. Indeed, Demi included multiple modes in almost every class that I observed. Sometimes, she assigned writing projects for students to develop during class on laptops. During this time, she circulated, primarily focusing on helping students to get the language right, but also sometimes addressing larger issues of expression. At other times, she had students work in pairs for conversation and complex speaking activities where one student had information that the other student wanted. She showed videos sometimes to give context, then had students complete the follow-up conversation task together.

For example, in one class I observed, Demi showed videos about giving and getting directions, followed by students needing to give and get directions with one another. In this listening comprehension activity, she showed each of four videos two times, clarifying and supporting the spoken German with frequent comments. The videos and voices were different, with different tasks using the same vocabulary and speed. Then, she handed out maps and tasks about giving directions from one place to another on the map, stating, 'You can't just say "rechts/links" ["right/left"], you have to say more like what you see, etc.'. Students were writing records of what they said as they spoke with one another, with almost 100% engagement as I observed the class. They ended the activity by handing in the paper at the end of class. During this time, again, Demi would circulate and answer questions. She used dialogues and other materials a tools and topics for discussion in German. Her assessments, too, included multiple parts focusing on listening, reading and writing.

Demi also regularly included complex units about cultural topics, giving ample multipart descriptions of what she expected of her students and contextualizing it extensively in the target cultures. One example was a project about a famous dead person in German. She used authentic materials such as German news videos in the upper-level classes, in parallel with German-dubbed English cartoon movies in the lower-level classes. She stopped the videos regularly to check for comprehension and ask additional questions in both English and German, and she would sometimes project the script on the board while replaying specific sections of dialogue. Students filled out worksheets during these viewings, and she prompted them when an important section of the video was coming up. Student engagement was almost 100% during these activities, particularly the German news videos at the upper levels. One other example of Demi's attention to teaching culture was in her sharing of current German music hits every Wednesday. She tried in those cases to have the German relate to a grammar structure or vocabulary. Throughout much of this work with authentic materials, she taught them strategies for deciphering unfamiliar vocabulary, saying things such as, 'Think about words you know that are contained in that'.

Demi did focus on teaching grammar and vocabulary as a regular part of her classes, often integrated in the skills- and culture-focused instructional activities. She used a German textbook from Germany to help guide some parts of her instruction. She gave her students packets for practicing targeted vocabulary, having students work individually and with nearby partners during class to complete them. She regularly corrected students and clarified her points about grammar, saying things like, 'Remember if you're going to use –ge, it goes at the end of a sentence'. She gave extensive comments on drafts of writing, asking students to address her comments as they were preparing their drafts. During one enrichment period, Demi tutored a German student in preparing for an upcoming test, asking him to refer back to what he knew about endings ('So you have the right ending but the wrong family.'). When she described the importance of reading in her classes, she justified her emphasis on that mode by contextualizing it in how it could help with teaching grammar, namely: 'You see the word order, you see the conjugations, you see the adjective ending, you see the capitalized letters'. Grammar framed the students' work even as they focused on the modes of communication.

Demi used English regularly in the classroom, especially in describing projects and more complex proficiency-focused tasks. She featured more German usage at the upper levels, although greetings and basic, frequently repeated instructions were in German in every class. Whenever there was a birthday, the class sang 'Happy Birthday' in German. Homework and guidelines were written in English for students to consult. When students were working on writing, Demi could often be observed translating things for them or prompting them through breaking down the sentences and the grammar structures that they were trying to use. She used German strategically in class, as she described, 'So even if it's just, you know, me giving my morning spiel, or giving instructions, the important thing is that they hear more of the target language from me'.

Demi was observably responsive to her students' needs in the classroom. She included breaks in the class when the ongoing task was very focused or intense. She noticed when students were off-task, and she would say things like, '10 minutes left in class – you shouldn't be packing up', and 'We have five minutes left, we are not packing up and sitting around for five minutes'. Although she was not afraid of correcting students in that way, she brought a friendly demeanor to her interactions with them, checking in regularly with them about family, community news and other personal aspects of their lives. During her classes, I heard her laugh merrily frequently, whenever something interesting or funny happened.

More formal learning-focused check-ins about student needs were also a part of Demi's teaching approach. She clarified regularly during class whenever there was confusion in the large or the small group. She walked around her classroom a lot, from front to back, to grab papers, open and shut shades, check on students who were working in different parts of the room. She used choral response as a common formative assessment to see if students were following along, explaining:

> I think of it as like the dipstick, you know, um I'm asking questions that I think they should know, boom, boom, boom, right off the bat, and if I'm getting either no answers, crickets, or a number of wrong answers. And then I realize, okay, they don't know what I think they know. And then, and then it's time to depart from the lesson plan.

Her willingness to put aside her lesson plan could be seen a few different times during the observed classes.

Themes and patterns in teaching and connection to beliefs

Differentiation and different approaches: 'Language classes need to be for everyone'

As a teacher of German, a language which was becoming less and less commonly taught in Iowa K–12 schools, Demi thought carefully about how to make her classroom a welcoming place for everyone. She explained that her beliefs over the years have changed about her responsibility for making success attainable for all of her students. She believed that language classes needed to be for everyone, and everyone needed to be provided with supports; students, for instance, needed to be provided with multiple ways to study. It was up to them at that point if they wanted to use the supports. She explained:

> I think [after a few years teaching German] I realized, oh, I need to be more careful about how many students are successful in my class. And really make sure that I was not having it be a class for the elite, rather everyone . . . should be able to have some level of success in my class. I'm not saying that everyone's going to get an A, but . . . really make it accessible.

This belief could be seen in many aspects of what Demi did in her classroom, including her work in teaching all modes of communication, her focus on engaging students with authentic texts and videos and her close attention to how students were experiencing her teaching. She preferred activities like reading that allowed her students to see 'the language, applied, and at their own speed' in comparison with listening, which required students to 'get it at the speed of the speaker'. Reading also, she explained, allowed students to 'go back as many times as you need, you can even get out a dictionary and look up words if you need to'.

As shown above in the explanation of Demi's teaching practices, she felt like many different activities were important to include in the language classroom. Teaching and explaining grammar were important to her, as she said, 'I still explain the grammar, I still make my students take notes'. At another time, she stated, 'The important thing is that they hear more of the target language from me'. In another statement, she said, 'Reading is the most beneficial'. These multifaceted perspectives on what was best for language learning fit with her beliefs about the importance of making language work for everyone in her classes. These different priorities might apply for different students, all with the goal of getting them to 'get it', to say, 'Oh my gosh! It just makes sense!' – which was, as she explained, 'just kind of the stuff that keeps me coming back'.

Macro-level planning: 'We're trying to push up into Intermediate-Low'

Demi, as the department chair, was sensitized to the need to do systemic curricular planning throughout the world language department. As we spoke, she argued that teachers needed time to plan and to coordinate curriculum, which is something that was not always provided sufficiently by schools. As the department head, she was frustrated by the fact that she did not get any extra planning period to guide the teachers in her department in further planning. She truly believed that standards and guidelines were important to classroom practice. She thought that the *World-Readiness Standards* (National Standards Collaborative Board, 2015) were vital to help with labeling and identifying what was already going on in the classroom, and that it was important for students to know about proficiency levels and to know where they were in their proficiency.

This was borne out in the classroom, where, as described above, the proficiency levels and the *World-Readiness Standards* (National Standards Collaborative Board, 2015) with their descriptors were posted on one wall of the classroom. She also included 'phrases or sentences that would be at that level, but in English', to make sure her students understood what the proficiency levels were. She said that she was being very specific in telling students what each level meant and where they were. On some specific assessments, for instance, she would say things such as, 'OK . . . we're trying to push up into Intermediate-Low, and to do that you want to personalize your responses'. Demi thus thought that the proficiency guidelines were vital to her teaching, to her assessment, and to how the students understood their learning. In giving examples of what different proficiency levels looked like, she offered students a window into the sometimes-mysterious process of language development. In bringing up the different proficiency levels and offering specific examples of how to move up in the assessments to the next proficiency level, she helped students see what they needed to do. Unsurprisingly, during an observation, I overheard a student saying, 'If you want to be novice-mid or novice-high', when talking with another student about completing some written work.

Demi's belief in the importance of standards and proficiency levels and making them a prominent part of her approach undoubtedly contributed to her focus on communication modes rather than grammar.

Factors influencing beliefs and practices

As can be seen above, field-determined guidelines like standards and proficiency levels clearly affected how Demi made her decisions in instruction. Her beliefs reflected those guidelines, and in turn, her instruction was formed around them. Interestingly, despite the prevalence of the standards in the field of world language education in the US, Demi was one of the only teachers in this study who mentioned them regularly. This straightforward relationship between the standards, Demi's beliefs and her practices was easy to trace.

It was less easy to identify other major factors that influenced Demi's beliefs and practices. One important group that did affect how Demi chose her materials and practices was her network of German teachers in the local area and across the country that connected via social media. Her local connections in her area of Iowa, which included several different German teachers, shared an online repository of lesson ideas to help when someone asked, as she said, 'Hey does someone have anything for this?'. She said that the teachers also planned to visit and observe one another later in the spring, to 'go around and just see what everybody else does'. As a teacher of a language that was only taught in a few neighboring districts, Demi made a strong effort to stay motivated in her collaborations with German teachers specifically.

She also connected with remote German teachers through social media. For instance, she found German teachers a few states away who adopted the same new textbook that she did. As she explained, 'And so we all kind of worked together in adopting this textbook. And it worked out fabulously'. Thus, she found supports for developing her curriculum even though she was alone as the German teacher in her school. She also talked about other ways that she connected with remote German teachers on 'three different German teacher groups'. Demi sought out any opportunity to work with German teachers, even when they were not near her or teaching the same courses as her. This process took effort on her part, but she clearly found it rewarding and important to stay engaged and motivated to get community and ideas. Her desire to 'know what they are doing' indicates a desire to stay connected with the latest things in her field.

Demi thought critically about the other teaching resources that she found through her professional connections, sometimes rejecting them if they seemed too far out of line with her beliefs. For instance, she talked multiple times during my observations and conversations about her consideration of using more Teaching Proficiency through Reading and Storytelling (TPRS) and comprehensible input in her classes. She said, 'I've done workshops on TPR and CI, and I really try to incorporate those things, but I have not switched over to . . . doing entirely that method'. She told stories of trying different instructional activities associated with those approaches, and she explained that they did not always 'go over very well', sometimes because she 'never instituted it', despite purchasing materials and organizing and presenting them to her students. In this case, she created a 'Free Voluntary Reading Library' with children's books that she had, but because she did not focus solely on comprehensible input in her classroom, her students were not going to be able to read them. She reported that the library remained largely untouched.

Looking across the Four Cases

These four teachers all shared the challenge of teaching languages other than Spanish in a state where Spanish was by far the most commonly taught language at 83% of enrollment (Iowa Department of Education, 2018). Evie and Molly, as teachers of French, relied on their textbooks and structured much of their instruction around grammar, games and positive interactions with their students. Despite these surface similarities, Evie depicted learning language as a fun enterprise, while Molly worked to help her students understand the struggles that they might face as learners. Toby, as a teacher of Chinese, worked in a block period schedule to engage his Chinese students with learning grammar structures and characters via project-based learning in an IB school. Demi, building on years of experience as a German teacher, worked to connect her teaching with the *World-Readiness Standards* (National Standards Collaborative Board, 2015) and the ACTFL Proficiency Guidelines (ACTFL, 2012). Thus, these four teachers brought new perspectives to our consideration of teacher beliefs and practices beyond the fact that they taught languages other than Spanish.

The fact that these four teachers did not teach Spanish often affected how they conceptualized their beliefs. All of the teachers recognized that they needed to make their classes accessible and attractive to students. Demi's explanation that she sought to make her class a place where all students could succeed was evidence of this. Even the nature of the language sometimes affected the ways that these teachers approached their languages. Notably, Toby believed in the importance of teaching characters to his students in Chinese, but he also recognized that this was a challenging enterprise. In some ways, as teachers who had to attract and retain students more aggressively than Spanish teachers in this US context, these four individuals had more of a reason to be responsive to students' needs than other teachers in larger programs.

Thus, learner beliefs and learner feedback, in fact, were prominent factors in how these teachers navigated the relationship between their own beliefs and practices. Recall here the studies by Phipps and Borg (2009), Kim (2011) and Nishino (2012), all of whom found that student learning and learner experiences had direct effects on teacher classroom practice. In the case of Evie, her own direct and indirect ways of questioning students shaped her practice enormously. Molly's concern about her students' development as world citizens, Toby's desire to pace his class more effectively for his students' learning, and Demi's hope that her classroom would be open to all learners all showed the major force that learners were on the teachers.

Institutional factors were less prominent in mediating the relationship between the teacher beliefs and practices for Evie, Molly, Toby and Demi. Evie and Molly both rarely mentioned how their institution affected their practice. Demi herself was a representative of her institutional constraints, having chosen to follow more precisely the guidelines established by ACTFL in their *World-Readiness Standards* (National Standards Collaborative Board, 2015) and Proficiency Guidelines (ACTFL, 2012). Toby differed from the other teachers, however, as he taught, like Gabriel (Chapter 6) in an IB school and with the input of a supervisor.

These four teachers have offered an important perspective on teaching at the K–12 world language classroom in the US, as teachers of languages other than Spanish. In some ways, they share the most in common with the singleton teachers in Chapter 4, who also did not have as many local colleagues to collaborate with. Toby's isolation, in fact, mirrors that of Lydia (Chapter 4). I now move to examine all 15 teachers together in Chapter 8, Conclusions.

Questions for Discussion and Reflection

(1) Out of the four teachers featured in this chapter, which one most resembles how you teach and/or world language teachers that you have had in the past?
(2) Demi's statement about the need to broaden the accessibility of language education resonates for all language teachers, regardless of language taught. How do you see that connecting with some of the questions that we are asking about teacher beliefs?
(3) These teachers of languages in departments where multiple languages are spoken often have to advocate for their programs while continuing to provide rigorous instruction. How might that affect their beliefs and practices?
(4) What type of support could be given to these teachers that does not currently exist in their schools?
(5) If you were their supervisor, what would you suggest to them?

8 Conclusions

The purpose of this study was to investigate in detail (1) how teacher beliefs relate to their practices and (2) how that relationship was mediated and moderated by their learners, institutional demands, equity and access to WL education and other factors. The previous chapters of this book have presented 15 stories of world language teachers in K–12 schools in Iowa in the US. These teachers have included individuals who are teaching at the elementary and middle/junior high school levels, who are the only language teachers in their district, who work on small teams in small districts, who work on large teams in large districts and who teach in large departments but are the only teachers who teach their language. Some of these teachers had to teach according to the clear guidelines and themes in International Baccalaureate programs and Advanced Placement classes, and others worked completely independently and with almost no specific requirements for their curricula. Some taught all levels in their school, while others only taught one or two classes and repeated them throughout their days.

In this chapter, I build from the information and conclusions about the teachers featured in this book. I structure this chapter in terms of the four different audiences I imagine might be reading this book: first, the research community and the book's contributions to scholarship; second, graduate students in language education or applied linguistics; third, postsecondary educators in language programs; and fourth, individuals training to be K–12 language teachers. I present discussion questions for each group at the end of each section.

Contributions to Scholarship

Teachers in this study expressed beliefs about a wide variety of components of world language teaching and learning. These expressed beliefs overlapped and interacted, and they were influenced by a variety of factors. Table 8.1 offers a count of the frequencies of what I determined were the key areas where teachers expressed beliefs across all 15 cases. In determining these numbers, I reread each chapter and each case and looked at the narratives presented in 'Themes and Patterns in Teaching and Connection to Beliefs', since I wrote those sections to identify the most prominent beliefs expressed by the teacher across the data sources.

This table illustrates that these teachers most commonly considered student behavior and engagement in expressing their beliefs. Language-focused course content was the next most common category of beliefs

Table 8.1 Frequency of notable mentions in general belief categories across all cases

Belief category	Number of notable mentions
Student behavior and engagement	13
Language-focused course content (grammar, input, output)	8
Student life skills (resilience, accountability)	6
Planning for instruction	5
Culture-focused course content	5
Differentiating for levels and language background	3
Research on language acquisition	2

expressed, and so forth. The table does not indicate that student behavior and engagement was the most important to teachers, since, as shown in Chapters 3 through 7, the teachers simultaneously held many beliefs, with some taking precedence for some teachers and others more central for others. I discuss this in more detail below in addressing the concept of core and peripheral beliefs in the data.

Recall here that this book takes the sociocultural, dialectical stance that beliefs cannot be separated from actions (Borg, 2017; Burns et al., 2015; Negueruela-Azarola, 2011). A decontextualized list of categories of beliefs like Table 8.1 offers a useful overview across the cases, but it is, as Borg (2017: 88) stated, 'not possible to adequately understand [beliefs] without reference to the interactions the teacher has with students, colleagues, professional learning, and institutional structures more generally over time'. In Chapter 2, I examined the research literature that defined beliefs with five guiding principles: teacher beliefs are dynamic; they can be identified as either core or peripheral; they are connected to emotion; they are connected to identity and they are socially constructed. I will now connect the data from each case to these concepts.

Teacher beliefs are dynamic

Beliefs, as Borg (2017) and Burns et al. (2015) argued, can change and transform over time. This characteristic of beliefs was certainly observable in the data for many teachers in this study. Several teachers told me the story of discovering a new approach to teach. Calvin's (Chapter 3) use of leveled readers in his classes, and his students' reactions, caused him to shift his beliefs about language learning and student engagement to a stronger consideration of comprehensible input via reading. Marlene (Chapter 5) similarly observed how using novels with her students engaged them and helped them with their language acquisition, and then her beliefs in the importance of reading in her classroom began to shift.

Some teachers described a similar transformation of their beliefs when exposed to different research about second language acquisition (SLA). Wade's (Chapter 4) growing awareness of the research on SLA led to him believing in new ways to approach language learning in his classroom, which then led to a shift in his practices. Caitlyn (Chapter 5) openly acknowledged the changing nature of her beliefs as a part of her continuous growth, self-evaluation and development, indicating that she was constantly considering what the research showed in order to refine her teaching.

Teachers also noted the influence of both their learner and institutional contexts on the dynamic changes over time in their beliefs. Several teachers told stories of the changes in their beliefs and the related practices when they changed careers, jobs or teaching responsibilities. Veronica (Chapter 5), for instance, addressed at length how she had to change how she thought about teaching grammar when she realized the needs of her students in her school. Although she had believed more in the centrality of providing comprehensible input in her previous teaching context, she realized in her current context, when she saw her students' lack of knowledge of important grammar concepts, that she also valued targeted grammar instruction. Diana (Chapter 6) noted in her interview that she brought all of her previous life experience to her work, which inevitably, as she argued, led to a change in her beliefs. Recall her statement here: 'Have my ideas changed? Yes . . . because my groups, my places have changed'. This notion that ideas or beliefs change based on context and student need appeared in many teachers' statements across all cases.

Teacher beliefs can be identified as either core or peripheral

As described in Chapter 2, the scholarship in the field has established that core beliefs are 'deeper' and 'more general' (Phipps & Borg, 2009: 387), and they might be more connected to directly observable actions in the classroom. Peripheral beliefs might be newer or not as well-supported, or they might change more in the face of student or contextual pressures (Oranje & Smith, 2018; Phipps & Borg, 2009).

Each teacher in the study was clearly able to articulate and illustrate a variety of beliefs. Some of these beliefs were more general and all-encompassing, including, for instance, beliefs about the importance of communication (Marlene, Chapter 5), giving students tools to succeed (Gabriel, Chapter 6) or creating and maintaining relationships with students (Bryanna, Chapter 4). I would argue that most of the beliefs shared within this study by the teachers were core beliefs.

Teachers did express some beliefs that were more peripheral, however. Sometimes, it was because of newer ideas or initiatives that they were beginning to institute in their classes. Demi (Chapter 7) spoke about the increasing importance of considering standards and proficiency levels in her context, something that was newer to her practice and therefore was not necessarily a core belief yet. Sarah (Chapter 3) identified yearly goals that shifted regularly, which in the observation year were to use the whole room, to be more culturally aware and to look more at student behaviors and her responses. Although goals and beliefs are not the same thing, her goals had a direct connection to beliefs about what was important in the language classroom. Since they were only described as yearly goals, her dedication to them as a core part of her classroom was not yet undetermined.

As beliefs are dynamic and changing, some of the teacher beliefs could be seen as in transformation between peripheral and core beliefs. One such belief would be the importance of SLA research in determining classroom practices. As teachers such as Wade (Chapter 4) and Caitlyn (Chapter 5) consulted research and incorporated it into their classrooms, their beliefs transformed and shifted from peripheral to core beliefs. Many of the teachers in the study consulted their students directly about how their classes were going via surveys and other means; their discoveries had the potential to shift their peripheral, newer beliefs about teaching to more proven, general and central core beliefs. Thus, not only did beliefs change over time as illustrated in the previous section, but they also changed in importance or in their nature as core or peripheral beliefs for some of these teachers.

Teacher beliefs are connected to emotion

Beliefs connect closely to other aspects of the social psychologies of the teachers, such as emotion and identity (Barcelos, 2015; Barcelos & Ruohotie-Lyhty, 2018). Teachers in this study often expressed positive emotions like excitement, motivation and relief when characterizing their beliefs about teaching. Evie's (Chapters 3 and 7) love of incorporating fun in her classroom, Caitlyn's (Chapter 5) enjoyment of teaching when getting positive feedback from students, Gabriel's (Chapter 6) energy and excitement as a point of pride in engaging his students – all were intertwined with their beliefs about language teaching and learning.

Other emotions expressed by teachers in the study could be mixed or predominantly negative. Boredom was something that several teachers mentioned as an emotion that they worked to avoid; Evie in Chapters 3 and 7, Abbie and Lydia in Chapter 4 and Marlene in Chapter 5 all repeated variations on the phrase, 'If I'm bored, my students are bored'. This avoidance of boredom for them and for their students shaped their beliefs about how best to teach. Isolation and loneliness were described by some of the teachers who were singletons in their districts (Chapter 4), by the teachers in small programs in Chapter 5, who found it hard to collaborate in small departments, and by teachers like Toby (Chapter 7), who was the only Chinese teacher. This loneliness affected how they sought out community with their students and other teachers, and it had an impact on how their beliefs changed or did not change about teaching. Isolated teachers did not have the outside influence on their beliefs as teachers who felt connected with and got ideas from communities of teachers. Teachers like Abbie (Chapter 4), Veronica (Chapter 5) and Diana and Gabriel (Chapter 6) all faced frustration, overwork and stress in finding materials that worked for their students. Teachers like the singletons in Chapter 4 had extensive teaching responsibilities with very little time provided to plan, and they also expressed stress and concern over being able to meet the needs of their students.

There is not a linear relationship between emotions and beliefs, as they are both contextual, embedded, complex and dynamic (Barcelos & Ruohotie-Lyhty, 2018). However, the emotions expressed by teachers in this study did connect with their beliefs about teaching in a variety of ways.

Teacher beliefs are connected to identity

Teacher beliefs, as a part of their cognition, have been shown to contribute to the development and change of their language teacher identity across contexts (Barkhuizen, 2017; Kubanyiova & Crookes, 2016). The teachers in this study, although not explicitly asked to reflect on their language teacher identity, often clearly indicated how their beliefs connected to who they thought they were in their professional role as a teacher, or 'who I am is how I teach' (Farrell, 2017: 184). Some examples of this included some teachers clearly defining their professional role identity as enforcers of classroom control (Lydia, Chapter 4) or student accountability (Bryanna, Chapter 4). Bryanna also identified as a community member as well as a teacher, a dual identity that she felt strengthened her professional role identity. This identity as a community member was the case for several of the other teachers working in smaller schools and communities like Abbie (Chapter 4). Demi (Chapter 7) saw an important part of her professional identity as being as an advocate for her German program. This investigation into beliefs thus naturally included some important reflections of how teacher professional role identity could be constructed by the participants.

Other aspects of language teacher identity that emerged in this study were closely related to the linguistic and cultural backgrounds of the teachers and the students in their classes. Thirteen out of 15 of the teachers in this study were US-born individuals whose first language was English and who had learned the target language through a combination of formal schooling and time abroad. Several of these teachers believed that it was important to connect with their non-HL students about the difficulties that they faced. Lydia (Chapter 4), Bryanna (Chapter 4), Evie (Chapters 3 and 7) and Toby (Chapter 7) all believed that it was important to communicate clearly with their students about the challenges of learning the language, often sharing their own experiences. Their identities as language learners as well as language teachers, in turn, helped them to enact their beliefs about connecting with students and helping students to understand the process, and sometimes the challenge, of language learning. Beliefs (importance of sharing challenges of learning language) reinforced aspects of their identity (successful language learner), which in turn helped them to enact other beliefs (connecting meaningfully with students).

Gabriel (Chapter 6) and Calvin (Chapter 3) self-identified as members of the target cultures and native speakers of the languages that they were teaching. The teachers' identities as native speakers came frequently into their discussions of their beliefs about teaching (Barcelos, 2015; Barcelos & Ruohotie-Lyhty, 2018). They both clearly considered their own professional identities as overlapping, intersecting and reinforcing their identities as native speakers of the language. Calvin, with no Spanish HLs in his classes, often referred to his own identity as a Colombian and a native speaker in contextualizing his beliefs about teaching. Recall his explanation that some teaching techniques seemed repetitive to him as a native speaker of the language, and so he avoided them as a result. Interestingly, his non-HL remarked positively on his status as a native speaker of the language, reiterating the predominant ideology that suggests that native speakers are ideal teachers of the language (Holliday, 2006; Llurda & Calvet-Terré, 2022; Moussu & Llurda, 2008; Ortega, 2019).

Both my observations of Gabriel and my interviews with him revealed that he foregrounded his identity as a Mexican and a native speaker in his beliefs and his classroom practices. He used examples from his experiences learning English, he explained his cultural practices in the home including his meals (eating 'tacos with mole'), and he regularly drew on his travel and life experiences as a multilingual citizen of the world in interacting with both his HL and non-HL students. Thus, this cultural and linguistic identity was closely bound with his beliefs about teaching language, and it strengthened how he put his beliefs into practice in his classes.

Teacher beliefs are socially constructed

Finally, teacher beliefs have been shown to be influenced by social groups and communities (Borg, 2017). In the data from this study, there are several different ways that this occurred for the teacher participants.

First, I can examine the relationship between teacher beliefs and learners that traced through almost all the different cases in the study. In Table 8.1, it shows that some of the most common beliefs across all the teachers had to do with their relationships with their students, whether that was related to their desires to develop classroom management, to encourage student engagement, to support students and differentiate instruction to address their needs or to help students develop life skills like resilience and grit. All of these beliefs related directly to the interactions that the teachers had with their students in the context of their classrooms and their schools.

This study thus echoes other work that has presented evidence that teachers were affected by their desire to build positive relationships or avoid negative interactions with their students, even when it meant that they had to act in a way that diverged from their beliefs (Borg, 1998; Breen *et al.*, 2001; Farrell & Bennis, 2013; Gatbonton, 2000). Interestingly, these other studies have not generally framed this interaction as being a social construction of teacher beliefs, perhaps because the relationship between teacher and student has a power differential that separates it from other social relationships, which are often depicted as relationships among equals or peers. Nonetheless, the ways that teachers enacted their beliefs in their classrooms occurred in many cases a result of their continued social interactions with students.

The institution has also functioned as a locus of social construction of beliefs for the teachers in this study. Institutional factors in teacher beliefs have been shown in this study to also be important, as in other studies in the field. Teachers in some schools with larger departments, as represented in Chapters 6 and 7 primarily, spoke about the importance of their colleagues in aligning their beliefs and their instructional practices. Diana and Gabriel (Chapter 6), as well as Evie (Chapters 3 and 7) and Demi (Chapter 7), all discussed the importance of their school colleagues in constructing their beliefs and practices. Lydia, Bryanna (Chapter 4) and Toby (Chapter 7) were influenced by their supervisors and instructional coaches, echoing the literature about institutional factors (e.g. Borg & Sanchez, 2020; Flores & Day, 2006; Kennedy & Kennedy, 1996; Priestley *et al.*, 2010).

Other communities were mentioned by other teachers as being important to them in determining their beliefs, largely on an *ad hoc* basis. Recall here the importance of online and regional gatherings of teachers to the singleton teachers like Abbie and Wade (Chapter 4) and Caitlyn, Veronica and Marlene (Chapter 5) in small programs, and Demi (Chapter 7) as a German teacher. Although little literature traces world language teacher communities like this and their influence on teacher beliefs, there is certainly evidence here that these communities were key to helping the teachers construct their beliefs through exchanging ideas, successes and reflections on teaching.

Questions for further discussion

(1) What is the most important or surprising contribution that you see this study making to the research on world language teacher beliefs?
(2) How would you construct a follow-up study to this work?

(3) How does this study relate to parallel research studies in, for instance, other locations, or with teachers working at other types of institutions or with other types of students?

Graduate Students

One of the audiences of this book is graduate students in language education, applied linguistics and other related fields. I have spent many years of my career either as a graduate student in these areas or as a faculty member in a research-intensive institution working closely with graduate students. Graduate students interested in conducting research (in the US, this might mean students in a PhD program or an MA program with a research focus) will certainly benefit from a close consideration of the preceding section of this chapter where I connect my findings to the scholarship in the field. Graduate students focused on teaching or practical applications of research (in the US, students in an EdD program, MAT or MEd program, certificate program or teaching-focused MA program) would benefit from the next sections where I address implications for instructors in a variety of contexts. However, I would also like to share some thoughts about how this book might provide insights to individuals who are still in the process of learning about our field.

Conceptual insights

This book addresses the conceptual notion of teacher beliefs and how they relate to practice. It is common as a novice researcher to seek out and rely on clear frameworks, tools and agreed-upon definitions that operationalize difficult constructs simply and directly. With some social psychological constructs in our field, notably language learning anxiety and language learning motivation, these frameworks, tools and definitions are widely used by researchers at all stages of career. Work by Elaine Horwitz, Robert Gardner and Zoltan Dörnyei has led the way in these areas. There are certainly advantages to having common definitions and especially tools in research. For instance, research can be more comparable across studies when a common definition is used, and a more consistent voice and set of inferences can be built. However, novice researchers might be less inclined to seek out new definitions or to challenge commonly accepted definitions or tools when one definition or tool dominates the scholarly discourse about a specific construct. Defining concepts precisely also inevitably bounds them and reduces the possibilities of connection with other concepts in the field.

Constructs in our field like language teacher beliefs, including language teacher and student identity, have a different type of history and structure to how researchers have approached them. The work of Simon Borg on teacher cognition, cited extensively throughout this book, has been essential in understanding teacher beliefs. His work is clearly oriented to an inclusive and multipart definition of teacher cognition, rather than a creation of a narrower model of the construct, as evidenced in much of his work but, most recently, his 2019 chapter in the *Second Handbook of English Language Teaching*. Research in teacher beliefs in the last twenty years of scholarship has adopted a sociocultural perspective that focuses on the situatedness of teacher beliefs, often in the form of in-depth case studies of a small number of teachers.

As such, this book provides one model to novice researchers for considering the concept of teacher beliefs. It is possible to identify teacher beliefs across a variety of data, including observational data, and then to examine patterns across teachers and contexts. I have illustrated how different factors have influenced the relationship between teacher beliefs and teacher practices. Finally, I have shown how the data and findings have connected back to the different ways that teacher beliefs have been defined in the field. My hope would be that graduate students reading this book would have a clearer idea of language teacher beliefs without feeling too limited by the ways that I have chosen to define them here.

Contextual insights

This book addresses the lived context of K–12 teachers of world language in the US. Some graduate student readers, based on their teaching background or where they are studying, might not be familiar with the ways that K–12 world language education is taught and learned in the US. In some cases, this information might simply be another context to consider in a broader path of studies, particularly for those graduate students in programs outside of the US. For students in the US with little to no background in K–12 US education, this book can offer some important insights into how language learning occurs at young ages in the context where they are studying. The information about US educational policy related to world language education provided in Chapter 1 should have been especially helpful to students in those cases.

For graduate students who have an extensive background in K–12 US world language education, this book offers an opportunity to practice their transformation from a teacher to a researcher. Indeed, I see this book as offering this opportunity for all novice researchers, especially those who have a background as a language educator in any context. It can be difficult for graduate students to make the shift from being a teacher to being an educational researcher (DiPardo, 1993). As I explained in my positionality statement in Chapter 2, my own teaching experience inevitably influenced how I considered the data that I was collecting in this study. However, I believe that looking at a great deal of data across contexts might help graduate students to distance themselves from comparisons and judgements, instead focusing on the central conceptual questions about teacher beliefs and practices that are the focus of this book.

Methodological insights

Finally, this book provides an example of how to conduct qualitative research in the form of multiple case studies. This methodological example can offer insights to graduate students interested in conducting their own research. The overview provided in Chapter 2 of all parts of the study's research design should be traceable throughout each chapter and each case. My interview questions, recruitment documents, and other study materials provided in that chapter can give students seeking to do their own research some materials that they can adapt to their own work. The choices that I made as a researcher to gather and analyze data, although perhaps not feasible for every researcher, can help novice researchers to navigate some of their own choices in the future.

Questions for further discussion

(1) Do you think that it is better to have a field generally agree on a definition for and a tool to measure concepts such as teacher beliefs, language learning anxiety or language learning motivation, or for there to be less consensus and more flexibility across the scholarship?
(2) What were some things that you learned about US K–12 schools in reading these chapters?
(3) Consider this book as a work of research/research design. How does it conform to the expectations that you had after reading the second part of Chapter 2? How credible is the study, now that you have read the data and the findings?
(4) What would you do differently, were you to design this study?
(5) How has this book informed your ideas about research and/or language teaching?

Postsecondary Language Educators

I wrote the original proposal of this book with the sage advice of colleagues working as postsecondary language educators in the US. Although I do not have experience teaching language at the postsecondary level, I habitually work closely with postsecondary language educators at my own university, as a part of my professional organizations and in the language teacher workshops that I have delivered. Although some of my postsecondary colleagues may have studied world language in this context, their experiences as students might have been very different from current practices. Other instructors may have become multilingual through home and community learning, in another country's educational system or via another educational process. Thus, in writing this, I have constantly considered what this book could offer to my colleagues at the postsecondary level.

First, this book offers contemporary and in-depth information about the structures, requirements, resources, policies and, of course, teacher beliefs that exist at the K–12 level of world language instruction in the US. The diversity of the types of programs, the approaches taken by the teachers to their teaching, and the overall experiences in K–12 programs are illustrated throughout this study. Postsecondary educators reading this book will gain a broader understanding of the students who might be entering their classes, as well as the thought process and experiences of their colleagues who are teaching younger students. This study has shown that, even within one school, world language classrooms might offer different learning opportunities to students depending on the teacher, their beliefs and their experiences. In some cases, students entering postsecondary classrooms might have had only one language teacher at all levels, suggesting that the transition to a different classroom context might be an exceptional challenge for them.

One area where the classrooms in this study differ greatly is in the assessment procedures, which has immediate bearing on the postsecondary context, particularly in terms of the placement procedures for university classes. K–12 teachers have been shown to hold different beliefs and carry out different practices about how and on what basis students should be assessed. Some examples are given across the different contexts. In light of this information, postsecondary educators should think about how their placement tests can be most useful to them.

Finally, a postsecondary educator who reads this book might better understand how to connect with their K–12 colleagues. They have undoubtedly seen themselves in some of the beliefs, experiences and emotions expressed by the teacher participants here. Many postsecondary institutions can identify key schools and districts that feed into their programs. I would hope that this book might offer some foundational knowledge that would help postsecondary educators to approach their K–12 colleagues to work with them to enhance the effectiveness of the transition from high school to college for their students.

Questions for further discussion

(1) How do the data in this study offer insights to what you see in your own language classrooms at your institution?
(2) What surprised you about the beliefs and practices of K–12 educators?
(3) Which of the 15 K–12 educators in this study did you identify with as an educator? Which one(s) did you feel yourself to be the most distant from? Why do you think that is?

K–12 World Language Teachers (Pre-Service and In-Service)

This book has allowed readers to visit 15 different classrooms. Although all K–12 teacher training programs in the US feature field experiences, and most teachers have the opportunity to visit other classes once they have started their own teaching careers, those experiences are often limited to visiting a small number of classrooms, and they may not include in-depth conversations with the host teacher about their outlook and beliefs. Both pre-service and in-service teachers can benefit from the extensive visits into the classrooms featured in this book, as well as the thoughts and experiences of their fellow teachers. All teachers can use this book as an opportunity to reflect. Additionally, I feel that three major implications for teachers, whether pre-service or in-service, arise out of the data in this study regarding the importance of professional development and teacher community, consulting students regularly and incorporating reflection throughout their practice.

Professional development and teacher community

First, the teachers in this book spoke at length about the importance of professional development and connection in community with other teachers. Some were struggling with finding professional development that worked for them in their schedules and lives, and they lacked teacher community within their schools. Others appreciated their school or departmental community of teachers and looked to them to develop their beliefs and practices. Some teachers worked to connect with other teachers and professional organizations outside of their schools, either regionally or online, to access professional development. Because schools in the US do not have state mandates or training requirements for in-service teachers, the participants in this study had very different supports available to them. Some worked closely with supervisors or instructional coaches, while others did not. All of them, however, wished for more support and more community to develop their skills as teachers, to align their beliefs with their practices and to continue to improve.

The implication here is that both pre-service and in-service teachers should consider the availability of professional development and teacher community in their jobs or potential future jobs. When professional supports and community are not available, they should consider seeking out online communities as did some of the participants in this study, simply to be exposed to new ideas and to have the opportunity to grow as educators. Those individuals who work as administrators or supervisors of K–12 world language teachers should also consider the importance with which professional development and teacher community emerged as a major component of this study.

Consulting students regularly

Teachers across this study reported on how they were influenced by their students in both their beliefs and practices. For this, they used three primary techniques: direct consultation with students via surveys or other direct questioning, observation of student behavior and engagement during class and assessment of student outcomes and learning. These different ways of checking in with students offered the teachers insights into the effectiveness of their teaching that in turn transformed their beliefs and practices, as evidenced throughout this book. Although not all of these might work for all teachers, these ideas offer important paths forward.

To directly check in with students, some teachers gave out periodic surveys, like Sarah (Chapter 3), Bryanna (Chapter 4), Caitlyn and Marlene (Chapter 5), Diana (Chapter 6), Molly (Chapter 7) and Evie (Chapters 3 and 7). For example, Sarah would ask students directly what she might do differently or how an activity could be conducted differently. Caitlyn explained how she gave her students a survey at the end of the quarter and the semester that asked them questions about her effectiveness as a teacher and their own ideas about how they were as language learners. These ways of directly asking students to reflect on their learning, although perhaps daunting in some ways, offered clear and simple data to teachers about their work. Teachers using this technique should also keep in mind that some students might be uncomfortable responding to direct questions about their engagement.

Other teachers talked about observing student positive engagement in their classes, a technique observed in other contexts (Borg, 1998; Breen *et al.*, 2001; Farrell & Bennis, 2013; Gatbonton, 2000). Calvin (Chapter 3) watched how students were doing during his lessons, assessing if they were still engaged. Wade and Abbie (Chapter 4) differed in their descriptions of how they planned for their classes, but they both spoke at length about how they watched their students and made changes accordingly on the spot. Gabriel (Chapter 6) was attentive to his students' nonverbal expressions and blurted comments, sometimes changing his lesson plan from class to class even if the classes were technically the same (e.g. Spanish 1). Indeed, almost all teachers described this practice as a part of their work. This finding fits with the overall conclusion that teachers were regularly affected by students, although this practice does potentially omit situations in which teachers failed to observe something. Students might have been struggling in a way that as not readily visible to teachers; other students might have been consciously hiding their lack of engagement.

Finally, some teachers used student outcome data to assess the effectiveness of their instructional practices, a technique that has been widely documented in the research literature (Borg, 1998; Farrell & Bennis, 2013; Farrell & Guz, 2019; Gatbonton, 2000; Graden, 1996). Veronica (Chapter 5) was a clear example of this, where she saw what the students' needs were based on their performance on her assessments, and she changed her practices as a result. As with the more informal observations of student engagement, this technique is best when it is systematic and planned rather than *ad hoc*, with teachers determining ahead of time how they would adjust their lessons based on student outcome data.

Incorporating reflection throughout their practice

Many teachers in this study spoke about setting goals, constantly self-evaluating and adhering to a growth mindset as a teacher. Those teachers often had close alignment between their beliefs and practices. Indeed, research has shown that teachers who regularly reflect on their own practice demonstrate greater alignment between their beliefs and their practices (Farrell & Ives, 2015; Farrell & Yang, 2019; Watson, 2015). Student interviews revealed that they also appreciated teachers who had demonstrated that they had reflected on what they were doing, and when they shared those reflections with the students. Many ways of reflecting on practice were exemplified in the different cases in this book.

K–12 world language teachers can take these examples and apply them to their own practice. For current pre-service or in-service teachers, some ways to think about their own beliefs might include a consideration of the concept of core and peripheral beliefs (Phipps & Borg, 2009). Teachers able to articulate their core beliefs can use them as a guide to make decisions in the classroom, while peripheral beliefs offer new avenues of exploration in instructional practice to see if they work.

K–12 world language teachers might also combine both professional development and teacher community and consultation with students to create some useful reflective practice. For instance, feedback from direct or indirect student consultation could be collected in order to identify areas of need for growth. Then, teachers can reflect on how they might address those areas in consultation with colleagues and the teaching community. Finally, teachers might attend conferences or participate in online groups that might help them to identify ways to proceed.

Questions for further discussion

(1) Which of the 15 K–12 educators in this study did you identify with as an educator? Which one(s) did you feel yourself to be the most distant from? Why do you think that is?
(2) What type of professional development would you like to engage with as a teacher? How can you focus this work on exploring your beliefs and the connection between your beliefs and practices?
(3) What do you see as your core beliefs as a world language teacher? What are some peripheral beliefs that you might hold right now?

(4) How do you currently reflect on your practice, and how would you like to reflect in the future?

Conclusion

This chapter connected the findings from the study with the different audiences for this book, hopefully offering some insights to all groups. Moving forward, this book is only as useful as its contributions to our scholarly and instructional communities. I hope that you will use it in your context to continue to develop better understanding about language education and language educators.

Appendix A: Teacher Interview Questions

Formal Interview Protocol

Opening questions:

(1) Tell me a little about you as a teacher. What do you love about teaching? Why did you become a teacher?
(2) Tell me about something that you think that you teach really well. What do you do? How do you know that you're teaching really well?
(3) Tell me about something that you struggle with in the classroom. What's a hard part of your job?

Describing their own teaching:

(1) How would you describe your own teaching style?
(2) How do you describe it to parents or administrators? Like at Back-to-School night, for instance?
(3) When you are observed in the classroom by a principal or peer, what do you want to be sure that they see? What kind of comments do they make to you about what they see?
(4) Tell me a story about something memorable that happened in your classroom this year.

Opinions, thoughts:

(1) What is your favorite activity to do with students?
(2) How do you believe that students learn language best? What activities do you think have the greatest impact on students' language development? Which activities do you think that they find most helpful?
(3) Right now, which period of your day is your favorite to teach? Why do you think that you enjoy that class so much? If you don't have – or want to identify a favorite – tell me about a class that you remember well from the past that you really enjoyed.
(4) Think about one of your best students – What makes that student stand out from the rest? What are they capable of doing that others cannot?

Learning and connecting about teaching:

(1) How much do you share what you do with other language teachers?
(2) Do you feel like you belong to a community of language teachers who influence how you teach?
(3) How do you continue to improve as a teacher?

Innovations:

(1) How do you know when to make changes to your curriculum or to depart from your lesson plan? How do you make that decision?
(2) What are new things or changes that you have started to do in your classroom?
(3) Tell me about the different ways that you use technology in the class – any kind of technology. Some examples might be for recording grades, communicating, sharing documents, accessing the internet for research, connecting with other teachers online, etc.
(4) What do you think are the advantages and disadvantages of using technology in the classroom?
(5) What do you think are the most important things to keep in mind when planning a lesson involving technology?
(6) What do you know about the Iowa World Language Competencies (IWLCs)? Do you use them in your planning? Do you use them in reporting on what you do?
(7) How has your practice changed since incorporating the IWLCs in your classroom?
(8) Have you changed in how you think about language teaching since starting in this career? Have you changed in how you teach?

Informal Interview Prompts

Themes addressed in questions about observed classes during passing periods:

- How do you feel the lesson(s) that I observed went? Do you feel that the lesson was successful? Did students learn/acquire what you had hoped? How did you know?
- Would you say that the lesson(s) I observed was/were representative of how you generally teach? If not, how were these lessons different?
- If you could reteach the lesson(s), what changes would you make and why?
- Can you tell me how the lesson(s) fit(s) into the broader context of the unit or series of lessons that you were teaching at the time?
- Is there anything that happened during the observation that you feel is important to discuss or explain in greater detail?

General questions:

- What are some big things going on right now at the school?
- What are teachers talking about these days?

Appendix B: Student Interview Questions

(1) I just want to start by talking generally about languages and language learning. What's your main reason for learning [language]?

(2) When did you start learning languages? What other languages have you studied?

(3) Talk to me about [language]. Do you think that it's good to know it? Why or why not?

(4) Talk to me about [language]-speaking people that you know. What are they like?

(5) In the future, do you think that you will use [language]? What do you think that you will use it for? What about other languages – do you want to study other languages?

*****

(6) Let's talk about your [language] class. Can you describe it to me? What are some things that you do a lot in that class?

(7) What are some of your favorite activities in that class?

(8) What are some of your least favorite activities?

(9) What do you think helps you learn the most in that class?

*****

(10) How long have you been taking [language] with your teacher?

- (If more than one year with the same teacher:) Have you noticed changes in how [he/she] has done things this year compared with previous years? What do you think of those changes?

(11) Talk to me about how you use technology in your [language] class. Do you ever use computers or the internet? What do you use it for?

(12) Do you know why your teacher teaches what [he/she] teaches? Does [he/she] share [his/her] objectives or goals for the class with you?

(13) Tell me some memories or stories about being in the class. It can be a good memory, or a bad memory, or both. Do you remember a time when you were frustrated, or really happy, or having a lot of fun?

Why do you think that you remember this so much? Are there any other things you really remember?

(14) Let's say a new student asked you about your [language] class. What would you tell them? Be honest – you can be positive or negative.

References

281 IAC 77. Iowa Administrative Code, Education Department [281] (2017) Chapter 77: Standards for teacher intern preparation programs. See https://www.legis.iowa.gov/law/administrativeRules/rules?agency=281&chapter=77&pubDate=01-04-2017.

281 IAC 79.8(256). Iowa Administrative Code, Education Department [281] (2017) Chapter 79: Standards for practitioner and administrator preparation programs. See https://www.legis.iowa.gov/law/administrativeRules/rules?agency=281&chapter=79&pubDate=01-04-2017.

ACTFL (n.d.) Assigning CEFR ratings to ACTFL assessments. See https://www.actfl.org/sites/default/files/reports/Assigning_CEFR_Ratings_To_ACTFL_Assessments.pdf.

ACTFL (2010a) *Foreign Language Enrollments in K-12 Public Schools: Are Students Prepared for a Global Society?* ACTFL.

ACTFL (2010b) Use of the target language in the classroom position statement. See https://www.actfl.org/advocacy/actfl-position-statements/use-the-target-language-the-classroom.

ACTFL (2012) ACTFL proficiency guidelines 2012. See https://www.actfl.org/resources/actfl-proficiency-guidelines-2012.

ACTFL (2014) Global competence position statement. See https://www.actfl.org/advocacy/actfl-position-statements/global-competence-position-statement.

ACTFL, Californians Together, Modern Language Association, National Association for Bilingual Education, National Association of English Learner Program Administrators, National Council of State Supervisors for Languages and TESOL International Association (2020) Guidelines for implementing the Seal of Biliteracy. See https://www.actfl.org/assessments/k-12-assessments/seal-of-biliteracy.

ACTFL/CAEP (2015) ACTFL/CAEP program standards for the preparation of foreign language teachers. See https://www.actfl.org/sites/default/files/caep/ACTFLCAEPStandards2013_v2015.pdf.

Al-Khatib, M.A. (2008) Innovative second and foreign language education in the Middle East and North Africa. *Encyclopedia of Language and Education* 4 (2), 227–237. https://doi.org/10.1007/978-0-387-30424-3_101.

Allen, L.Q. (2002) Teachers' pedagogical beliefs and the standards for foreign language learning. *Foreign Language Annals* 35 (5), 518–529. https://doi.org/10.1111/j.1944-9720.2002.tb02720.x.

American Councils for International Education (ACIE) (2017) *The National K-12 Foreign Language Enrollment Survey Report. ACIE with ACTFL, CAL, MLA and NCSSFL.* See https://www.americancouncils.org/sites/default/files/FLE-report-June17.pdf (accessed December 2023).

Anya, U. and Randolph, L.J. (2019) Diversifying language educators and learners. *The Language Educator* 14 (4), 23–27.

Aro, M. (2016) Authority versus experience: Dialogues on learner beliefs. In P. Kalaja, A.M.F. Barcelos, M. Aro and M. Ruohotie-Lyhty (eds) *Beliefs, Agency and Identity in Foreign Language Learning and Teaching* (pp. 27–47). Palgrave Macmillan.

Assen, J.H.E., Meijers, F., Otting, H. and Poell, R.F. (2016) Explaining discrepancies between teacher beliefs and teacher interventions in a problem-based learning environment: A mixed methods study. *Teaching and Teacher Education* 60, 12–23. https://doi.org/10.1016/j.tate.2016.07.022.

Avant (2017) Avant STAMP results—National averages 2016–2017. See https://d3itqxtdxl1nz0.cloudfront.net/pdfs/STAMP-National-Averages-Update-2017.pdf.

Baggett, H.C. (2016) Student enrollment in world languages: L'Égalité des chances? *Foreign Language Annals* 49 (1), 162–179. https://doi.org/10.1111/flan.12173.

Baker, A. (2014) Exploring teachers' knowledge of second language pronunciation techniques: Teacher cognitions, observed classroom practices, and student perceptions. *TESOL Quarterly* 48 (1), 136–163. https://doi.org/10.1002/tesq.99.

Bale, J. (2014) Heritage language education and the 'national interest'. *Review of Research in Education* 38 (1), 166–188. https://doi.org/10.3102/0091732X13507547.

Barcelos, A.M.F. (2017) Identities as emotioning and believing. In G. Barkhuizen (ed.) *Reflections on Language Teacher Identity Research* (pp. 145–150). Routledge.

Barcelos, A.M.F. and Kalaja, P. (2013) Beliefs in second language acquisition: Teacher. *The Encyclopedia of Applied Linguistics*. https://doi.org/10.1002/9781405198431.wbeal0083.

Barcelos, A.M.F. and Ruohotie-Lyhty, M. (2018) Teachers' emotions and beliefs in second language teaching: Implications for teacher education. In J.D.M. Agudo (ed.) *Emotions in Second Language Teaching* (pp. 109–124). Springer.

Barkhuizen, G. (2017) Language teacher identity research. In G. Barkhuizen (ed.) *Reflections on Language Teacher Identity Research* (pp. 1–11). Routledge.

Basturkmen, H. (2012) Review of research into the correspondence between language teachers' stated beliefs and practices. *System* 40 (2), 282–295. https://doi.org/10.1016/j.system.2012.05.001.

Bateman, B.E. and Wilkinson, S.L. (2010) Spanish for heritage speakers: A statewide survey of secondary school teachers. *Foreign Language Annals* 43 (2), 324–353. https://doi.org/10.1111/j.1944-9720.2010.01081.x.

Bazeley, P. (2013) *Qualitative Data Analysis: Practical Strategies*. SAGE.

Bell, T.R. (2005) Behaviors and attitudes of effective foreign language teachers: Results of a questionnaire study. *Foreign Language Annals* 38 (2), 259–270. https://doi.org/10.1111/j.1944-9720.2005.tb02490.x.

Berbeco, S. (2016) Foreign language education in America. In S. Berbeco (ed.) *Foreign Language Education in America* (pp. 1–16). Palgrave Macmillan. https://doi.org/10.1057/9781137528506_1.

Bernat, E. (2008) Beyond beliefs: Psycho-cognitive, sociocultural and emergent ecological approaches to learner perceptions in foreign language acquisition. *Asian EFL Journal* 10 (3), 7–27. See http://www.asian-efl-journal.com/September_2008.pdf?q=your-home-issue-44-september-2008-chinese#page=7.

Borg, S. (1998) Teachers' pedagogical systems and grammar teaching: A qualitative study. *TESOL Quarterly* 32 (1), 9–38. https://doi.org/10.2307/3587900.

Borg, S. (2003) Teacher cognition in language teaching: A review of research on what language teachers think, know, believe, and do. *Language Teaching* 36 (2), 81–109. https://doi.org/10.1017/S0261444803001903.

Borg, S. (2006) *Teacher Cognition and Language Education: Research and Practice*. Continuum.

Borg, S. (2017) Teachers' beliefs and classroom practices. In P. Garrett and J.M. Cots (eds) *The Routledge Handbook of Language Awareness* (pp. 222–237). Routledge.

Borg, S. (2019) Language teacher cognition: Perspectives and debates. In X. Gao (ed.) *Second Handbook of English Language Teaching* (pp. 1149–1170). Springer Link.

Borg, S. and Sanchez, H.S. (2020) Cognition and good language teachers. In C. Griffiths and Z. Tajeddin (eds) *Lessons from Good Language Teachers* (pp. 16–27). Cambridge University Press.

Bouabré, C.K. (2019) Current state of foreign language instruction in US K-12 Christian schools. *Journal of Research on Christian Education* 28 (3), 239–259. https://doi.org /10.1080/10656219.2019.1703848.

Brecht, R.D. (2007) National language educational policy in the nation's interest: Why? How? Who is responsible for what? *The Modern Language Journal* 91 (2), 264–265. https://doi.org/10.1111/j.1540-4781.2007.00543_8.x.

Breen, M.P., Hird, B., Milton, M., Oliver, R. and Thwaite, A. (2001) Making sense of language teaching: Teachers' principles and classroom practices. *Applied Linguistics* 22 (4), 470–501. https://doi.org/10.1093/applin/22.4.470.

Brown, A.V. (2009) Students' and teachers' perceptions of effective foreign language teaching: A comparison of ideals. *The Modern Language Journal* 93 (1), 46–60. https://doi .org/10.1111/j.1540-4781.2009.00827.x.

Burke, B.M. (2013) Looking into a crystal ball: Is requiring high-stakes language proficiency tests really going to improve world language education? *The Modern Language Journal* 97 (2), 531–534. https://www.jstor.org/stable/43651654.

Burns, A., Freeman, D. and Edwards, E. (2015) Theorizing and studying the language-teaching mind: Mapping research on language teacher cognition. *The Modern Language Journal* 99 (3), 585–601. https://doi.org/10.1111/modl.12245.

Carreira, M. and Kagan, O. (2018) Heritage language education: A proposal for the next 50 years. *Foreign Language Annals* 51 (1), 152–168. https://doi.org/10.1111/flan.12331.

Center for Applied Second Language Studies (CASLS) (2010) What proficiency level do high school students achieve? See https://casls.uoregon.edu/wp-content/uploads/pdfs /tenquestions/TBQProficiencyResults.pdf.

Chou, A. (2019) The 2019 National Seal of Biliteracy Report. See https://sealofbiliteracy .org/research/2019-National-Seal-of-Biliteracy-Report.

Commission on Language Learning (2017) America's languages: Investing in language education for the 21st century. American Academy of Arts & Sciences. See https://www .amacad.org/language.

CCSSO's Interstate Teacher Assessment and Support Consortium (2013) *InTASC Model Core Teaching Standards and Learning Progressions for Teachers 1.0.* Council of Chief State School Officers. See https://ccsso.org/sites/default/files/2017-12/2013_INTASC _Learning_Progressions_for_Teachers.pdf.

Council of Europe (2020) *Common European Framework of Reference for Languages: Learning, Teaching, Assessment. Companion Volume.* COE. See https://rm.coe.int/common -european-framework-of-reference-for-languages-learning-teaching/16809ea0d4.

Davin, K.J. and Heineke, A.J. (2017) The Seal of Biliteracy: Variations in policy and outcomes. *Foreign Language Annals* 50 (3), 486–499. https://doi.org/10.1111/flan.12279.

Davin, K., Troyan, F.J., Donato, R. and Hellman, A. (2011) Research on the Integrated Performance Assessment in an early foreign language learning program. *Foreign Language Annals* 44 (4), 605–625. https://doi.org/10.1111/j.1944-9720.2011.01153.x.

Davin, K.J., Rempert, T.A. and Hammerand, A.A. (2014) Converting data to knowledge: One district's experience using large-scale proficiency assessment. *Foreign Language Annals* 47 (2), 241–260. https://doi.org/10.1111/flan.12081.

de Brey, C., Musu, L., McFarland, J., Wilkinson-Flicker, S., Diliberti, M., Zhang, A., Branstetter, C. and Wang, X. (2019) *Status and Trends in the Education of Racial and Ethnic Groups 2018.* US Department of Education, National Center for Education Statistics. See https://nces.ed.gov/pubs2019/2019038.pdf.

Devlin, K. (2018) Most European students are learning a foreign language in school while Americans lag. Pew Research Center, 6 August. See https://www.pewresearch.org/fact-tank/2018/08/06/most-european-students-are-learning-a-foreign-language-in-school-while-americans-lag/.

DiPardo, A. (1993) When teachers become graduate students. *English Education* 25, 197–212. https://www.jstor.org/stable/40172814.

Dolci, R. (2015) On America's foreign language education policy and the 'foreign language deficit'. In R. Dolci and A.J. Tamburri (eds) *Intercomprehension and Plurilingualism: Assets for Italian Language in the USA* (pp. 1–27). Calandra Institute.

Donato, R. and Tucker, G.R. (2007) K-12 language learning and foreign language educational policy: A school-based perspective. *The Modern Language Journal* 91 (2), 256–258. https://www.jstor.org/stable/4626006.

Egnatz, L. (2016) The high school challenge. In S. Berbeco (ed.) *Foreign Language Education in America* (pp. 66–84). Palgrave Macmillan. https://doi.org/10.1057/9781137528506_4.

Ellis, D. (2016) The STARTALK experience. In S. Berbeco (ed.) *Foreign Language Education in America* (pp. 85–114). Palgrave Macmillan. https://doi.org/10.1057/9781137528506_5.

Farrell, T.S. (2017) 'Who I am is how I teach': Reflecting on language teacher professional role identity. In G. Barkhuizen (ed.) *Reflections on Language Teacher Identity Research* (pp. 183–188). Routledge.

Farrell, T.S. and Lim, P.C.P. (2005) Conceptions of grammar teaching: A case study of teachers' beliefs and classroom practices. *TESL-EJ* 9 (2). See https://eric.ed.gov/?id=EJ1065837.

Farrell, T.S. and Bennis, K. (2013) Reflecting on ESL teacher beliefs and classroom practices: A case study. *RELC Journal* 44 (2), 163–176. https://doi.org/10.1177/0033688213488463.

Farrell, T.S. and Ives, J. (2015) Exploring teacher beliefs and classroom practices through reflective practice: A case study. *Language Teaching Research* 19 (5), 594–610. https://doi.org/10.1177/1362168814541722.

Farrell, T.S. and Guz, M. (2019) 'If I wanted to survive I had to use it': The power of teacher beliefs on classroom practices. *TESL-EJ* 22 (4). See https://eric.ed.gov/?id=EJ1204614.

Farrell, T.S. and Yang, D. (2019) Exploring an EAP teacher's beliefs and practices in teaching L2 speaking: A case study. *RELC Journal* 50 (1), 104–117. https://doi.org/10.1177/0033688217730144.

Flores, M.A. and Day, C. (2006) Contexts which shape and reshape new teachers' identities: A multi-perspective study. *Teaching and Teacher Education* 22 (2), 219–232. https://doi.org/10.1016/j.tate.2005.09.002.

Gabillon, Z. (2013) A synopsis of L2 teacher belief research. Belgrade International Conference on Education, 14–16 November, Serbia. See https://shs.hal.science/halshs-00940593/ (accessed December 2023).

García, O. (2014) US Spanish and education: Global and local intersections. *Review of Research in Education* 38 (1), 58–80. https://doi.org/10.3102/0091732X13506542.

Gardner, R.C. (1985) *Social Psychology and Second Language Learning: The Role of Attitudes and Motivation*. Edward Arnold.

Gatbonton, E. (2000) Investigating experienced ESL teachers' pedagogical knowledge. *Canadian Modern Language Review* 56 (4), 585–616. https://doi.org/10.3138/cmlr.56.4.585.

Glisan, E.W. and Foltz, D.A. (1998) Assessing students' oral proficiency in an outcome-based curriculum: Student performance and teacher intuitions. *The Modern Language Journal* 82 (1), 1–18. https://doi.org/10.1111/j.1540-4781.1998.tb02587.x.

Glynn, C. (2012) The role of ethnicity in the foreign language classroom: Perspectives on African American students' enrollment, experiences, and identity. Unpublished doctoral dissertation, University of Minnesota, Minneapolis.

Glynn, C. and Wassell, B. (2018) Who gets to play? Issues of access and social justice in world language study in the US. *Dimension: Journal of the Southern Conference on*

Language Teaching 2018, 18. See https://www.scolt.org/wp-content/uploads/2019/08/2 _Dimension2018.pdf.

Graden, E.C. (1996) How language teachers' beliefs about reading instruction are mediated by their beliefs about students. *Foreign Language Annals* 29 (3), 387–395. https://doi .org/10.1111/j.1944-9720.1996.tb01250.x.

Griffiths, C. (2007) Language learning strategies: Students' and teachers' perceptions. *ELT Journal* 61 (2), 91–99. https://doi.org/10.1093/elt/ccm001.

Hawkey, R. (2006) Teacher and learner perceptions of language learning activity. *ELT Journal* 60 (3), 242–252. https://doi.org/10.1093/elt/ccl004.

Heineke, A.J. and Davin, K.J. (2020) Prioritizing multilingualism in US schools: States' policy journeys to enact the Seal of Biliteracy. *Educational Policy* 34 (4), 619–643. https://doi.org/10.1177/0895904818802099.

Holliday, A. (2006) Native-speakerism. *ELT Journal* 60 (4), 385–387. https://doi.org /10.1093/elt/ccl030.

Holmes, A.G.D. (2020) Researcher positionality – A consideration of its influence and place in qualitative research – A new researcher guide. *Shanlax International Journal of Education* 8 (4), 1–10. See https://eric.ed.gov/?id=EJ1268044.

Horwitz, E.K. (1985) Using student beliefs about language learning and teaching in the foreign language methods course. *Foreign Language Annals* 18 (4), 333–340. https://doi .org/10.1111/j.1944-9720.1985.tb01811.x.

Hu, Y. (2007) China's foreign language policy on primary English education: What's behind it? *Language Policy* 6 (3), 359–376. https://doi.org/10.1007/s10993-007-9052-9.

Huebner, T. and Jensen, A. (1992) A study of foreign language proficiency-based testing in secondary schools. *Foreign Language Annals* 25 (2), 105–115. https://doi .org/10.1111/j.1944-9720.1992.tb00518.x.

Ingold, C. and Hart, M.E. (2010) Taking the 'L' out of LCTLs: The STARTALK experience. *Russian Language Journal/Русский язык* 60, 183–198. https://www.jstor.org /stable/43669182.

Iowa Board of Educational Examiners (n.d.) Native language teaching authorization. See https://boee.iowa.gov/license-authorization/native-language-teaching-authorization.

Iowa Code, Section 256.11.5.f. (2023) Department of Education, educational standards. See https://www.legis.iowa.gov/DOCS/ACO/IC/LINC/Section.256.11.pdf.

Iowa Department of Education (2018) The annual condition of education report: 2018. See https://educateiowa.gov/sites/default/files/documents/2018ConditionOfEducation .pdf.

Johnson, K.E. (2009) *Second Language Teacher Education: A Sociocultural Perspective.* Routledge.

Johnson, K.E. and Golombek, P.R. (2020) Informing and transforming language teacher education pedagogy. *Language Teaching Research* 24 (1), 116–127. https://doi .org/10.1177/1362168818777539.

Kalaja, P. and Barcelos, A.M.F. (2019) Learner beliefs in second language learning. *The Encyclopedia of Applied Linguistics.* https://doi.org/10.1002/9781405198431 .wbeal0082.pub2.

Kalaja, P., Barcelos, A.M.F. and Aro, M. (2017) Revisiting research on L2 learner beliefs: Looking back and looking forward. In P. Garrett and J.M. Cots (eds) *The Routledge Handbook of Language Awareness* (pp. 222–237). Routledge.

Kennedy, C. and Kennedy, J. (1996) Teacher attitudes and change implementation. *System* 24 (3), 351–360. https://doi.org/10.1016/0346-251X(96)00027-9.

Kern, R.G. (1995) Students' and teachers' beliefs about language learning. *Foreign Language Annals* 28 (1), 71–92. https://doi.org/10.1111/j.1944-9720.1995.tb00770.x.

Kim, S. (2011) Exploring native speaker teachers' beliefs about learning and teaching English. *English Teaching* 66 (2), 123–148. See http://kate.bada.cc/wp-content /uploads/2015/01/kate_66_2_6.pdf.

Kissau, S., Adams, M.J. and Algozzine, B. (2015) Middle school foreign language instruction: A missed opportunity? *Foreign Language Annals* 48 (2), 284–303. https://doi.org/10.1111/flan.12133.

Kubanyiova, M. and Crookes, G. (2016) Re-envisioning the roles, tasks, and contributions of language teachers in the multilingual era of language education research and practice. *The Modern Language Journal* 100 (S1), 117–132. https://doi.org/10.1111/modl.12304.

Kumaravadivelu, B. (1991) Language-learning tasks: Teacher intention and learner interpretation. *ELT Journal* 45 (2), 98–107. https://doi.org/10.1093/elt/45.2.98.

Li, M. (2017) Power relations in the enactment of English language education policy for Chinese schools. *Discourse: Studies in the Cultural Politics of Education* 38 (5), 713–726. https://doi.org/10.1080/01596306.2016.1141177.

Llurda, E. and Calvet-Terré, J. (2022) Native-speakerism and non-native second language teachers: A research agenda. *Language Teaching*, 1–17. https://doi.org/10.1017/S0261444822000271.

Mackey, A., Al-Khalil, M., Atanassova, G., Hama, M., Logan-Terry, A. and Nakatsukasa, K. (2007) Teachers' intentions and learners' perceptions about corrective feedback in the L2 classroom. *International Journal of Innovation in Language Learning and Teaching* 1 (1), 129–152. https://doi.org/10.2167/illt047.0.

Mason, A. and Payant, C. (2019) Experienced teachers' beliefs and practices toward communicative approaches in teaching English as a foreign language in rural Ukraine. *TESOL Journal* 10 (1), e00377. https://doi.org/10.1002/tesj.377.

Merriam, S.B. and Tisdell, E.J. (2015) *Qualitative Research: A Guide to Design and Implementation* (4th edn). Jossey-Bass.

Met, M. and Brandt, A.M. (2017) Foreign language learning in K-12 classrooms in the USA. In N. Van Deusen-Scholl and S. May (eds) *Second and Foreign Language Education* (pp. 357–370). Springer International.

Moeller, A.J., Theiler, J.M. and Wu, C. (2012) Goal setting and student achievement: A longitudinal study. *The Modern Language Journal* 96 (2), 153–169. https://doi.org/10.1111/j.1540-4781.2011.01231.x.

Moussu, L. and Llurda, E. (2008) Non-native English-speaking English language teachers: History and research. *Language Teaching* 41 (3), 315–348. https://doi.org/10.1017/S0261444808005028.

National Foreign Language Center and National Security Agency (NFLC & NSA) (2020a) STARTALK 2020: Longitudinal impact report, student participants 2007–2019. See https://startalk.umd.edu/public/system/files/docs/startalk2020_studentandparent longitudinalsurveyreport.pdf.

National Foreign Language Center and National Security Agency (NFLC & NSA) (2020b) STARTALK 2020: Longitudinal impact report, teacher participants 2007–2019. See https://startalk.umd.edu/public/system/files/docs/startalk2020_teacherlongitudinal surveyreport.pdf.

The National Standards Collaborative Board (1998) *The Standards for Foreign Language Learning in the 21st Century*. ACTFL.

The National Standards Collaborative Board (2015) *World-Readiness Standards for Learning Languages* (4th edn). ACTFL.

Negueruela-Azarola, E. (2011) Beliefs as conceptualizing activity: A dialectical approach for the second language classroom. *System* 39 (3), 359–369. https://doi.org/10.1016/j.system.2011.07.008.

Nishino, T. (2012) Modeling teacher beliefs and practices in context: A multimethods approach. *The Modern Language Journal* 96 (3), 380–399. https://doi.org/10.1111/j.1540-4781.2012.01364.x.

Oranje, J. and Smith, L.F. (2018) Language teacher cognitions and intercultural language teaching: The New Zealand perspective. *Language Teaching Research* 22 (3), 310–329. https://doi.org/10.1177/1362168817691319.

O'Rourke, P., Zhou, Q. and Rottman, I. (2016) Prioritization of K–12 world language education in the United States: State requirements for high school graduation. *Foreign Language Annals* 49 (4), 789–800. https://doi.org/10.1111/flan.12232.

Ortega, L. (2019) SLA and the study of equitable multilingualism. *The Modern Language Journal* 103, 23–38. https://doi.org/10.1111/modl.12525.

Pajares, F. (1993) Preservice teachers' beliefs: A focus for teacher education. *Action in Teacher Education* 15 (2), 45–54. https://doi.org/10.1080/01626620.1993.10734409.

Pan, L. and Block, D. (2011) English as a 'global language' in China: An investigation into learners' and teachers' language beliefs. *System* 39 (3), 391–402. https://doi.org/10.1016/j.system.2011.07.011.

Pavlenko, A. (2003) 'Language of the enemy': Foreign language education and national identity. *International Journal of Bilingual Education and Bilingualism* 6 (5), 313–331. https://doi.org/10.1080/13670050308667789.

Phillips, J.K. and Abbott, M. (2011) *A Decade of Foreign Language Standards: Impact, Influence, and Future Directions*. Report of Grant Project #P017A080037, Title VII, International Research Studies, US Department of Education to the American Council on the Teaching of Foreign Languages.

Phipps, S. and Borg, S. (2009) Exploring tensions between teachers' grammar teaching beliefs and practices. *System* 37 (3), 380–390. https://doi.org/10.1016/j.system.2009.03.002.

Pillow, W. (2003) Confession, catharsis, or cure? Rethinking the uses of reflexivity as methodological power in qualitative research. *International Journal of Qualitative Studies in Education* 16 (2), 175–196. https://doi.org/10.1080/0951839032000060635.

Priestley, M., Edwards, R., Priestley, A. and Miller, K. (2012) Teacher agency in curriculum making: Agents of change and spaces for manoeuvre. *Curriculum Inquiry* 42 (2), 191–214. https://doi.org/10.1111/j.1467-873X.2012.00588.x.

Pufahl, I. and Rhodes, N.C. (2011) Foreign language instruction in US schools: Results of a national survey of elementary and secondary schools. *Foreign Language Annals* 44 (2), 258–288. https://doi.org/10.1111/j.1944-9720.2011.01130.x.

Pufahl, I., Rhodes, N.C. and Christian, D. (2000) Foreign language teaching: What the United States can learn from other countries. US Department of Education's Comparative Information on Improving Education Practice Working Group 4.

Rahman, M.M., Singh, M.K.M. and Pandian, A. (2018) Exploring ESL teacher beliefs and classroom practices of CLT: A case study. *International Journal of Instruction* 11 (1), 295–310. See https://eric.ed.gov/?id=EJ1165221.

Rey Agudo, R. (2021) Can we rid academic departments of the F-word? *Inside Higher Ed*, 6 April. See https://www.insidehighered.com/views/2021/04/07/academe-shouldnt-automatically-call-languages-other-english-foreign-opinion.

Ritz, C. and Sherf, N. (2021) World language programming and leadership in K–12 Massachusetts public schools. *Foreign Language Annals* 54 (2), 476–504. https://doi.org/10.1111/flan.12519.

Robertson, W.B. and Yazan, B. (2022) Navigating tensions and asserting agency in language teacher identity: A case study of a graduate teaching assistant. *Linguistics and Education* 71, 101079. https://doi.org/10.1016/j.linged.2022.101079.

Sparks, R.L., Luebbers, J. and Castañeda, M.E. (2017) How well do US high school students achieve in Spanish when compared to native Spanish speakers? *Foreign Language Annals* 50 (2), 339–366. https://doi.org/10.1111/flan.12268.

Tarone, E. and Allwright, D. (2006) Second language teacher learning and student second language learning: Shaping the knowledge base. In D.J. Tedick (ed.) *Second Language Teacher Education: International Perspectives* (pp. 5–24). Lawrence Erlbaum.

Teacher Effectiveness for Language Learning Project (n.d.) Teacher Effectiveness for Language Learning framework. See http://www.tellproject.org.

Tedick, D.J. (2009) K–12 language teacher preparation: Problems and possibilities. *The Modern Language Journal* 93 (2), 263–267. https://www.jstor.org/stable/40264056.

Tedick, D.J. (2013) Embracing proficiency and program standards and rising to the challenge: A response to Burke. *The Modern Language Journal* 97 (2), 535–538. https://www.jstor.org/stable/43651655.

Terry, R.M. (2016) *A History of ACTFL.* ACTFL.

US Department of Education (n.d.a) Our Nation's English learners: What are their characteristics? See https://www2.ed.gov/datastory/el-characteristics/index.html.

US Department of Education (n.d.b) Teacher shortage areas database. See https://tsa.ed.gov/#/home.

Vyn, R., Wesely, P.M. and Neubauer, D. (2019) Exploring the effects of foreign language instructional practices on student proficiency development. *Foreign Language Annals* 52 (1), 45–65. https://doi.org/10.1111/flan.12382.

Wan, W., Low, G.D. and Li, M. (2011) From students' and teachers' perspectives: Metaphor analysis of beliefs about EFL teachers' roles. *System* 39 (3), 403–415. https://doi.org/10.1016/j.system.2011.07.012.

Wang, S.C. and Green, N. (2008) Heritage language students in the K-12 education system. In J.K. Peyton, D.A. Ranard and S. McGinnis (eds) *Heritage Languages in America: Preserving a National Resource* (pp. 167–196). Center for Applied Linguistics.

Watson, A.M. (2015a) Conceptualisations of 'grammar teaching': L1 English teachers' beliefs about teaching grammar for writing. *Language Awareness* 24 (1), 1–14. https://www.tandfonline.com/doi/abs/10.1080/09658416.2013.828736.

Watson, A.M. (2015b) The problem of grammar teaching: A case study of the relationship between a teacher's beliefs and pedagogical practice. *Language and Education* 29 (4), 332–346. https://doi.org/10.1080/09500782.2015.1016955.

Wiebe, G. and Kabata, K. (2010) Students' and instructors' attitudes toward the use of CALL in foreign language teaching and learning. *Computer Assisted Language Learning* 23 (3), 221–234. https://doi.org/10.1080/09588221.2010.486577.

Wesely, P.M. (2009) The language learning motivation of early adolescent French immersion graduates. *Foreign Language Annals* 42 (2), 270–286. https://doi.org/10.1111/j.1944-9720.2009.01021.x.

Wesely, P.M. (2010) Language learning motivation in early adolescents: Using mixed methods research to explore contradiction. *Journal of Mixed Methods Research* 4 (4), 295–312. https://doi.org/10.1177/1558689810375816.

Wesely, P.M. and Plummer, E. (2017) Situated learning for foreign language teachers in one-to-one computing initiatives. *CALICO Journal* 34 (2), 178–195. See https://files.eric.ed.gov/fulltext/EJ1143357.pdf.

Wesely, P.M., Vyn, R. and Neubauer, D. (2021) Teacher beliefs about instructional approaches: Interrogating the notion of teaching methods. *Language Teaching Research*. https://doi.org/10.1177/1362168821992180.

Wiley, T., Moore, S.C. and Fee, M.S. (2012) A 'languages for jobs' initiative. Renewing America: Policy Innovation Memorandum No. 24. Council on Foreign Relations. See https://www.files.ethz.ch/isn/146207/Policy_Innovation_Memo24_ForeignLanguage.pdf.

Woods, D. and Çakır, H. (2011) Two dimensions of teacher knowledge: The case of communicative language teaching. *System* 39 (3), 381–390. https://doi.org/10.1016/j.system.2011.07.010.

Index